W9-BVI-694

This CD and the software included on it have been designed to run on Windows 95 and NT 4.0.

Please see the CD-ROM appendix for more information on how to install or run any of the software included on this CD.

Minimum Suggested System Requirements

▶ Computer: Pentium IBM PC-compatible

▶ Memory: 16MB of RAM

▶ Platform: Windows 95 or NT 4.0

▶ Hardware: 2X CD-ROM drive

CD Start Instructions

1 Place the CD-ROM in your CD-ROM drive.

2 From the CD-ROM root directory (usually D) run SETUP.EXE.

3 Follow the onscreen instructions to complete the install process.

HOW to Program

Delphi 3

HOW _to_ Program

Delphi 3

F R A N K · E N G O

Ziff-Davis Press
An imprint of Macmillan Computer Publishing USA
Emeryville, California

Publisher	Stacy Hiquet
Associate Publisher	Steven Sayre
Acquisitions Editor	Lysa Lewallen
Development Editor	Nancy Warner
Copy Editor	Udonia Annis
Technical Reviewer	Matt Eliot
Production Editor	Madhu Prasher
Proofreader	Timothy Loughman
Cover Illustration and Design	Megan Gandt
Book Design and Layout	Bruce Lundquist
Indexer	Ted Laux

Ziff-Davis Press, ZD Press, and the Ziff-Davis Press logo are trademarks or registered trademarks of, and are licensed to Macmillan Computer Publishing USA by Ziff-Davis Publishing Company, New York, New York.

Ziff-Davis Press imprint books are produced on a Macintosh computer system with the following applications: FrameMaker®, Microsoft® Word, QuarkXPress®, Adobe Illustrator®, Adobe Photoshop®, Adobe Streamline™, MacLink®Plus, Aldus® FreeHand™, Collage Plus™.

Ziff-Davis Press, an imprint of
Macmillan Computer Publishing USA
5903 Christie Avenue
Emeryville, CA 94608

ISBN 1-56276-526-4

Manufactured in the United States of America

10 9 8 7 6 5 4 3 2 1

In memory of my sister Susan

Table of Contents

Introduction   xv

Part I Programming in Delphi

Chapter 1: The Road Ahead   3

Getting Started with Delphi   5

The Delphi Environment   5

Exercise: Creating a Simple Program   6

Closing a Form 8

Renaming Components 8

Coding Event Procedures 9

Working with Dialog Boxes   10

Adding Comments 12

Using Constants 13

Working with Data Types   14

Component Basics   15

Using Labels 15

Adding Edit Components to Forms 16

Properties of Edit Components 17

Aligning Controls 18

Adding Multiple Components of the Same Type 18

Setting the Tab Order 19

Exercise: Creating a Sales Tax Calculator   20

Working with Units   23

Deleting Object References   26

Managing Projects   26

Summary   27

Chapter 2: Creating Interfaces   29

Standard Components in Delphi   29

Working with List Boxes 29

Displaying Combo Boxes 32

Using Check Boxes 33

Displaying Mutually Exclusive Choices to Users 35

Using Scroll Bars 37

Event Handlers 39

Validating Program Options at Run-Time   41

Enabling and Disabling Controls 41

Showing/Hiding Components 42

Dressing Up Interfaces   42

Showing Bitmaps in Buttons 43

Displaying Button Hints 43

Inherited Properties of Controls   45

Overriding Inherited Defaults 45

Creating a Picture Viewer 46

Summary   49

Chapter 3: Working with Forms   51

Creating Multiform Applications   51

Displaying Forms   51

Unit References   52

Managing Units   54

Changing the Appearance of Forms   55

Executing Cleanup Code 56

Reference Controls on Other Forms 56

Creating a Tabled Notebook Style Interface   58

The Delphi IDE 59

The Object Repository 59
Using Component Templates 61
Configuring Palettes 62
Adding ActiveX Components to Forms 62

Common Programming Mistakes 63

Bad or Non-relational Designs 63
Stacking Controls on Forms 63
Using Literals Instead of Constants 65
Lack of indentation or Spacing 66
Hard Coded Paths 67
Using Long Names 67
Coding Large Procedures 67
Repeating of Copying Blocks of Code 68
Using the GOTO Statement 68
Using Non-Standard Forms 68

Exercise: Building a Multi-Page Dialog 68

Summary 70

Chapter 4: Programming Standards 73

Writing Expressions 73

Real Number Arithmetic 75
Order of Precedence 76

Using the If Statement 77

Complex Conditional Expressions 78

Using the Case Statement 80

Working with Loops 82

The For Loop 82
The While Loop 83
The Repeat..Until Loop 84

Working with Types 84

Enumerated Types 84
Subrange Types 86
Array Types 88
Record Types 90

Exercise: Encrypting a Message 92

Summary 93

Chapter 5: Working with Procedures and Functions 95

Object Pascal Syntax 96
User-Defined Procedures and Functions 97
Coding Procedures and Functions 98
The Body of a Subroutine 98
Coding User-Defined Functions 100
Passing Parameters 101

Placement of Procedures and Functions 103

Positioning Subroutines 104

Accessing the Delphi Programmers' Library 106

Commonly Used Delphi Procedures and Functions 107

The Abs Function 107
The Copy Function 108
The ExtractFileName Function 109
The ExtractFilePath Function 109
The FileGetDate Function 110
The Sleep Function 111
The UpperCase Function 112
The TrimLeft and TrimRight Functions 113
The ParamStr Function 113
Other Delphi Procedures and Functions 115

Exercise: Defining Hotspots on a Form 115

Summary 117

Chapter 6: Creating Menus   119

Using the Menu Designer   119

Creating Menu Items   120

Adding Separator Bars in a Menu   120

Defining Accelerator Keys on a Menu   121

Adding Shortcut Keys to a Menu   121

Creating Submenus   122

Editing Menu Items   123

Programming Menu Controls   123

Using Menu Templates   124

Saving Menu Templates   124

Controlling Menu Items at Run-Time   125

Enabling and Disabling Menu Items   126

Displaying Check Marks and Bullets in Menus   127

Creating Pop-Up Menus   127

Exercise: Creating a Drop-Down Menu System   128

Summary   133

Chapter 7: Dealing with Errors   135

Overview of the Debugger   135

Types of Errors   135

Errors the Debugger Can Help With   136

Using the Debugger   136

Debugging Techniques   136

Running to the Cursor   137

Tracing and Stepping over Code in a Project   137

Controlling the Flow of Execution   138

Using Breakpoints   138

Setting Conditional Breakpoints   139

Monitoring Values of Expressions   140

Removing or Disabling Watch Expressions   141

Setting Test Values   141

Debugging Applications in Delphi 3.0   142

Viewing Calls to Subroutines   142

Resource Protection and Error Handling   142

Resource Protection Handlers   142

Writing Exception Handlers   143

Reraising Exceptions   145

Exercise: Using Exception Handlers   147

Summary   148

Chapter 8: Working with Databases   151

Building Database Applications in Delphi   151

Quick Start   151

A Close Look   155

Using the DBRichEdit Component   156

Using Data Modules   157

Writing Code to Maintain Databases   159

Working with Datasets   159

Using the MoveBy Method   160

Finding Information in Tables   160

Performing Faster Searches   161

Adding Records to a Table   163

Editing Table Records   166

Using the SetFields Method to Update Records   167

Deleting Table Records   168

Checking for Empty Datasets   168

Using Bookmarks   169

Exercise: Creating a Table   170

Summary   173

Chapter 9: Using Structured Query Language 175

Fundamentals of SQL 175

Starting InterBase Windows Interactive SQL 176

Adding a Table to the Database 176
Inserting Records into a Table 178
Performing Queries 179
Updating Records and Table Definitions 180
Removing Table Records 181
Specifying Ranges 181

Using the Query Component 182

Exercise: Running Queries From Delphi 182

Writing Code to Execute Queries 183
Sorting a Dataset 184
Checking for Null and Inequality 186
Performing Interactive Queries 187
Database Manipulation Routines of the Library 188

Summary 188

Chapter 10: Building Reports 191

Creating a Simple Report 191

Formatting Reports 192
Editing Report Headings and Columns 193
Changing Columns 193
Inserting Fields 193
Inserting Summary Fields 194
Formatting Headings 195
Setting Filters 196
Adding Derived Fields 197
Creating File Links 199
Editing Links 200
Saving Reports 200

Printing Reports from Delphi 200

Summary 201

Chapter 11: Developing Multimedia Applications 203

The MediaPlayer Component 203

Playing Audio 204
Playing Video 207

Graphics and Multimedia 208

The Image Control 208
Sizing Graphics 209
Working with Color Palettes 209
Avoiding Color Palette Conflicts 210
Third-Party Voodoo Solutions 211
Multimedia Routines of the Library 211

Distributing Applications on CD-ROMs 212

Building the Pre-Master 213
Building the Glass Master 214
Writing Code to Access CDs 214

Exercise: Playing a Video from Delphi 214

Summary 215

Chapter 12: Building User-Defined Components 217

Why Create Components? 217

Building Components 217

Defining a New Component 218
Generating the Unit 219
Registering Components 220
The Visual Component Library 221

Exercise: Creating a Sample Component 221

Testing Components without Installing 225
Testing the Enlarge Method 226
Installing Components 228

Summary 229

Chapter 13: Delphi and the Internet 231

A Brief History 231

Developing Internet Applications in Delphi 231

Creating Web Viewers 232

Retrieving an HTML Document 233

Canceling an HTML Operation 234

Sending E-Mail over the Internet 237

Making an FTP Connection 240

Getting Directory Information from an FTP Server 242

Adding Directory Items to a Tree 244

Accessing UNIX Hosts 247

Other Internet-Related Issues 247

Using TCP/IP 247

Making a TCP Connection 248

Getting Network News 248

Packages and the Internet 249

Exercise: Creating an E-Mail Application 249

Summary 253

Part 2 The Library

Chapter 14: Database Routines 257

AddField 257

DisplayQueryRecs 259

IsEmpty 260

LoadQuery 261

SortTable 262

Chapter 15: Multimedia Routines 265

BlockShadow 266

ColorMsg 267

CustomCursor 269

DisplayDirImages 270

MessageBlink 273

PlayVideoFile 274

PlayWaveFile 275

ShowHotSpot 276

ShowScrSaver 279

ShowTNail 283

SlowPrint 285

SoundEnabled 286

TickerTape 287

TileBitmap 289

TransparentButton 290

Chapter 16: Rich Edit Routines 295

OpenRichEdit 295

SaveRichEdit 297

SetAlignment 299

SetBoldFace 301

SetBullet 301

SetBlockStyle 303

SetItalics 304

SetUnderline 304

UndoChange 305

Chapter 17: Spreadsheet Routines 307

CreateChart 307

DrawObject 309

FormatWorksheet 310

PrintWorksheet 313

Chapter 18: String Routines 317

IsNumVal 317

StrCenter 318

StrDeleteAll 320

StrExtractCmd 321

StrFormatUpper 322

StrReplaceAll 324

StrReverse 325

StrRightChar 326

StrStripSpaces 327

Chapter 19: String Grid Routines 331

ClrStrGrid 331

InitStringGrid 332

OpenStringGrid 333

SaveStringGrid 334

WeeklySchedule 335

Chapter 20: System Routines 337

ChangeSearchPath 337

CheckPentium 338

FileCopyList 339

WinDir 341

Chapter 21: Utility and Web Connectivity Routines 343

BrowseWebPage 343

ComparePaths 345

ConvertFraction 346

DecryptMsg 347

EncryptMsg 348

GetDay 350

GetFTPDir 351

NextControl 354

SearchListItem 355

SendEMailMsg 356

ShowHelpTopic 358

Appendix A: What's on the CD 360

Installing the CD 360

Troubleshooting the Install Program 360

Appendix B: Using the Formula One Component 362

Performing Calculations 362

Using Conditional Operators 362

Writing Code to Interface with Spreadsheet 363

Determining the Active Cell 363

Reading Cell Ranges 364

Saving and Retrieving Worksheets 365

Index 367

Acknowledgments

Special thanks to Lysa Lewallen, Richard J. Smith, Gary Tischler, John Maolucci, Matt Eliot, Mike Donnelly, Udonia Annis, Stuart Torzewski, Renee Wilmeth, Nancy Warner, and the members of Ziff-Davis Press for their hard work and support.

Introduction

In the tradition of the best-selling *How to Program* series, this book provides a clear and straightforward approach to learning Delphi. Part 1 covers the basics. In this section, readers will learn how to develop Delphi applications using the easy-to-follow examples and step-by-step tutorials. Assuming no prior knowledge of programming, *How to Program Delphi 3* provides up-to-date information on the latest Delphi 3.0 enhancements. Special emphasis is placed on developing database applications, working with SQL, connecting to the Internet, and accessing multimedia devices.

Part 2 covers the developers' library included with this book. The general categories of library routines include database, multimedia, Rich Text Edit, spreadsheet, string and string grid routines, plus system/utility and Web connectivity procedures and functions. Each routine is listed in a standard format that includes its syntax, parameters, return values, remarks, and at least one coding example. The routines listing in Part 2 can be used for the professional development of new software—free from royalty obligations—provided that you agree to the terms in the licensing agreement and also not use the library to develop a competing reusable code system.

The Library

Below are listed the contents of the developers' library organized by type of routine.

Database Routines

- ▶ AddField—Adds a new field to a table structure.
- ▶ DisplayQueryRecs—Displays the results of a query on a grid.
- ▶ IsEmpty—Returns **True** if a table is empty.
- ▶ LoadQuery—Loads and executes a saved query.
- ▶ SortTable—Sorts records in a table.

Internet Routines

- ▶ BrowseWebPage—Loads and displays an HTML document.
- ▶ GetFTPDir—Returns directory information from an FTP server.
- ▶ SendEMailMsg—Sends a message over the Internet.

▶ SetListViewHeadings—Prepares a ListView component for the display of file information read from an FTP server.

Multimedia Routines

▶ DisplayDirImages—Shows the next/previous graphic in a directory.

▶ PlayWaveFile—Plays a .WAV (wave) audio file.

▶ PlayVideo—Plays an .AVI file.

▶ ShowHotSpot—Defines a hotspot on a form or image control (automatically displays hand pointer when mouse cursor is over it).

▶ SoundEnabled—Returns **True** if a sound card is installed.

▶ TickerTape—Displays an animated scroll message within a simulated ticker tape machine.

▶ TransparentButton—Displays a transparent button over a user-defined graphic.

Rich Text Edit Routines

▶ OpenRichEdit—Loads a RichEdit document from disk.

▶ SaveRichEdit—Saves a RichEdit document to a file.

▶ SetAlignment—Sets the paragraph alignment of a selected block.

▶ SetBoldFace—Boldfaces a selected block.

▶ SetBullet—Inserts or removes a bullet from a RichEdit document.

▶ SetFontStyle—Sets the font style of a selected block.

▶ SetItalics—Italicizes a selected block.

▶ SetUnderline—Underlines a selected block.

▶ UndoChange—Reverses the last edit operation in a RichEdit document.

Spreadsheet Routines

▶ CreateChart—Creates a graph from a selected range in a worksheet.

▶ DrawObject—Inserts a drawing object into a Formula One worksheet.

▶ FormatWorksheet—Formats a cell range in a Formula One worksheet.

▶ PrintWorksheet—Prints a Formula One worksheet.

Screen Routines

▶ BlockShadow—Displays a message with a block shadow effect.

▶ ColorMessage—Shows a message with each letter in a different color.

▶ CustomCursor—Displays a user-defined mouse cursor.

▶ DelayMessage—Shows a message with a delayed effect.

▶ MessageBlink—Shows a message with three dots blinking after it.

▶ ShowScrSaver—Displays a customizable screen saver.

▶ ShowTNail—Loads a bitmap onto a form and proportionally reduces its size for viewing purposes.

▶ TileBitmap—Tiles the screen with a user-defined graphic.

String Routines

▶ IsNumeric—Returns **True** if a string contains a numeric value.

▶ StrCenter—Correctly centers a variable length string on a form at run-time.

▶ StrDeleteAll—Deletes all occurrences of a character from a string.

▶ StrExtractCmd—Extracts and returns an argument from a command string.

▶ StrFormatUpper—Capitalizes the first letter of each word in a string.

▶ StrReplaceAll—Replaces all occurrences of a character in a string with another character.

▶ StrReverse—Returns a string with its characters reversed.

▶ StrRightChar—Returns the rightmost character from a string.

▶ StrStripSpaces—Removes blank spaces from a string.

String Grid Routines

▶ ClrStrGrid—Clears a string grid.

▶ InitStringGrid—Initializes a string grid.

▶ OpenStringGrid—Restores a string grid saved with SaveStringGrid.

▶ SaveStringGrid—Saves a string grid to a file.

▶ WeeklySchedule—Displays a weekly time schedule on a string grid.

System Routines

▶ ChangeSearchPath—Changes the drive letter of a search path from a CD-ROM path to the equivalent path on a local hard drive.

▶ CheckPentium—Reports whether a Pentium processor is faulty.

▶ FileCopyList—Copies a list of files in a directory to an alternate drive.

▶ WinDir—Returns the Windows or Windows\System directory.

Utility Routines

▶ ComparePaths—Compares two directories and creates a list of files that are not common between paths.

▶ ConvertFraction—Converts a decimal to a fraction.

▶ GetDay—Returns the current day of the week.

▶ NextControl—Enables tabbing with the Enter key.

▶ SearchListItem—Searches a list box and returns the closest match to keys typed in an edit component.

▶ ShowHelpTopic—Displays context-sensitive Help for an application.

Security Routines

▶ DecryptMsg—Decrypts a string encrypted with EncryptMsg.

▶ EncryptMsg—Encrypts a string for security purposes.

Over the entran
temple a
was a famous in

Part 1
Programming in Delphi

Chapter 1:   The Road Ahead

Chapter 2:   Creating Interfaces

Chapter 3:   Working with Forms

Chapter 4:   Programming Standards

Chapter 5:   Working with Procedures and
             Functions

Chapter 6:   Creating Menus

Chapter 7:   Dealing with Errors

Chapter 8:   Working with Databases

Chapter 9:   Using Structured Query Language

Chapter 10: Building Reports

Chapter 11: Developing Multimedia Applications

Chapter 12: Building User-Defined Components

Chapter 13: Delphi and the Internet

Getting Started
with Delphi

The Delphi
Environment

Working with
Dialog Boxes

Working with Data
Types

Component Basics

Working with Units

Deleting Object References

Managing Projects

Chapter 1
The Road Ahead

We live in a world full of objects. The chairs we sit in, the desks we work at, the cars we drive in are all examples of objects. Each type of object has characteristics that separate it from other types of objects. A desk, for example, has legs, a hard top, some drawers, and other smaller components such as nuts, bolts, and brackets that are used to assemble the whole. If we were to lay out the main characteristics of a desk, we might come up with something like this:

My Desk = Object

Characteristics are:

1 Top

4 Legs

6 Drawers

6 Handles

In addition to its characteristics, an object can also be described according to the class it belongs to. For example, a desk can be classified as an object of type Office Equipment just like a rake or a hoe could be categorized as Gardening Equipment.

Computers are really no different than this. In Windows, for instance, virtually everything on the screen makes up a different object. Figure 1.1 shows examples of some common Windows objects we use every day.

The objects in Figure 1.1 appear to look very different, but they all have one thing in common: Objects have properties that control their appearance and behavior. For example, when you click on the Start button in Windows 95, a pop-up list of program options appears (see Figure 1.2).

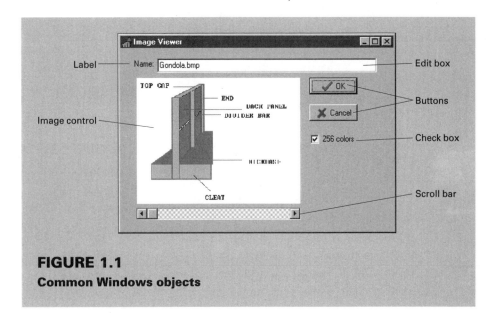

FIGURE 1.1
Common Windows objects

Choosing an item subsequently from this menu then causes another action to take place. Thus the Start button automatically "knows" that when it is clicked, it should perform the following tasks:

▶ Show button inverted to make it look as if it were physically pressed.

▶ Display a list of choices to the user in a pop-up window.

In addition to the actions that it performs, the Start button also has properties that make it appear the way it does. From a simple observation, we can see the button has at least the following properties:

▶ A Caption property that shows the Start prompt

▶ An Icon property that shows the Windows logo

▶ A Left property and a Top property to determine its relative horizontal and vertical position on the screen

▶ A Width property and a Height property to indicate the size of the button

▶ A Foreground Color property and a Background Color property

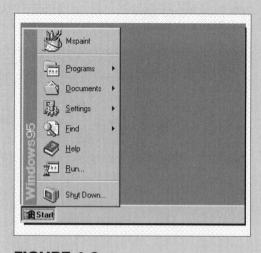

FIGURE 1.2
The Start menu in Windows 95

In short, objects have properties that can be customized to control the way they look and respond. This flexible system provides the ability to take a generic object such as a command button, customize it and use the same button object in other programs. For example, notice the resemblance between the Start button in Windows 95 and the Go button in CompuServe 3.0 (see Figure 1.3). Although one has an icon and is a little bigger than the other, both have a 3D look, use the same basic colors and are inverted when they are selected. As you might expect, this is no coincidence. These buttons are used in many Windows applications and for a good reason: Programmers do not waste time reinventing the wheel. Once an object has been programmed, there is no need to reprogram it. The same object can easily be reused in other programs.

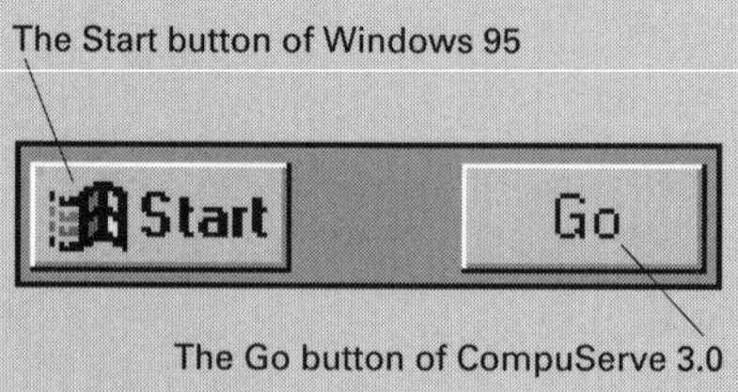

The Start button of Windows 95

Start   **Go**

The Go button of CompuServe 3.0

FIGURE 1.3
Button objects

Not surprisingly, Delphi, being a Windows-based application, makes heavy use of objects. Although the concept of object-oriented programming may seem a little abstract at first, Delphi makes working with objects easy. Even if you have never written a program before, you can quickly create rich and robust applications in Delphi using its visual design tools. In this chapter, you will learn how to produce simple Delphi applications that make use of standard Windows objects.

Getting Started with Delphi

The following discussion assumes that you have already installed Delphi on your system. Because the best way to learn Delphi is to use it, please install it now, if you have not already done so. You will want to have Delphi running as you work through this chapter.

To start Delphi,

1 From the Start menu, choose the Programs item.

2 Move the mouse pointer to the Borland Delphi 3.0 folder.

3 Choose the Delphi 3.0 icon to start the program.

The Delphi Environment

When you first load Delphi, the screen is divided into several parts. At the top of the screen, drop-down menus provide access to the program's commands. The toolbar in the upper-left corner provides quick access to many commonly used menu items. Figure 1.4 shows the toolbar and what each of its buttons does.

In the middle of the screen you will notice there is a window that shows the caption Form1 (see Figure 1.5). This is the default form. You use forms in Delphi to place the graphical objects that make up the way a program appears when it runs.

Above the form is a palette that displays the type of objects that can be added to forms. These visual tools, known as components, provide the means for creating applications in Delphi. Fundamentally speaking, there are only three steps in creating a Delphi application:

1 Select the components you wish to add to a form from the Component Palette (see Figure 1.6).

2 Customize each component by setting its properties with the Object Inspector (see Figure 1.7).

3 Write the short blocks of code that tell the program what to do after a component is selected.

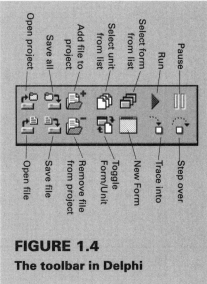

FIGURE 1.4
The toolbar in Delphi

Enough said. It is time to get your feet wet. In the following exercise, you will create a simple application that demonstrates the program development process. After performing this exercise, you should be able to:

▶ Add button components to forms.

▶ Customize the property settings of components.

▶ Create event handlers.

▶ Compile and run programs.

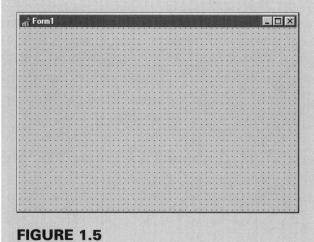

FIGURE 1.5
The default form

Exercise: Creating a Simple Program

1 From the Component Palette, add a button to the form by double clicking on the button icon (see Figure 1.8). Delphi automatically centers the button on the form.

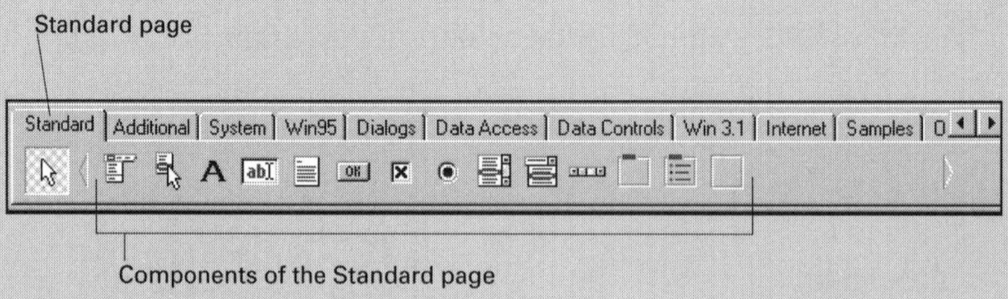

Standard page

Components of the Standard page

FIGURE 1.6
The Component Palette

2 Move the button to where it appears roughly in Figure 1.9 by clicking on the component and holding the left mouse button down while dragging the object to its new location (the same way you would move an icon in Windows).

3 Using the Object Inspector, change the default caption that appears on the button from Button1 to OK. Do this by clicking on the button once to make sure it is selected. Then click on the Caption property in the Object Inspector (see Figure 1.10). Afterwards, type **OK** to overwrite the existing caption.

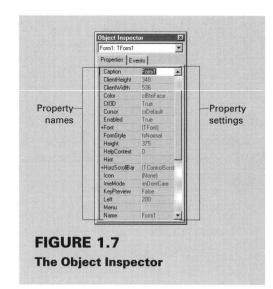

Property names

Property settings

FIGURE 1.7
The Object Inspector

Note *The Caption property of a button is merely a label that appears on the component. By changing this property, you do not actually rename the component. For this, you must set the Name property.*

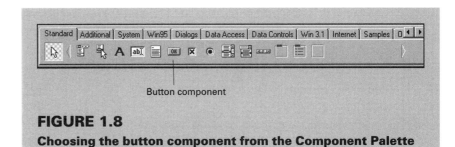

Button component

FIGURE 1.8
Choosing the button component from the Component Palette

4 Double-click on the button you added to the form to open the Code Editor. This is where you enter the lines of code that will tell the program what to do when someone clicks on the button to run the program. In the Code Editor, type the following lines between the **begin** and **end** reserved words:

```
ShowMessage ('Hello World!');
Close;
```

Be sure to include the single quotes around the message and to include the semicolon at the end of the line. Object Pascal, which Delphi uses as its base language, is not case sensitive. Therefore, you can enter this code in all caps, in lowercase, with an initial capital letter or in any combination in between.

Congratulations! You have just created your first Delphi program. To see how it works, choose the Run command from the Run menu. Delphi will now automatically compile the program to generate the run-time code it needs to execute the project[1]. Note that you could also execute the program by choosing the Run button from the toolbar or by pressing F9.

Note that if you receive an error message at this point, you will have to fix the problem before the program will run. Since the program contains only two lines of code, finding the error should not be too hard. Often a simple typo or forgotten symbol is the culprit.

Once you have the program running, click on the OK button. A small dialog box now appears showing the *Hello World!* message (see Figure 1.11). This dialog box is *modal*, which means that until you click on the OK button,

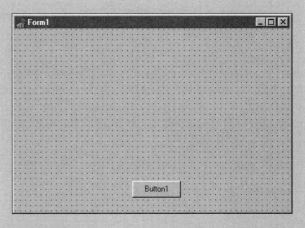

FIGURE 1.9
Positioning the button component on the form

Caption property

FIGURE 1.10
The Caption property of a button component

---

[1] When Delphi compiles an application, it translates the computer statements you write into executable code that the computer can understand. Since computers really only know one language (binary) this translation is necessary for Delphi to interpret the English-like commands you enter into a program.

no other task in the program can be performed. Although this may sound like a limitation, modal dialog boxes are actually quite useful. Since the user must click on the OK button before proceeding, it is more likely that a message appearing in a modal dialog box will be read. Thus you can use modal dialog boxes to show important messages and to capture the user's attention when necessary.

After you have read the message, click on the OK button to close the dialog box. The program will now end its run. Control now returns back to Delphi.

FIGURE 1.11
A simple dialog box

Closing a Form

The Close method, as you might expect, simply causes the form to unload (thereby ending the run of the program). Delphi automatically terminates a running program when the main form is closed. Notice here we slipped in another term: a *method*. A method is a pre-defined language element in Object Pascal that causes an action to occur on an object. In this case, the object that the Close method acts upon is a form. Thus when the Close method executes, the form is given an instruction to unload itself.

You may wonder what would happen if you forgot to include the Close method in the program. How would the program ever end? By default, every Delphi form has an icon in the upper-left corner that shows a list of form-specific options when you click on it (see Figure 1.12). By selecting the Close command from this menu, the form will automatically unload itself.

Renaming Components

In the preceding exercise, the default name of the Button1 component was used to simplify the example. Delphi automatically assigns names in numeric order to components when you add them to a form. For example, the first button component placed on a form is given the name Button1, the next one is called Button2, and so on. Although renaming button components is not mandatory, it is strongly recommended that you change these default names so that you will remember the purpose of each one. It is easier to understand and remember

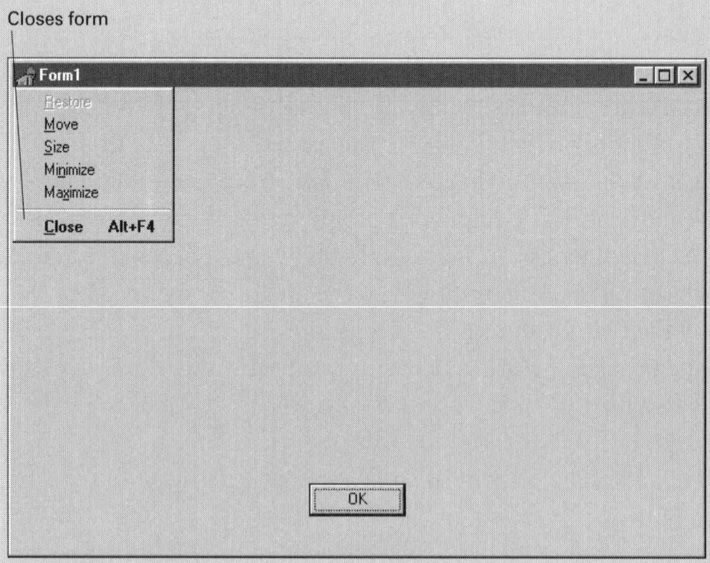

Closes form

FIGURE 1.12
The Control Box menu of a form

their functions if you assign more descriptive names, such as btnOK, btnCancel, and btnHelp. Notice the use of the *btn* component prefix. By using prefixes to distinguish among different kinds of components, your programs will be easier to read and maintain.

Using the Object Inspector, try changing the name of the component from Button1 to btnOK. Do this by clicking on the Name property and then typing in the new value. Note that when you click on this property, Delphi automatically highlights the existing value so that any key entered will erase the old name. If you accidentally change a property's value, however, you can easily restore its original setting by pressing the Escape key before pressing Enter or clicking on another property.

> **Note** *If you need to, you can use the vertical scroll bar in the Object Inspector to scroll up and down in the property list to see properties.*

You may wonder how Delphi knew that you wanted to change the name of the button and not the form or possibly other components that might appear on it. Since the button was the last component you were working with on the form before you double-clicked on the component to edit its associated code, this component remains the currently selected object in the Object Inspector. Aside from this, you can easily tell which component on the form has focus (that is, attention) by looking at the name that appears in the upper-left corner of the Object Inspector. Before you renamed it, the name was Button1. Figure 1.13 shows how the Object Inspector should appear now with the new name.

Notice that the btnOK button has another name next to it in the Object Inspector. This name is the class name of the object. Going back to our earlier discussion, you may recall that objects can be classified by the kinds of objects they are. For example, a desk can be classified as an object of type Office Equipment. Similarly, a button can be classified by the type of component that it is. By convention, Delphi precedes each class name with a capital T. Thus a button component is an object of type TButton.

Likewise, the class name of a form is TForm. Since this is getting a little ahead of ourselves, we will come back to this discussion at a later time. For now, it is enough to know that each component you place on a form has a class name and that each class has properties and methods that apply specifically to the type of object it is.

FIGURE 1.13
The Object Inspector after setting the Name property

> **Note** *In Chapter 12, you will learn more about classes and how to generate your own user-defined components.*

Coding Event Procedures

Unlike more traditional development systems, Delphi is *event driven*—meaning that it does not simply execute the code in a program one line at a time until it runs out of instructions. Instead, it waits for *events* to occur in the program and then executes the code associated with those events. What is an event? Virtually any action initiated by the user or by the operating system creates an event. For example, the following are all events:

▶ Clicking on a button

▶ Moving the mouse pointer over an object

▶ Selecting an item from a menu

▶ Retrieving a file

▶ Printing a document

▶ Sending a file via modem

Earlier in this chapter, you learned how to generate an event handler. When you double click on a component to enter the Code Editor, Delphi creates an event procedure that is linked to the component. For example:

```
procedure TForm1.Button1Click(Sender: TObject);
begin

end;
```

Between the **begin** and **end** block, any code you add to the procedure will execute when the user clicks on the button at run-time. Inside the parentheses, information is passed to the event handler as a *parameter*. Put simply, a parameter is a value passed to a procedure. Although this is not a full definition of a parameter, it will do here for our purposes. In Chapter 5, you will learn how to work with parameters. For now, simply keep in mind that event handlers are the means for Delphi programs to interact with users.

It is very important to understand the difference between *design-time* and *run-time*. At design-time, you add components to forms, set their properties, and create event handlers. At run-time, you use the buttons and other components on a form to interact with the program.

Working with Dialog Boxes

Earlier you saw how to display messages using the ShowMessage procedure in the exercise for creating a simple program. Delphi also provides an easy way of retrieving input from users using a similar routine called the InputBox function. Like ShowMessage, InputBox appears to the user as a modal dialog box (see Figure 1.14). The following example shows how it can be applied:

```
procedure TForm1.Button1Click(Sender: TObject);
var
  Response: String;
```

```
begin
   Response := InputBox('Welcome to my program',
                'What is your name?', '');
end;
```

The **var** reserved word declares a *variable* that will hold the answer the user supplies. A *variable* is a name you define that is used by Delphi as a reference to store a value that can change in a program. Thus, *Response* is a variable that will contain the answer the user enters when the program runs. *Response* is declared as type String.

A *string* is a special data type that holds non-numeric information. For example, a name is a string because it contains a succession of characters that are s-t-r-u-n-g together.

The prompt that the InputBox function shows is user-definable and can be customized in many ways. In the preceding example, the string *Welcome to my program* appears in what is called the *title bar* of the box (see Figure 1.15). The second string after the comma shows the actual prompt that will be displayed to the user:

```
What is your name?
```

After the second comma, a set of single quotes appears (that is, ''). This empty string is where you would place a default value that will be assigned to the *Response* variable if the user does not type an answer. For example, the following code assigns *Guest User* to the *Response* variable if the user does not type in another name:

```
var
   Response: String;
begin
   Response := InputBox('Welcome to my program', 'What is your name?',
                'Guest User');
end;
```

Notice that in order to make an assignment, you must precede the equal sign with a colon. When used together like this, these two symbols create what is known as the

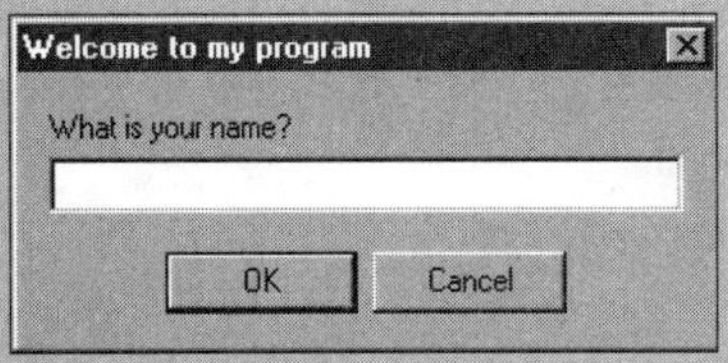

FIGURE 1.14

The InputBox function dialog box

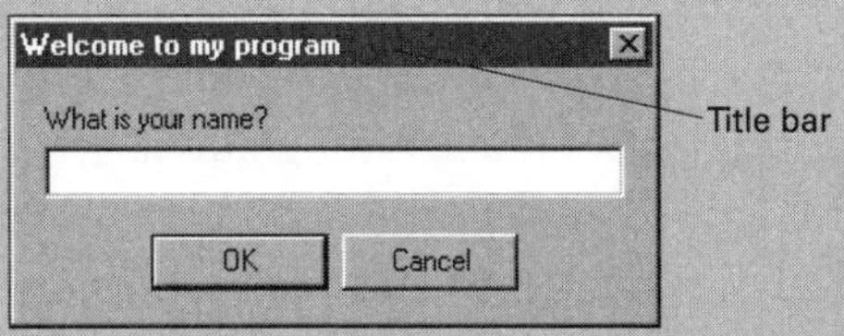

FIGURE 1.15

The title bar of the InputBox dialog

assignment operator. The variable that you assign the answer to must be of the same type as the value it is being assigned. Thus it would be wrong to try to assign a number to the *Response* variable since *Response* has been declared as a string.

If you need to make an assignment that requires the use of numbers, there are several ways you can do this. For whole numbers, you declare a variable as type Integer. For example:

```
procedure TForm1.Button1Click(Sender: TObject);

var
  x: Integer;

begin
  { Initialize x }
  x := 1;
  x := x + 6;
end;
```

Notice that the **var** reserved word must appear before the **begin** in the procedure. Variable x is declared as type Integer in the declaration section of the event handler. Between the **begin** and the **end** block, an assignment is made to the variable. Variable x is initialized as 1 using the assignment operator. Afterwards, 6 is added to x to give it a new value of 7.

Adding Comments

Notice the words appearing above the first assignment inside the braces. This is a comment. When Delphi encounters a comment in a program, it simply ignores everything between the beginning and ending braces. Comments are useful for describing what a program does.

> **Note** *Some programmers make the mistake of assuming comments are not important. Nothing could be further from the truth! Even if you understand everything in your programs, six months from now, you may not remember anything about the code unless you take the time to add comments.*

Another important point about comments is that they are not intended to appear *after the fact*. Comments must be added to programs as you write code or else they serve little purpose. In some cases, you may find that it is hard to remember what a routine does even a few days after writing it. Without comments, key points to understanding the logic in a program may be forgotten forever. To sum things up, comments are important; use them!

Delphi also permits two other ways in which comments can be entered into a program. In addition to braces, you can use a pair of beginning and ending parentheses together with asterisks to denote a comment. For example:

```
(* Comment text appears here and can be stretched across
   multiple lines *)
```

Another way to add a comment is to use two forward slashes like this:

```
ShowMessage ('Hello World!');   //  Comment text added here
```

The latter method is useful when you want to add a comment to the end of a line. Note that if you use this method, however, you cannot extend the comment over multiple lines in a program. Which method of adding comments is better depends on your point of view. There is no single correct method for adding comments to a program. Some developers feel it is best to stick with a single commenting style. However, this is entirely up to you.

```
(*==================== * Comments * ====================*)
(*   If you like to dress up your programs to make them  *)
(*   visually more appealing and easier to read, feel    *)
(*   free to experiment!                                  *)
(* =====================================================*)
```

Using Constants

Like comments, *constants* are an important feature that are often neglected by some programmers. A constant is a name that you assign to a value that does *not* change in a program. For example:

```
const
   SectionSize = 15Ø; // inches
```

SectionSize in this example is a constant that indicates the number of inches in a shelving section. By incorporating constants in an application, your program will be easier to read and maintain. Without constants, mystery numbers appearing in code can be quite bewildering. For example, can you tell what the following code does?

```
procedure TForm1.Button1Click(Sender: TObject);

{ Compute total widgets }

var
   TotalWidgets: Integer;
```

```
begin
  TotalWidgets := 8 + 2;
end;
```

Although this code contains a comment, it is still not easy to understand the procedure because no constants were used. However, if the procedure were rewritten the following way, you would at least have some clue as to what the mystery numbers 8 and 2 meant in the preceding example:

```
procedure TForm1.Button1Click(Sender: TObject);

{ Compute total widgets }

const
  StandardWidgets = 8;
  Spares = 2;

var
  TotalWidgets: Integer;
begin
  TotalWidgets := StandardWidgets + Spares;
end;
```

Working with Data Types

Previously in this chapter, you learned how to define Integer and String type variables. Delphi also provides other data types you can use in programs. Table 1.1 summarizes the data types used most often in Delphi. In later chapters, you will learn when to use these data types and how to apply them in typical business applications.

TABLE 1.1 BASIC DATA TYPES IN DELPHI.

Type	Range	Size in Bytes
Boolean*	1 byte	1
Byte	0 to 255	1
Char	1 byte	1
Comp	-2^{63} to $2^{63}-1$	8
Double	5.0×10^{-324} to 1.7×10^{308}	8
Extended	3.4×10^{-4932} to 1.1×10^{4932}	10
Integer**	-2,147,483,648 to 2,147,483,647	2
LongInt	-2,147,483,648 to 2,147,483,647	4
Real	2.9×10^{-39} to 1.7×10^{38}	6
ShortInt	-128 to 127	1
Single	$\pm 1.5 \times 10^{-45}$ to 3.4×10^{38}	4
String	1 to 2 GB	variable
Word	0 to 65535	2

* Logical True/False.

** In a 32-bit application, Integer and LongInt have the same range.

Component Basics

Previously, you created a simple program that made use of a button component. In addition to command buttons, a program can contain many other types of components. Each tab on the Component Palette contains a different category of objects. The Standard Page contains the graphical controls used most often in programs. Figure 1.16 shows the Standard Page and its associated buttons. An explanation of what each of these buttons does is presented in Chapter 2. In the following section, you will see how to incorporate two components from the Standard Page on forms (the label component and the edit component). Afterwards, you will learn the Delphi tools available that make working with forms easier.

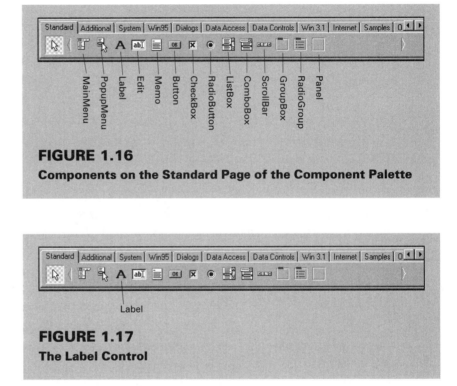

FIGURE 1.16
Components on the Standard Page of the Component Palette

Using Labels

Label components allow you to display prompts and messages to users. You use label components to display strings that you do not want the user to modify at run-time. To add a label to a form, double click on the Label button in the Component Palette (see Figure 1.17).

FIGURE 1.17
The Label Control

Once a label control (that is, component) has been added to a form, it appears with its default caption (Label1, Label2, Label3, and so on). To change the string that the component displays, first make sure the label has focus by clicking on it once. Several black squares appear around the outer perimeter of the control. These are size handles which you use to resize components. By clicking on any of these size handles and dragging the outer borders of the control, the label will stretch vertically or horizontally.

> **Note** *You can also add components to a form using the View | Component List command in Delphi.*

Label components are typically initialized at design-time. In many cases, you only need to set the Caption property of the label using the Object Inspector. Occasionally, it becomes necessary to change the caption of a label at run-time. To do this, you assign a string to the Caption property of the label like this:

```
Label1.Caption := 'Computing totals, please wait...';
```

The period placed between Label1 and Caption is a separator that informs Delphi that Caption is a property of Label1. In addition to setting the label's caption, you can also read the value it contains. To do this, you assign the Caption property of the label to a variable. Since the Caption property of a label control is a string, the value that it contains must be assigned to a variable that is of the same type. For example, the following code sets a string variable equal to the Caption property of Label1:

```
procedure TForm1.btnOKClick(Sender: TObject);


{ Assign label's caption to variable S }


var
  S: String;
begin
  S := Label1.Caption;
end;
```

For simplification, many of the examples in this chapter use the default names of components. However, labels, like other components, have a Name property that can be set to reference the control more easily. When referring to labels, this book often uses an *lbl* prefix to denote labels. For example:

```
lblMessage.Caption := 'Printing file...';
```

Tip *Although it is not mandatory to change the default names given to labels, you will find as a general rule that if you must reference a label at run-time, it is a good idea to change the default name given to the control. Otherwise it becomes very difficult to determine which label is which on the form.*

Adding Edit Components to Forms

The edit component provides an easy way of obtaining input from users. Edit components appear to the user as input boxes. Thus a group of edit components on a form can be used to create a custom data entry view. To place an edit component on a form, you select the Edit button from the Component Palette (see Figure 1.18). Once added to a form, the Text property of an edit control retrieves the value the user inputs. To get this value, you assign the Text property of the control to a string. For example:

```
procedure TForm1.btnOKClick(Sender: TObject);


{ Read text box and assign answer to
  variable S}
```

```
var
  S: String;
begin
  S := Edit1.Text;
  ShowMessage ('The value you typed was ' + S);
end;
```

By default, the Text property of an edit Component is equal to the name of the control. Since there is no reason for the user to see this value, typically you use the Object Inspector to delete the default value of the Text property at de-sign-time. Occasionally, it becomes necessary to clear the Text property of an edit control at run-time. For example, you can automatically

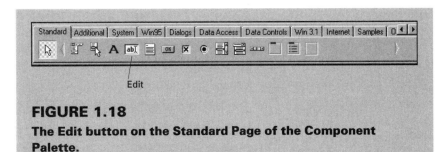

Edit

FIGURE 1.18
The Edit button on the Standard Page of the Component Palette.

clear a password from an edit component if the user types the wrong password. To ac-complish this, you set the Text property of the component to a null string:

```
Edit1.Text := '';
```

Likewise, if you need to display a message to the user, you could also set the Text property to an initialized string. For instance, the following assignment sets the Text property of Edit1 to the default path where the program will look for data files:

```
Edit1.Text := 'c:\myapp\data';
```

By displaying the path to the user in an edit component, the user can modify the default path and supply a new one. Thus, edit components provide an easy way of ac-quiring information and interacting with users.

Properties of Edit Components

Edit components also have other useful properties. The MaxLength property deter-mines the maximum number of characters the user can enter into the control. This property is useful for validating input and making sure the user does not enter a string that is too long. For example, if the MaxLength property is set to 25 characters and the user tries to enter more characters than are permitted, an error sound will be played.

Note *The actual sound you will hear is dependent on the default error sound listed in the Windows Control Panel.*

Another useful property that edit components have is the PasswordChar property. By default, any keys typed in an edit component at run-time are visible to the user. By setting the PasswordChar property to a value other than its default, the control will suppress the display of characters typed and show only the PasswordChar. For example, if you set PasswordChar to an asterisk, then only asterisks will appear in the control when the user enters the password.

Edit components also have many other useful properties. This chapter covers the basics of the control. In later discussions, you will learn how to apply its other properties in developing more advanced applications.

Aligning Controls

When working with controls, often it becomes necessary to align components on a form. Delphi lets you automatically align components using its built-in alignment features. To align controls on a form:

1 Select the controls you want to align by dragging the mouse over the range. To do this, you must first click on the form to give it focus. Once this is done, you can select the controls by holding the left button down as you drag.

2 Press the right mouse button to display the context-sensitive pop-up menu of control options (see Figure 1.19).

3 Choose the Align... command. The Alignment dialog box will appear (see Figure 1.20).

4 Choose the alignment configuration you wish to use.

Components can be aligned on a form in relation to one another or to the form itself. Figure 1.21 shows several different possibilities that can be achieved.

Adding Multiple Components of the Same Type

Another useful feature of Delphi's form designer is its ability to repeat the last control added to a form. This feature is particularly useful when you need to add several components of the same type. For example, if you know you are going to have multiple buttons on a form, you can easily redraw this component without having to choose it each time from the Component Palette.

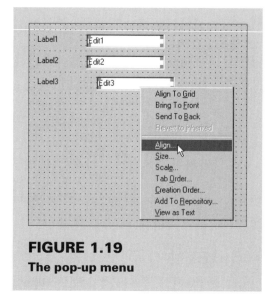

FIGURE 1.19
The pop-up menu

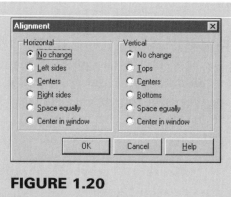

FIGURE 1.20
The Alignment dialog box

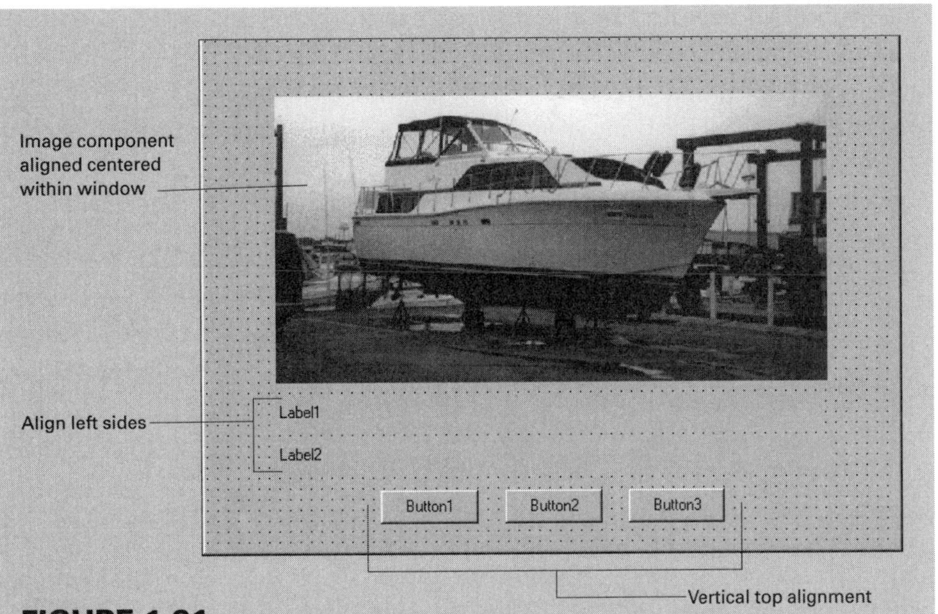

Image component
aligned centered
within window

Align left sides

Label1

Label2

Button1   Button2   Button3

Vertical top alignment

FIGURE 1.21
Aligning components on a form

To repeat the last component added to a form:

1 Hold the Shift key down.

2 From the Component Palette, choose the control you wish to add.

3 Release the Shift key.

4 Click on the form where you want the first occurrence of the component to appear.

5 Click on the form where you want the next occurrence of the control to appear. Repeat this step for each occurrence of the component you wish to add.

6 When you have finished, click on the picture of the arrow pointer that is on the left end of the Component Palette to stop adding components to the form.

Setting the Tab Order

The *tab order* is the order in which components on a form receive focus when you press the tab key. Delphi automatically sets the tab order according to the order in which controls were added to the form. Since forms often change during the design process, there is no guarantee that the order in which components were added will match the expected tab order. Therefore, it often becomes necessary to reset the tab order.

There are two ways to adjust the tab order of components. Using the Object Inspector, you can set the TabOrder property of each component. The first control in the tab order should be set to 0. Another way is to right-click the form (or any component on the form). A pop-up list of component options will appear. From the pop-up menu, choose the Tab Order... command. Afterwards, the Edit Tab Order dialog box will appear showing you a list of all the components on the form that can receive focus.

To change the order of a component in the Edit Tab Order dialog box, use the mouse to drag the name of the component to where you want it to appear in the tab order list. If you do not like dragging, you can also reset the tab order by clicking on a component name in the list and choosing the up or down arrow buttons.

> **Note** *You can also access the Edit Tab Order dialog box by selecting the Tab Order... command from the Edit menu.*

Exercise: Creating a Sales Tax Calculator

In the following exercise, you will learn how to work with label controls and edit components. After this exercise you should be able to:

▶ Create an interface using label components and edit controls.

▶ Get input from users.

▶ Perform simple calculations.

▶ Convert data types.

1 From the File menu, choose New.... The New Items dialog box now appears (see Figure 1.22). Click on OK to accept the default choice and thereby create a new application. Before starting a new project, Delphi will prompt you first to save the current project. Click on No.

2 Using the Component Palette, add five label components, three edit components and two button components to the form. Place each object roughly where they appear in Figure 1.23.

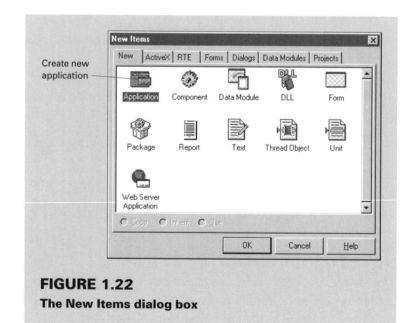

FIGURE 1.22
The New Items dialog box

3 Use the Object Inspector now to set the properties of each object as follows:

Component	Property	Value
Label1	Caption	Item Name:
Label2	Caption	Item Cost:
Label3	Caption	Total Units:
Label4	Caption	Amount Due:
Label5	AutoSize	False
	Name	lblTotal
	Caption	(null string)
Edit1	Name	ItemName
	Text	(null string)
Edit2	Name	ItemCost
	Text	(null string)
Edit3	Name	TotalUnits
	Text	(null string)
Button1	Name	btnOK
	Caption	OK
Button2	Name	btnCancel
	Caption	Close
Form1	Position	poScreenCenter

Figure 1.24 shows how the form should look when you are done. If it does not look this way, go back and double check the properties of each component.

4 Double click on the OK button and add the missing lines of code into the procedure below. Don't worry if you do not understand all that is going on here. In Chapters 4 and 5, you will learn how to perform arithmetic operations and how to work with functions.

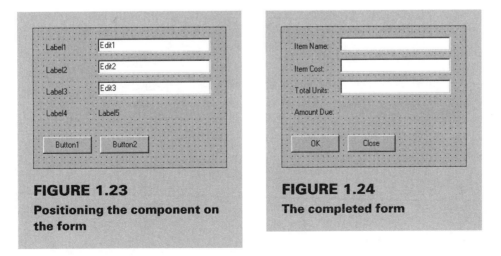

FIGURE 1.23

Positioning the component on the form

FIGURE 1.24

The completed form

```
procedure TForm1.btnOKClick(Sender: TObject);

{ Compute sales tax for item }

const
  SalesTax = 0.07;
var
  Cost, SalesTotal: Extended;
  Units: Integer;
begin
  Cost := StrToFloat(ItemCost.Text);
  Units := StrToInt(TotalUnits.Text);
  SalesTotal := ((Cost * Units) + (Cost * Units) * SalesTax);
  lblTotal.Caption := FloatToStr(SalesTotal);
end;
```

5 Using the Toggle Form/Unit button on the toolbar, switch back to the form (see Figure 1.25).

6 Double click on the Close button and add the following lines:

```
{ End session }

Close;
```

7 Run the program by pressing the F9 shortcut key. If you receive an error message, go back and compare each line listed in Steps 4 and 6 to what you typed. If Delphi reports an error in a message box informing you that the program has caused an *exception error*, don't worry, you will not blow smoke out of your speakers. However, before the program will run successfully, you must find the error, fix it, and then use the Program Reset command from the Run menu to rebuild the project.

Note *Exception errors are explained in Chapter 7, "Dealing with Errors."*

8 Once you have the program running, use the following data to test the program:

Item Name: Widget

Item Cost: 25.50

Total Units: 4

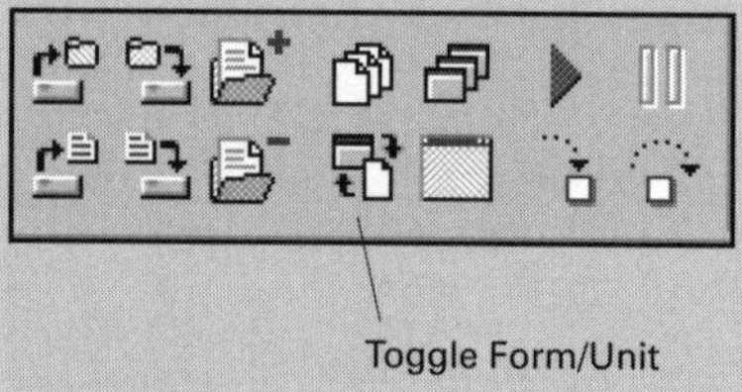

Toggle Form/Unit

FIGURE 1.25
The Toggle Form/Unit button of the toolbar

9   Click on OK to compute the sales tax for the item. The answer now appears in the lblTotal label.

10   Choose the Close button to end the session.

Working with Units

Throughout this chapter, you have seen examples of how Object Pascal can be used in programs. By entering code instructions in event handlers, you define the actions that occur on a form at run-time. Behind the scenes, Delphi creates the necessary associations to link the program instructions you enter in the Code Editor to forms. At the most basic level, Delphi uses a special file called a *unit* to make these associations. When you enter Object Pascal code into the Code Editor, you are actually working in a unit.

Where did this unit come from? Delphi automatically creates a new unit each time you begin a new session or create a new project. In the process, it establishes the necessary links to associate forms with units. This system has its advantages and its disadvantages. From an experienced programmer's perspective, Delphi frees you from having to worry about routine tasks that require you to write unnecessary code. This means, however, that there is going to be some code in the program that the beginner will not understand at first. Examples of such coding are as follows:

```
unit Unit1;

interface

uses
  Windows, Messages, SysUtils, Classes, Graphics, Controls, Forms,
  Dialogs;

type
  TForm1 = class(TForm)
  private
    { Private declarations }
  public
    { Public declarations }
  end;

var
  Form1: TForm1;

implementation
```

```
{$R *.DFM}

end.
```

This is what the default unit Delphi creates looks like. Although you do not need to understand all of this now, a quick overview is provided here to help you get started. If after reading through this discussion you are still confused, don't worry. By the time you have finished reading this book, you will have mastered units.

The first line of the default unit simply declares the unit name and follows it by the required semicolon:

```
unit Unit1;
```

By default, the unit is given the name Unit1. You can of course rename the unit. However, there is no need to change the name of the unit in the program. Instead, you use the File | Save As... command in Delphi to rename the file. Since units are really Object Pascal source code files, they are given a .PAS file extension. If you omit this extension when saving the file, Delphi will automatically assign the correct one.

After the unit declaration is a line that begins with **interface**. The **interface** section of a unit tells Delphi what objects, variables, procedures, and so on are accessible to other units. If you do not define variables in this section, they will not be accessible to other units. Following the **interface** reserved word is an optional **uses** clause. If a unit contains a **uses** clause in the **interface** section, it must appear immediately after the **interface** reserved word. The **uses** clause specifies which units the current unit is accessing.

The default unit is given access to the most common units needed in applications. For now, it is not so important that you know what each of these does. What is important is that you realize that this is how your programs can gain access to other units and thereby include important code and definitions needed to make your programs work.

The **type** reserved word comes next. Put simply, the **type** reserved word creates the association necessary for the form to exist within the unit. The **private** section of the **type** specifies whether the properties of the form will be accessible (**public**) or not accessible (**private**) to other units. For example:

```
type
  TForm1 = class(TForm)
  private
    { Private declarations }
  public
    { Public declarations }
  end;
```

Below the **type** reserved word comes a **var** in the unit. Here a name is given to the form to give it a memory address. Although the form has already been declared as an object type, Delphi still requires the **var** declaration to associate the form's name with a memory address. Confused? Don't worry, we're almost done with this chapter. Chapter 2 and most discussions thereafter will be considerably easier.

```
var
    Form1: TForm1;
```

The final part of a unit is called the **implementation** section. This is where the code you enter for event handlers appears. For instance, going back to the first exercise where you placed a button on the form and entered some code into a procedure, Delphi adds the following boldfaced lines into the unit:

```
unit Unit1;

interface

uses
   Windows, Messages, SysUtils, Classes, Graphics, Controls, Forms,
   Dialogs;
type
   TForm1 = class(TForm)
     Button1: TButton;
     procedure Button1Click(Sender: TObject);
   private
     { Private declarations }
   public
     { Public declarations }
   end;

var
   Form1: TForm1;

implementation

{$R *.DFM}

procedure TForm1.Button1Click(Sender: TObject);
begin

end;
```

```
end.
```

> **Note** *These lines are boldfaced purely for reference here. Delphi does not actually apply the boldface style.*

Notice the new declarations for the Button1 object in the **interface** section. Delphi adds this automatically. Also note that it adds the correct procedure heading for the event handler in the **implementation** section.

One final note about units. The very last line of every unit must contain a period after the **end** reserved word. If you accidentally remove this period, the program will not run until you fix the problem. However, Delphi can usually detect this error and you will most likely not stumble if you receive such an error message.

Deleting Object References

With all this automatic handling going on, one might wonder, how does a person remove an object from a form that is no longer needed?

Before you can delete a component on a form, you must take into account any event handlers associated with that control. For example, if you entered some code in the click event of a button, then you must manually remove the code by pressing Ctrl+Y to delete each line inside the procedure. Or if you prefer, you can erase the code using the Edit | Cut command. Don't worry about removing the procedure headings, Delphi will handle this for you.

Once you have removed all the code inside the event handlers, switch to Form View and delete the component by pressing the Del key. Once you have done this, Delphi will remove all references to the component from the unit the next time you compile or run the program (including those listed in the **interface** section). If you do not remove the component this way, you will have to manually remove all the object's references from the unit yourself.

> **Note** *Before you can cut text using the Edit | Cut command, you must first select the range with a mouse.*

Managing Projects

Delphi saves all the units, forms, and related files of an application as a project. As mentioned before, units have a .PAS file extension. When saving a project, Delphi will prompt you first to name any files that have not been previously named. To save a project, from the File menu choose the Save Project As... command. If you do not specify the file extension, Delphi will automatically add a .DPR (Delphi Project File) extension to the name. Forms (which have a .DFM file extension), are automatically named using the base name of the .PAS file.

For example, if the name of the unit is MYUNIT.PAS, the form's corresponding name will be MYUNIT.DFM. Similarly, when you compile a project, Delphi automatically generates one .DCU (Delphi Compiled Unit) for each unit in the project. But the most important file that it creates is the executable (.EXE) file. The executable file allows you to run your program as a stand-alone application.

To derive the name of the executable file, Delphi uses the name of the project. Thus, if the project is called MYPROG.DPR, the executable name will be MYPROG.EXE. Executable files produced by Delphi do not require a run-time library (unless you use packages, discussed below). Thus Delphi applications are typically easier to install than programs written in other development systems.

The packages feature allows you to compile your application so that it can take advantage of code-sharing and reduce the executable size of an application. By default, Delphi now compiles applications using packages. For more information on this subject, see Chapter 12, "Creating User-Defined Components," and Chapter 13, "Delphi and the Internet."

Summary

In this chapter you have learned how to create applications in Delphi. Specifically, you have learned how to:

- ▶ Add components to forms.

- ▶ Set their properties via the Object Inspector.

- ▶ Create event handlers.

- ▶ Execute projects.

- ▶ Display modal dialogs and input boxes.

- ▶ Work with standard components like command buttons, label controls, and edit components.

- ▶ Align components on forms.

- ▶ Repeat the last control added to a form.

- ▶ Set the tab order of controls.

- ▶ Work with units.

- ▶ Perform simple calculations.

- ▶ Convert data types.

- ▶ Save projects.

Standard
Components in
Delphi

Validating Program
Options at Run-
Time

Dressing Up
Interfaces

Inherited
Properties of Controls

Chapter 2
Creating Interfaces

In Chapter 1, you learned how to create simple interfaces in Delphi using buttons, labels, and edit components. Delphi also has many other controls you can use to create interfaces. In this chapter, you will learn how to incorporate some of these tools in applications. In addition, you will learn how to enable/disable controls, show/hide components, display help hints next to controls, and incorporate graphics in applications.

Standard Components in Delphi

Already you have seen how to generate simple programs in Delphi using buttons, labels, and edit components. Although simple to use, these three controls provide a strong foundation for developing Windows applications. In addition to these controls, Delphi provides several other components on just the Standard page of the Component Palette alone. Table 2.1 summarizes the graphical controls available on the Standard Page. In the following section, you will learn how to build projects using these controls.

Working with List Boxes

The TListBox component displays a list of selectable items. At run-time, the items that appear in the list can be chosen by clicking on a list item or by using the keyboard. The sample application LBOXPRJ.DPR, shown in Figure 2.1, demonstrates how to use list boxes. When the project loads, the FormCreate method executes to initialize the list. At the start of each session, Delphi automatically calls this method to create the main form:

```
procedure TForm1.FormCreate(Sender: TObject);

begin

    .     .     .
    .     .     .

end;
```

TABLE 2.1   COMPONENTS ON THE STANDARD PAGE OF THE COMPONENT PALETTE

Component	Description
MainMenu	Adds a menu bar with drop-down menus to a form.
PopupMenu	Associates a pop-up menu with a form.
Label	Displays text on a form that cannot be modified by the user.
Edit	Displays an input box that can be used for the purpose of entering data and modifying strings.
Memo	Displays a multi-line editing area where memos can be created and modified.
Button	Adds a push-button to a form.
CheckBox	Creates a toggle switch that displays a check mark in a box when the control is selected.
RadioButton	Draws an option button on a form that shows mutually exclusive choices to users.
ListBox	Creates a scrollable list of entries.
ComboBox	Creates a drop-down list of items the user can choose from. The list also contains an attached edit box where the user can type an entry to make a selection from the list.
ScrollBar	Draws a control that can be used to scroll other components such as windows or forms.
GroupBox	Draws a control that permits grouping of other components.
RadioGroup	Adds a container object to a form that displays groups of radio buttons.
Panel	Displays a panel on a form that can be used to hold other components and to create toolbars.

By default, when you double click on a form at design-time, Delphi places you inside the FormCreate event handler of that form. From there, you can enter any initialization code that the program must execute upon startup.

In order to understand how the list is initialized, it is important to realize that a property of an object can also itself be an object. For example, the Items property of a list box is actually an object, too. Since it is an object, the Items property has methods you can use to add, insert, or delete list elements. The following example shows how to add the text from an edit control to a list box:

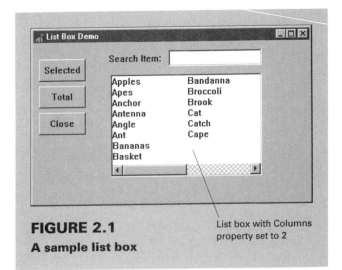

FIGURE 2.1
A sample list box

List box with Columns property set to 2

```
ListBox1.Items.Add (Edit1.Text);
```

The LBOXPRJ.DPR project uses the Add method of the Items object to initialize the list using a similar technique. However, instead of reading the text from an edit component, the items added are specified in the OnCreate event handler of the form:

```
procedure TForm1.FormCreate(Sender: TObject);
```

```
{ Fill list with search items }

begin

  ListBox1.Items.Add ('Apples');
  ListBox1.Items.Add ('Apes');
  ListBox1.Items.Add ('Anchor');
  ListBox1.Items.Add ('Antenna');
  ListBox1.Items.Add ('Angle');
  ListBox1.Items.Add ('Ant');
  ListBox1.Items.Add ('Bananas');
  ListBox1.Items.Add ('Basket');
  ListBox1.Items.Add ('Bandanna');
  ListBox1.Items.Add ('Broccoli');
  ListBox1.Items.Add ('Brook');
  ListBox1.Items.Add ('Cat');
  ListBox1.Items.Add ('Catch');
  ListBox1.Items.Add ('Cape');

end;
```

Once the list has been initialized, the user can choose an item from the list. To determine which element has been selected by the user, the following code can be used:

```
procedure TForm1.Button1Click(Sender: TObject);
var
  CurrentItem: Integer;
begin
  CurrentItem := ListBox1.ItemIndex;
end;
```

The ItemsIndex property returns the position of the currently selected item in the list. Like the tab order of controls, the list begins at 0 not 1. Since it is more likely that you will want to see the actual text of the item the user has selected, the position that the ItemIndex property returns can also be assigned as an index to the Items property to retrieve the user's selection:

```
ShowMessage (ListBox1.Items[ListBox1.ItemIndex]);
```

Note that this example does not take into account what would happen if no item in the list was selected. When this occurs, the program will generate an exception error that will cause it to terminate if no error checking is done. To avoid this, you can place the ShowMessage procedure in a **try..except** block like this:

```
try
   ShowMessage (ListBox1.Items[ListBox1.ItemIndex]);
except
   on EStringListError do
      ShowMessage ('No item selected.');
end;
```

This code will permit the program to show an error message to the user in case an exception error occurs. It will also provide a way for the program to continue running even after the error has occurred. Exception errors and information on how to write exception handlers are discussed in Chapter 7.

Column and MultiSelect Properties

The TListBox component has many other useful properties and methods. By setting the Columns property to a number other than 0, the items in a list box will wrap around into multiple columns. The TListBox component also has a MultiSelect property. When this property is set to **True**, you can select multiple items from a list by holding the Shift key down while making the selection (to select a continuous range of items) or by holding the Control key down while making the selection (to select a non-continuous range of items).

Sorting Properties

Another useful feature of the TListBox component is the Sorted property. By setting this property to **True** at run-time, the list will appear sorted when the program starts. By sorting list elements, you can better organize information. For example, if the list contains state abbreviations, it is much easier to locate a particular state's abbreviation when you know the elements are ordered alphabetically.

Displaying Combo Boxes

Like list boxes, combo boxes let you display a list of choices on a form. Unlike list boxes, however, combo boxes have an attached edit box that you can use to make selections. In addition, combo boxes save room on forms since the list does not actually appear until you open it. Figure 2.2 shows how combo boxes appear on a form both before and after the list is opened.

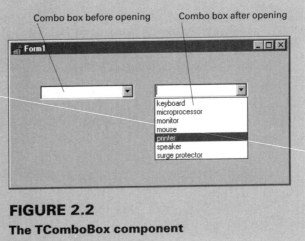

FIGURE 2.2
The TComboBox component

Combo boxes share many of the same properties, methods, and events as list boxes. For example, you can sort a combo box by setting its Sorted property to **True** and you can also add items to the list using the same method demonstrated before for list boxes. The following code demonstrates how to initialize a combo box when the program runs:

```
procedure TForm1.FormCreate(Sender: TObject);

{ Initialize combo box }

begin
  ComboBox1.Items.Add('Item 1');
  ComboBox1.Items.Add('Item 2');
  ComboBox1.Items.Add('Item 3');
  ComboBox1.Items.Add('Item 4');
  ComboBox1.Items.Add('Item 5');
end;
```

To determine what value the user types in a combo box, you use the Text property to read this value:

```
procedure TForm1.Button1Click(Sender: TObject);

{ Read combo box }

begin
  ShowMessage (ComboBox1.Text);
end;
```

When you click on an item in a combo box, the item selected automatically appears in the edit box of the control. Therefore, the preceding example to read the Text property also works to get the current item selected in the list.

Using Check Boxes

Another useful control available on the Standard page of the Component Palette is the TCheckBox control. Check boxes allow you to present program options to users. By clicking on the box at run-time, a check mark appears inside the control (see Figure 2.3). Clicking on the check box a second time will deselect the control, thereby removing the check mark.

For example, the Find Text dialog box in Delphi uses check boxes to determine whether the search should be case sensitive or not and whether whole-word matching should be used in the search (see Figure 2.4).

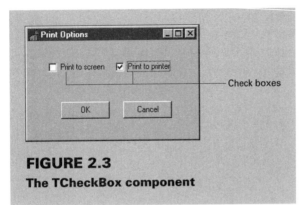

FIGURE 2.3

The TCheckBox component

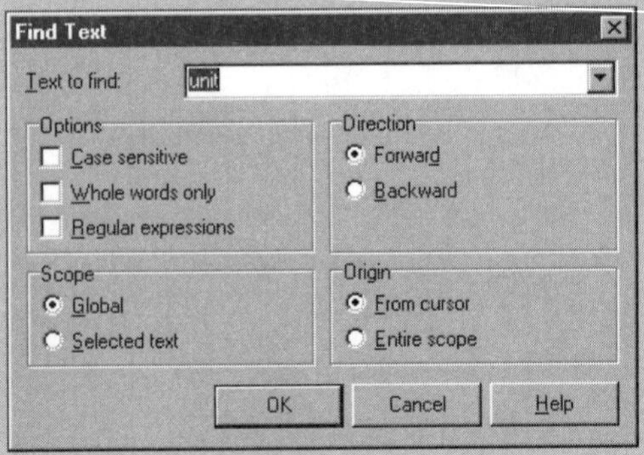

FIGURE 2.4

The Find Text dialog box

To determine whether a check box is selected, you test the value of the Checked property. For example:

```
if CheckBox1.Checked then
    ShowMessage ('Check box selected')
else
    ShowMessage ('Check box not selected');
```

The **if** statement tests whether the check box has been selected by the user. If so, the message *Check box selected* is displayed in a message box. If not, control next branches to the **else** clause and the *Check box not selected* message is shown instead.

When you click on a check box, an OnClick event occurs thereby executing any code associated with the OnClick event handler of the control:

```
procedure TForm1.CheckBox1Click(Sender: TObject);

{ Display user's choice immediately
  when check box is selected }

begin
  if CheckBox1.Checked then
      ShowMessage ('Check box selected')
  else
      ShowMessage ('Check box not selected');
end;
```

This code will immediately show a status message indicating whether or not the control has been selected when the user clicks on the check box. Since more often than not check boxes are used in combination with other controls on a form, you typically would place the code to test the status of the check box in the OnClick event of a button:

```
procedure TForm1.Button1Click(Sender: TObject);

{ Display user's choice when button
  is selected }

begin
  if CheckBox1.Checked then
     ShowMessage ('Check box selected')
  else
     ShowMessage ('Check box not selected');
end;
```

Displaying Mutually Exclusive Choices to Users

Like check boxes, radio buttons permit you to display program options to users (see Figure 2.5). Radio buttons are different, however, in that only one radio button on a form or container object can be selected at a time. Thus radio buttons are useful for displaying mutually exclusive options to users.

The Caption property of a radio button determines the string that the component displays. The Checked property determines the status of the control. This next example shows how to determine whether a radio button is selected:

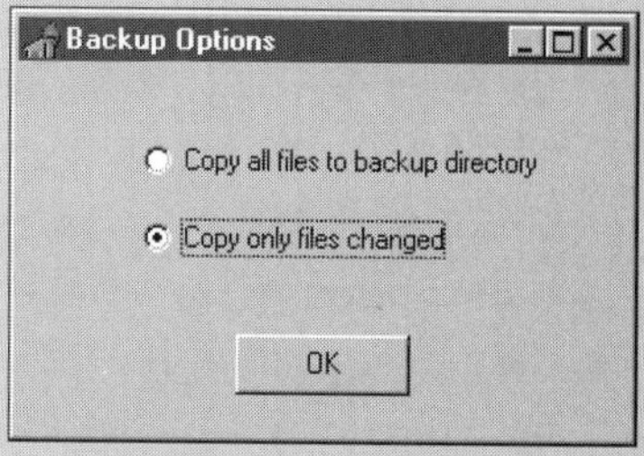

FIGURE 2.5
The TRadioButton component

```
procedure TForm1.RadioButton1Click(Sender: TObject);

{ Show which radio button is selected }

begin

  if RadioButton1.Checked then
     ShowMessage ('RadioButton1 selected')
  else
     ShowMessage ('RadioButton2 selected');

end;
```

Using an **if** statement again, this code checks to see which radio button on the form is selected. When RadioButton1 is chosen, the first message is displayed; otherwise, the second message is displayed.

> **Note** *Although check boxes and radio buttons are similar, they are not the same. Keep in mind that you should only use radio buttons when the choices you present are mutually exclusive. Otherwise, if multiple selections are considered valid, be sure to use check boxes instead.*

Grouping Radio Buttons

Radio buttons can also appear on other container objects such as GroupBoxes, Panels or ScrollBoxes. By adding radio buttons to one of these containers, the container object becomes the *parent*. Thus if you move the GroupBox on the form, the components it contains will also move with it. To make a GroupBox or other container object a parent, you must first place the container object on the form. So long as the container object has focus, any objects you select from the Component Palette will automatically be added to the container.

Multiple container objects can also be added to forms to create different groups of mutually exclusive options. Figure 2.6 shows an example of how this can be done. On the form there are two groups of radio buttons. The first set of radio buttons is contained in a GroupBox. The second set is on a panel. If the radio buttons were simply placed on the form, the action of choosing one radio button would have the same effect as deselecting all the others (since radio buttons always work together in groups). With the controls placed inside containers, you can select a radio button from one group without deselecting the radio buttons of the other.

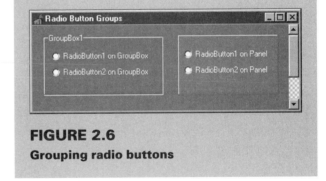

FIGURE 2.6
Grouping radio buttons

Using the TRadioGroup Component

The Standard Page also contains one other container object called the TRadioGroup component. This control is often the source of confusion because of its name. Unlike other container objects, you cannot select radio buttons from the Component Palette and place them on a TRadioGroup component. The reason for this is that TRadioGroup uses a different method to implement radio groups.

Instead of adding radio buttons from the Component Palette, you create the radio buttons on a TRadioGroup control by defining the name of each radio button in the TRadioGroup's Items property. To do this, you use the Object Inspector to set these values. When you double click on the Items property of a TRadioGroup component, the String List editor appears (see Figure 2.7). Each line that you type in this window will define a new radio button that will appear on the TRadioGroup.

After defining the groups of radio buttons, you can check which radio button the user selects at run-time by testing the value of the ItemIndex property. For example:

```
procedure TForm1.RadioGroup1Click(Sender: TObject);

{ Show which radio button on RadioGroup1
  is selected }

begin

  if RadioGroup1.ItemIndex = 0 then
    ShowMessage ('First radio button selected')
  else
    ShowMessage ('Second radio button selected');

end;
```

Using this technique, a central handler can be made to handle all the actions that apply to the radio group. Thus by using a TRadioGroup component as a container object, you can simplify and better control radio button groups.

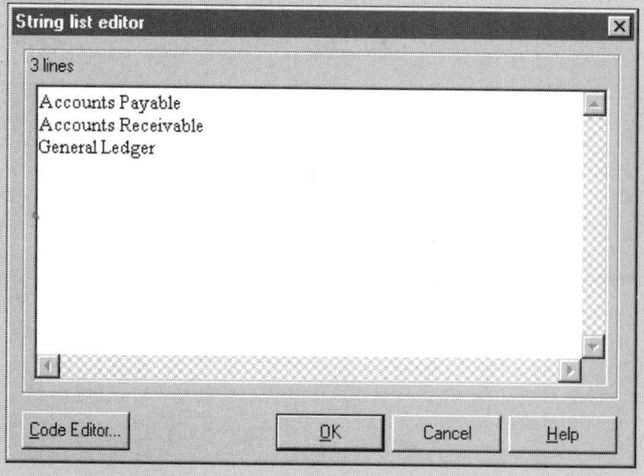

Using Scroll Bars

The TScrollBar component is a multi-purpose control often used to scroll windows and other controls. Many components in Delphi already have scroll bars built into them. A list box, for example, automatically appears with scroll bars if there are too many items in the list to appear within the boundaries of the control.

Although scroll bars are typically used to scroll windows, you can also use them for other purposes. For example, the CHGCOLOR.DPR project uses a scroll bar to set the color of a form (see Figure 2.8).

FIGURE 2.7
The String List editor

When the user clicks on one of the scroll arrows, an OnScroll event occurs. Inside the OnScroll event handler, the following code is used to change the intensities of the RGB (Red, Green, Blue) attributes:

```
procedure TForm1.ScrollBar1Scroll(Sender: TObject; ScrollCode:
        TScrollCode; var ScrollPos: Integer);

var
```

```
  Red, Green, Blue: Integer;
begin

  { Set red intensity to current scroll
    bar value }

  Red := ScrollPos;

  { Read other colors from edit
    components }

  Green := StrToInt (Edit1.Text);
  Blue := StrToInt (Edit2.Text);

  { Set form color to current RGB value }

  Form1.Color := RGB(Red, Green, Blue);

  { Set label caption to current scroll
    bar value which represent also the
    current red intensity }

  lblRed.Caption := IntToStr (ScrollPos);

end;
```

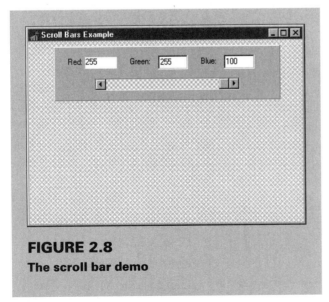

FIGURE 2.8
The scroll bar demo

The red intensity is determined by the *ScrollPos* parameter which Delphi passes to the handler each time the OnScroll event fires. The green and blue intensities are read from two edit components. When the user clicks on the scroll bar, the color of the form is set to the current RGB color. Choosing the left button on the scroll bar causes the red intensity to be reduced. Choosing the right button on the scroll bar causes the red intensity to become greater. The Min and Max properties of the scroll bar determine the range of return values of the component. By default, the values of these properties are:

Min = 0

Max = 100

For the change form color demo, these properties have been set to 1 and 255 to reflect the scale of all possible red intensities. After each time the scroll bar is clicked, the value of the current red intensity is also displayed in a label by setting the Caption property of the label equal to the current value of *ScrollPos:*

```
lblRed.Caption := IntToStr (ScrollPos);
```

Event Handlers

Like buttons on a form, when you click on a radio button, check box, or scroll bar, you are placed in the Code Editor in the default event handler for that control. The default handler for most controls is usually the OnClick event handler. However, when you click on a scroll bar, you end up instead inside the OnChange event handler:

```
procedure TForm1.ScrollBar1Change(Sender: TObject);
begin

end;
```

As you might expect, the code that you insert inside the OnChange event handler of a scroll bar will execute whenever the value of the scroll bar changes at run-time. Notice, however, that in the case of the color change demo, the code to set the form color was placed in the OnScroll event handler instead. So how do you define the proper header declaration for this event? In cases where you need to enter code for a control that is not placed in the default handler of that control, you need to use the Object Inspector to associate the code with the proper event. By looking at Figure 2.9 you will notice that the Object Inspector has two tabs at the top of it.

The first tab permits you to view the properties of an Object. By default, the Object Inspector shows the properties of a control first. The other tab is the Events tab. By clicking on this tab, the Object Inspector now displays a list of events for the control (see Figure 2.10).

To define the code that will be associated with the OnScroll event, you double click on this event name in the list (see Figure 2.11).

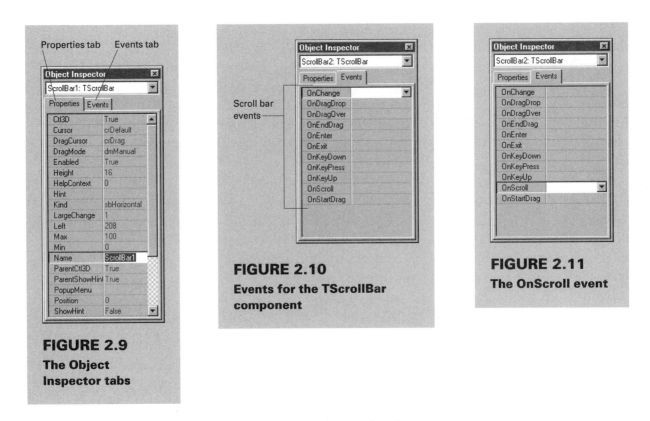

FIGURE 2.9
The Object Inspector tabs

FIGURE 2.10
Events for the TScrollBar component

FIGURE 2.11
The OnScroll event

The Code Editor now opens showing the OnScroll event handler:

```
procedure TForm1.ScrollBar1Scroll(Sender: TObject; ScrollCode:
        TScrollCode; var ScrollPos: Integer);
begin

end;
```

Here you can insert any code that needs to be performed when an OnScroll event occurs. For example, try entering the code for the scroll bar color demo here. You will find that there is often much to be learned by mimicking the examples in this book. To rebuild the scroll bar color demo, first add a panel to the form and set its Width property to 353 pixels and its Height property to 81 pixels. Afterwards, add the components in Figure 2.12 to the panel and set their properties as shown in Table 2.2.

Note *In order to place components on a panel, you must make sure the panel has focus before adding the components. If the panel does not have focus, click on it once to give it focus. You can tell which component on a form has focus by looking at its borders. If the control shows size handles, it means the component has focus.*

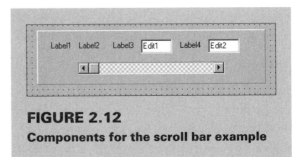

FIGURE 2.12
Components for the scroll bar example

Be sure to enter the code for the scroll bar in the OnScroll event. This is important because the OnChange event is not supplied with position information for the scroll bar. When you are done, press the F9 key to run the program. Notice that the color of the form changes from medium blue to bright magenta as you move the scroll bar from left to right. You can also achieve other color combinations by changing the default starting values of the green and blue intensities.

TABLE 2.2 PROPERTY SETTINGS FOR THE SCROLL BAR COLOR EXAMPLE

Component	Property	Value
Panel	Caption	(null string)
Label1	Caption	Red:
Label2	AutoSize	False
	Caption	(null string)
	Color	clWhite
	Name	lblRed
Label3	Caption	Green:
Label4	Caption	Blue:
Edit1	Text	1
Edit2	Text	255
ScrollBar	Min	1
	Max	255

Validating Program Options at Run-Time

In order to be a good programmer, you need more than just an understanding of how components work. You have to be able to think like end-users. Since the typical end-user of a program is not a computer programmer, it is important to make the software you write intuitive enough for the designated audience to understand. A great deal of this involves anticipating the kinds of mistakes the user will make.

Some operations that are perfectly valid under normal circumstances are invalid in others. For example, you cannot save information to a file if that file is not already open. Part of a programmer's job is to recognize that these kinds of errors can and do happen and that as the developer of an application, you must make every possible effort to prevent invalid choices from being made in the program.

Delphi provides a number of ways to prevent users from selecting invalid program options. One way, as you have already seen, is to use an **if** statement to check conditions in the program; if certain conditions are not met, then the user is not allowed to perform the operation. For example, if the user has not saved his or her work, then don't allow that user to quit the program until he or she has been notified of the problem. Using an **if** statement to prevent a user from performing an invalid operation is an acceptable approach. However, there is an easier way to validate user actions. If a certain button needed to perform a command were either disabled or invisible, then the user could not possibly choose the invalid option. Let's take a look at both possibilities.

Enabling and Disabling Controls

By default, components are usually enabled when you add them to a form. In some cases, you may wish to prevent the user from gaining access to a certain feature in the program until a valid selection can be made. In this situation, you can easily disable the control by setting its Enabled property to **False**. For example:

```
Button1.Enabled := False;
```

Likewise, you can re-enable the component at a later time once a certain condition is met. For instance, after a file has been opened you can enable the Add, Change, and Delete buttons:

```
procedure TForm1.btnOpenClick(Sender: TObject);

{ Enable editing buttons when file is opened }

begin
   .    .    .

   .    .    .
   btnAdd.Enabled := True;
   btnSave.Enabled := True;
   btnDelete.Enabled := True;
end;
```

Showing/Hiding Components

Using a similar technique, it is also possible to completely hide components that you do not wish the user to see until a certain condition is met:

```
btnPrint.Visible := False;
```

This feature might be useful also when a form has too many components on the screen at one time and causes the user to be confused. For example, in Microsoft Word 6.0, if you were to view at once all the toolbars the program has, there would be no room left on the screen to type!

To make a component visible after hiding it, you simply set its Visible property back to **True**:

```
btnPrint.Visible := True;
```

Dressing Up Interfaces

Now that you have had a taste of what Delphi can do, it is time to explore some of its wider possibilities. Standard components are useful but sometimes they can lack the extra appeal that makes a program stand out. Fortunately, Delphi is rich in controls that help make programs look better. In the following section, you will learn how to display graphics in buttons and how to provide help hints next to components.

Showing Bitmaps in Buttons

The Additional page of the Component Palette provides an enhanced button component called a BitBtn that permits you to display a small bitmap in the control (see Figure 2.13). A *bitmap* is a graphic file saved in .BMP format. You can use Microsoft Paintbrush or the Delphi Image Editor to create these graphics.

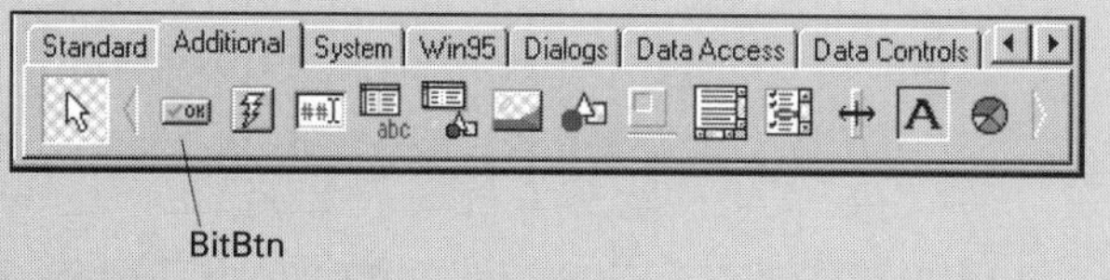

By default, when you place a TBitBtn component on a form, the button appears without a graphic. The TBitBtn component has several predefined images that the control can display. To show one of these pictures, you set the Kind property to one of the following:

bkOK	bkCancel
bkYes	bkNo
bkHelp	bkClose
bkAbort	bkRetry
bkIgnore	bkAll

FIGURE 2.13
The TBitBtn component

The sample project, BTNPRJ.DPR, shows how the Kind property effects a TBitBtn component when you set it (see Figure 2.14). This example is included on the CD. Before you can access it, you must install the sample projects (see Appendix A). If you run the program, you will notice that the Close button automatically unloads the form when you click on it. In addition, by setting the property to bkOK, that button will automatically become the default button to execute if you press Enter while no other button on the form has focus. Similarly, if you set the Kind property of one of the buttons to bkCancel, pressing the Escape key will automatically execute the OnClick event of that button.

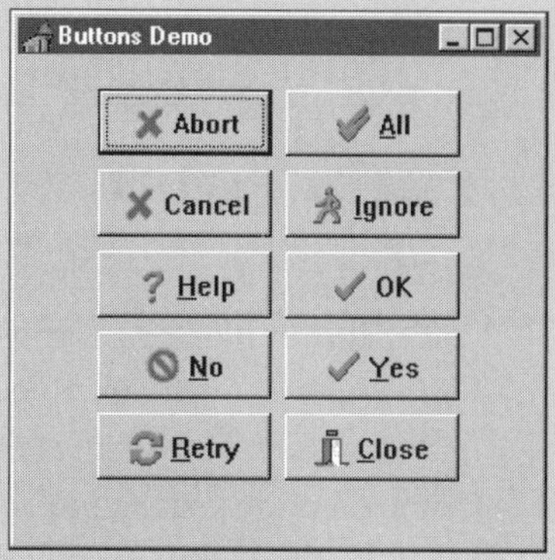

In addition to the standard bitmaps a TBitBtn can display, you can also specify a small custom bitmap using the Glyph property. If you wish to change the graphic in the button as the program runs, you can specify up to four bitmaps using the NumGlyphs property. For example, before the control is selected, you can show a picture of a book cover. Then once you click on the button, the graphic can be changed to a picture of an open book.

FIGURE 2.14
The BTNPRJ.DPR project

Displaying Button Hints

Another useful technique for making a program both look and seem more professional is to show help hints by components. In Delphi, for example, when you move the mouse pointer over the toolbar or Component Palette, help hints appear so that you know what purpose each button serves.

Traditionally, adding code like this to a program meant a great deal of work since you had to test the position of each screen element in the program that had a help hint and then interrupt whatever was going on in the program to display the appropriate message. With objects, however, adding help hints is a snap. Since each component on a form already "knows" its position and when it has focus, you can very easily write code to take advantage of this. In other words, there is no need to write the low-level code to display help hints in Delphi. Instead, you simply set the HelpHint property of each component to **True** to indicate that help hints should be displayed and then define the messages that each component will show. For example:

```
procedure TForm1.FormCreate(Sender: TObject);

{ Define help hint for button }

begin
  btnOK.ShowHint := True;
  btnOK.Hint := 'Click here to begin search';
end;
```

At run-time, when the user moves the mouse pointer over the button, a help hint will appear next to the component (see Figure 2.15). You can also customize the way the hint appears with the following code:

```
Application.HintColor := clAqua;
Application.HintPause := 200;
```

The Application variable is an object variable of type TApplication. Delphi automatically defines this object variable when you create a new project. Application has several useful properties that you can use to acquire information about running projects. In addition, this is how you specify the HelpHint color and amount of time to wait before displaying a help hint. In this example, the hint will appear after 200 milliseconds (or ¼ of a second) and will display to the user with black text on an aqua background.

You may wonder where the clAqua constant came from. Delphi provides this definition in the Graphics unit it includes in every project (by adding it to your **uses** clause). Other standard colors you can specify include clBlack, clBlue, clDkGray, clFuchsia, clGray, clGreen, clLime, clLtGray, clMaroon, clNavy, clOlive, clPurple, clRed, clSilver, clTeal, clWhite, and clYellow.

FIGURE 2.15
Displaying help hints

Inherited Properties of Controls

While working with colors and Delphi forms, it is important to understand the concept of *inheritance*. When you place a component on a form, it automatically inherits certain properties of that form. For example, if you add a label to a form and set the background color of that form to clBlue, the background color of the label will also appear blue. Thus you can quickly change the background color of a form and all the labels on it in a single color assignment.

Overriding Inherited Defaults

Although inheritance has its definite advantages, sometimes you don't want to inherit certain properties of the container object. For example, if you change the Font property of a form, by default, all the labels and edit controls on it will also inherit the same font (see Figure 2.16). While this may look interesting for a game, you certainly don't want your accounts payable program looking like it came from a three-ring circus. Delphi solves this problem with three properties:

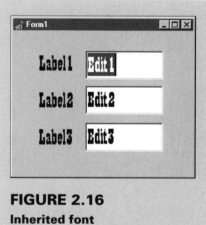

FIGURE 2.16
Inherited font

▶ ParentColor: Specifies whether a component will use its own color attributes or those of its parent.

▶ ParentFont: Specifies whether a component will use its own font attributes or those of its parent.

▶ ParentShowHint: Specifies whether to enable help hints based on a component's ShowHint property or on the ShowHint property of its parent. That is, when a component's ParentShowHint property is set to **True**, the component will display a help hint if its parent's ShowHint property is also **True**. Otherwise, the component will act independently of its parent and display a help hint regardless of its parent ShowHint property as long as its own ShowHint property is set to **True**.

The ParentColor and ParentFont properties are simple enough concepts to grasp. However, the notion of the ParentShowHint property can be a little confusing at first. Basically, if you set the ParentShowHint property to **True**, the component will only show its hint if you also set the ShowHint property of its parent to **True**. There are two reasons for doing this. First, if you set the ParentShowHint property to **True**, once you set the ShowHint property of the parent to **True**, you can define a help hint for each control with one line of code instead of two. Since all the components on a form by default use the ShowHint property of the parent, setting this property to **True** will allow all the components to display hints by simply defining the hint that each control will show:

```
procedure TForm1.FormCreate(Sender: TObject);

{ Display help hints for three buttons }
```

```
begin
  Form1.ShowHint := True;
  btnOK.Hint := 'Click here to begin';
  btnHelp.Hint := 'Click here for Help';
  btnClose.Hint := 'Click here to quit';
end;
```

The second reason why you might want to use the ParentShowHint property is to disable all the help hints. So long as you leave the ParentShowHint property set to its default (**True**), you can turn off all the help hints in a program by setting the parent's ShowHint property to **False**. This can be a configuration option for experienced users who may not wish to see the help hints.

Creating a Picture Viewer

In the following exercise, you will learn how to display images in Delphi. After this lesson, you should be able to:

▶ Load bitmaps in an image control.

▶ Display files in a directory.

▶ Add enhanced buttons to a form.

1 From the File menu, choose the New... menu option.

2 From the New Items dialog, double click on Application to create a new project.

3 Using the Object Inspector, set the properties of the form as follows:

Property	Value
Height	224
Width	383
Position	poScreenCenter

Note *When you set the Position property of a form to poScreenCenter, the form will not actually be centered on the screen until you run the program.*

4 From the Component Palette, choose the Additional tab (see Figure 2.17).

5 The Additional page of the Component Palette contains two

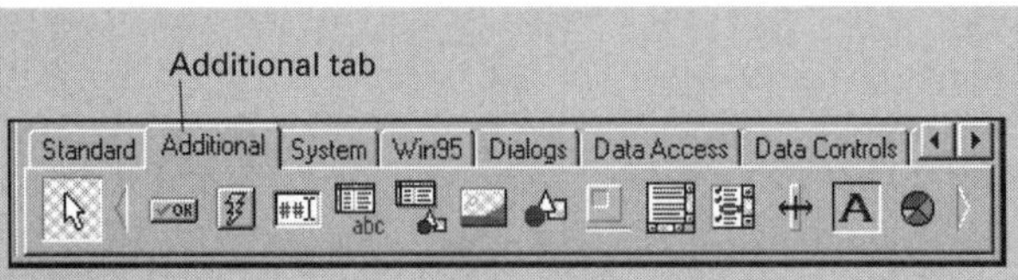

FIGURE 2.17
The Additional tab on the Component Palette

components you will be needing for this exercise (see Figure 2.18).

Add two BitBtns controls and an image component to the form. Place the three objects roughly where they appear in Figure 2.19.

Note *You may have to click the leftward pointing arrow on the Additional page in order to see this component.*

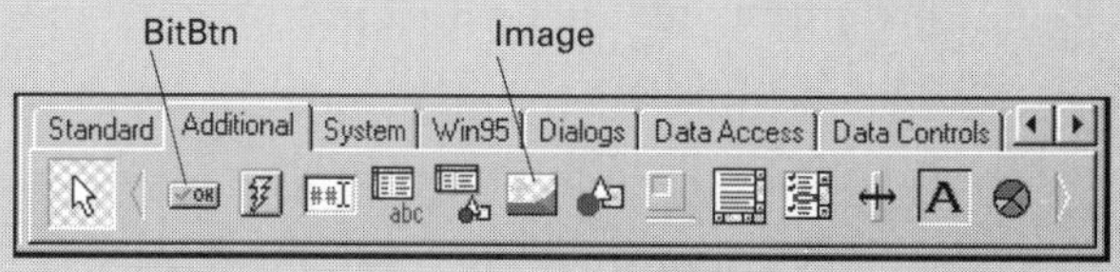

6 Using the Object Inspector, set the Stretch property of the image component to **True**. This will re-size the graphics when they are loaded to the size of the image component.

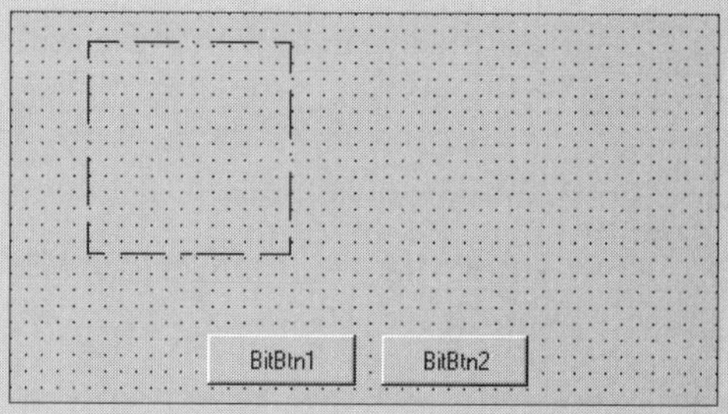

7 Using the right arrow button on the Component Palette, click until you see the Win 3.1 tab (see Figure 2.20).

8 Click on the Win 3.1 tab to view the component options for this page.

9 From the Win 3.1 page of the Component Palette, double click on the FileListBox button to add this component to the form. Figure 2.21 shows what the associated button for this control looks like in the Component Palette.

1Ø Place the FileListBox component on the form where it appears in Figure 2.22.

11 Set the Mask property of the FileListBox component to *.BMP.

Note *After setting this property, the file names in the file list box will temporarily disappear (since the current directory contains no bitmaps).*

12 Click on the BitBtn1 button to give it focus.

13 Using the Object Inspector, set the Kind property of this button to bkOK.

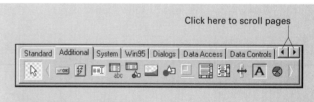

FIGURE 2.18
Components on the Additional page for the sample exercise

FIGURE 2.19
Positioning the components on the form

FIGURE 2.20
Scrolling the pages of the Component Palette

FIGURE 2.21
The TFileListBox component

14 Click on the BitBtn2 button to give it focus.

15 Using the Object Inspector, set the Kind property of this button to bkClose.

16 Double click on the BitBtn1 button. This will open the Code Editor.

17 Insert the following line between the **begin** and **end** reserved words:

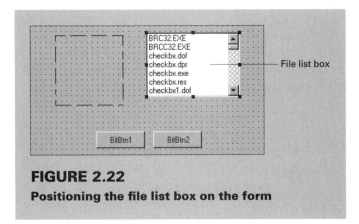

FIGURE 2.22
Positioning the file list box on the form

```
Image1.Picture.LoadFromFile (FileListBox1.FileName);
```

Note *This code will load the files that appear in the file list box when the program runs and display them in the image component.*

18 Click on the Toggle Form/Unit button on the toolbar to view the form.

Note *If you do not remember what this button looks like, you can determine which button is the Toggle Form/Unit button by reading the help hints that appear when you move the mouse pointer over the toolbar.*

19 Double click on the form to Open the Code Editor. The OnCreate event handler for the form should now appear. Be sure to click on the internal area of the form and not the title bar (see Figure 2.23). This is important because you cannot open the Code Editor by clicking on the form's title bar.

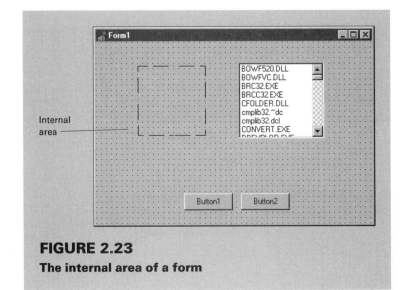

FIGURE 2.23
The internal area of a form

20 Insert the following line between the **begin** and **end** reserved words:

```
FileListBox1.Directory := 'C:\Windows';
```

Note *This code assumes that Windows is installed on your system in C:\Windows. If this is not the case, be sure to specify the correct path here.*

21 Run the program by either pressing the F9 shortcut key or by choosing the Run button on the toolbar.

22 From the file list box, click on the first file name in the list to select the file. The name of this file should now appear highlighted.

23 Now click on the OK button to view the file. You should see the first bitmap stored in your Windows directory appear in the image component.

24 Click on the second file name in the file list box to select the next file you want to view.

25 Now click on OK again to see the second bitmap. Repeat the preceding steps for any graphics you wish to view.

26 When you are done, choose the Close button to end the session. Notice how the BitBtn component automatically unloads the form even though no code has been added to its OnClick event handler.

Summary

In this chapter, you have learned how to work with the components on the Standard page of the Component Palette. In addition, you have also learned how to:

- ▶ Enable/Disable controls on a form.
- ▶ Show/Hide components.
- ▶ Display bitmaps in buttons.
- ▶ Show help hints next to components.
- ▶ Override inherited properties of controls.
- ▶ Create a directory picture viewer.

Creating Multiform
Applications

Creating a Tabbed
Notebook Style
Interface

The Delphi IDE

Common Programming
Mistakes

Exercise: Building
a Multi-page Dialog

Chapter 3
Working with Forms

In Chapter 2, you learned how to work with components from the Standard, Additional, and Win 3.1 pages of the Component Palette. So far, however, all the projects you have created have been limited to a single form. In this chapter, you will learn how to create multiform applications and also how to build custom dialog boxes. In addition, you will learn how to build tabbed notebook style applications and how to take full advantage of the tools the Delphi IDE has to offer.

Creating Multiform Applications

In Chapter 1, you learned how to display modal dialog boxes using the ShowMessage procedure and InputBox function. By adding components to a form, you can also create your own custom dialog boxes. At the start of each session, Delphi automatically creates the main form for an application. Since forms are limited in space, eventually components have to be placed on other forms. To add a form to a project, choose the New Form command from the File menu or click on the New Form button from the toolbar (see Figure 3.1).

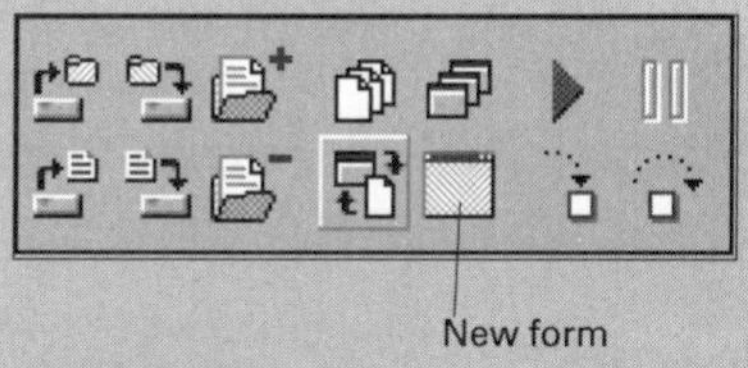

New form

FIGURE 3.1
The New Form button on the toolbar

Displaying Forms

Once you add a form to a project, it appears much the same way as the main form. By default, Delphi assigns the name Form2 to this form and links it to a unit called Unit2. You can add components to Form2 just like the main form. However, Delphi will not display this form unless you create an event handler to do this. There are two ways to display forms in Delphi:

▶ Modally: The form must be closed by the user before work can be done on another form.

▶ Nonmodally: Access to work on different forms is permitted at the same time.

As you have seen in Chapter 1, modal dialog boxes have their advantages and disadvantages. The major advantage of modal dialog boxes is that you can prevent the user from working in another window while an important operation is being performed. For example, when you choose the File | New command in Delphi, the New Items dialog box appears (see Figure 3.2). Since this dialog appears modally on the screen, the user must explicitly choose an option from the New Items dialog box before any other operation is permitted. If the user tries to click outside the New Items dialog box, an error sound will play through the speakers. Thus by restricting the user's access in the program to the current window, the New Items dialog box provides a way of validating conflicting menu options simply by not allowing the user to perform any other command until a choice has been made.

Although modal dialog boxes have their definite advantages, most of the time you will probably not want to use them because too many modal dialog boxes in a program can make an application difficult to use. In addition, many programs require that several dialog boxes be accessible to the user at the same time. For instance, in Delphi, you can add controls to forms using the Component Palette, change their properties with the Object Inspector, and edit units in the Code Editor simultaneously. To switch to another window, you simply click on that window to give it focus. Imagine how much harder it would be to develop projects if you had to close a window every time you used it. For this reason, it is often better not to make your dialog boxes modal unless you are sure it is necessary. If you decide that a particular window must be displayed modally, you can easily change this later.

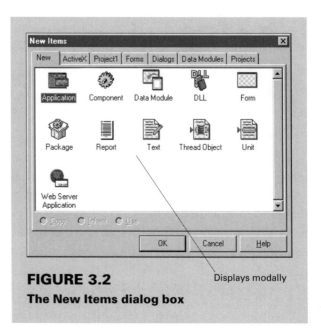

FIGURE 3.2
The New Items dialog box

Displays modally

To display a form nonmodally, you use the Show method to make it visible. For example:

```
Form2.Show;
```

Unit References

When referencing another form with the Show method, it is important to keep in mind the relationship between forms and units. Without the unit, a form cannot exist. As you saw in Chapter 1, Delphi automatically adds the necessary code to declare forms in units. When you use the Show method to display another form, you are actually referencing an object contained within another unit. Therefore, the unit being referenced must be included in the **uses** clause of the current unit. If you forget to add the unit name, Delphi will alert you to the problem and automatically add the correct reference, if you like. For example:

```
  .     .     .
implementation

uses Unit2;
```

```
{$R *.DFM}

procedure TForm1.Button1Click(Sender: TObject);

{ Display another form  }

begin
  Form2.Show;
end;
```

Notice that Delphi automatically adds a second **uses** clause to the unit. By placing the new **uses** clause in the **implementation** section of the unit, you avoid a common error called a *circular unit reference*. This error will occur whenever you have two units that reference each other and when both units list each other in their **interface** sections. For example, if Unit1 references Unit2 in its **interface** section like this:

```
unit Unit1;

interface

uses
  Windows, Messages, SysUtils, Classes, Graphics, Controls,
  Forms, Dialogs, Unit2;
  .     .     .
```

and Unit2 references Unit1 the following way:

```
unit Unit2;

interface

uses
  Windows, Messages, SysUtils, Classes, Graphics, Controls,
  Forms, Dialogs, Unit1;
  .     .     .
```

a circular unit reference error will result when you try to compile the program. To avoid this problem, place the reference to one or both of the units in the **implementation** section of a unit like this:

```
  .     .     .
implementation
```

```
uses Unit2;
```

Tip *Instead of manually specifying the name of the unit you wish to refer-
ence, use the File | Use Unit... command to automatically add the correct
unit reference to the program.*

Once you add the name of the unit to the **uses** clause, the Show method can be applied to display the form nonmodally:

```
Form2.Show;
```

If you wish to display the form modally instead, use the ShowModal method. For
example:

```
 .    .    .

implementation

uses Unit2;

{$R *.DFM}

procedure TForm1.btnOKClick(Sender: TObject);

{ Display form modally }

begin
  Form2.ShowModal;
end;
```

This code will display Form2 modally when the user
clicks on the btnOK button on Form1.

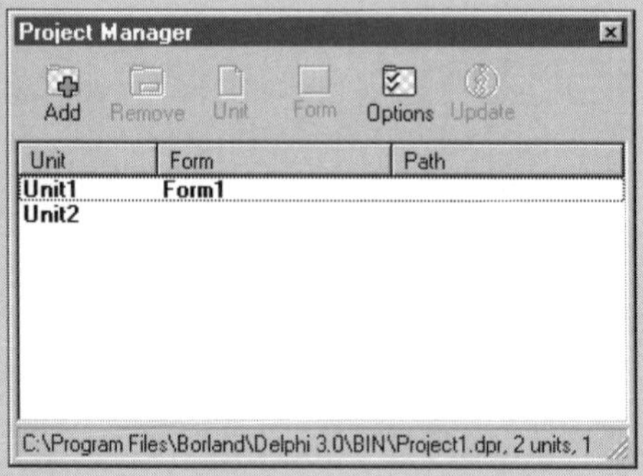

Managing Units

When working with a project that contains multiple
forms, it is important to know how to toggle between
them. One way to do this is to choose the View | Project
Manager command. The Project Manager not only can
switch tasks but also makes working with the files of a
project easier. Figure 3.3 shows the Project Manager.

Another way to switch between files is to use the View
| Units... command (Ctrl+F12). By double clicking on a
form at design-time, you will notice that Delphi adds a

FIGURE 3.3
The Project Manager

tab for each unit in a project, providing a third way to view units (see Figure 3.4).

Changing the Appearance of Forms

One of the great advantages of Delphi is the flexible way in which it can display dialogs. In Chapter 1, you learned that Delphi automatically provides a way of closing forms using a built-in menu on every form called the Control (or System) menu. Sometimes, however, you do not want users to have access to certain properties of a form. For example, if you want to make sure the user always exits a form by clicking on the Close button, you need to disable the built-in System menu. To do this, set the BorderStyle property to one of the following:

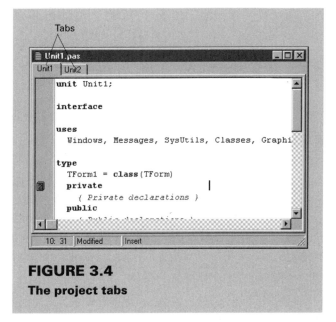

FIGURE 3.4
The project tabs

▶ bsDialog

▶ bsSizeToolWin

▶ bsToolWindow

When you set the BorderStyle property of a form to bsDialog, Delphi disables the Minimize and Maximize buttons, removes the form's System menu and makes the form not resizable. This setting is useful for modal dialogs which rarely need access to these options.

The BorderStyle options bsSizeToolWin and bsToolWindow are useful for creating toolbars. When either of these options is set, the form will appear without a System menu and with a narrow title bar. The two border styles work basically the same, except that the bsSizeToolWin option permits you to resize the window and the bsToolWindow setting does not.

> **Note** *When you change the BorderStyle property of a form at design-time, the form will not appear in the new BorderStyle until you run the program.*

When the BorderStyle property is set to bsNone, the form appears without any title bar, system menu, or beveled border. The bsNone style is useful for screen saver applications and for programs that make use of full screen graphics. You have to be careful when using this setting because there is no way to end the run of the program if you do not place a Close button on the form. When running in the design environment, you can stop a running program by choosing the Program Reset option from the Run menu in Delphi. Alternately, you can press Alt+F4 to close the form.

The bsSingle property option makes the form appear like Delphi's default form style (bsSizable), only the form cannot be resized.

> **Tip** *If you need to have a form appear in front of other forms, but do not want to make it modal, set the FormStyle property to fsStayOnTop.*

Executing Cleanup code

As a precaution, it is a good idea to have a backup procedure for executing cleanup code on a form in case the form is accidentally unloaded. To do this, you place the necessary cleanup code in the OnClose event handler. Alternatively, you can place the code in the OnCloseQuery event handler to allow better control over how the form is unloaded. If the user has not completed a necessary operation, such as filling in a required value in an edit box or saving his or her work, you can prevent the form from unloading by setting the CanClose parameter to **False**:

```
procedure TForm1.FormCloseQuery(Sender: TObject; var CanClose:
Boolean);

{ Don't allow user to close form if customer number has
  not been specified }

begin

  if CustNumber.Text = '' then begin
    ShowMessage ('Please fill in Customer Number');
    CanClose := False;
    end;

end;
```

In addition to the OnClose and OnCloseQuery events, a form generates an OnDeactivate event when the user switches to another running program, and an OnDestroy event when the main form is unloaded. By placing the cleanup code in the appropriate handlers, you can provide a fail-safe way of handling form closing/ deactivation errors.

Referencing Controls on Other Forms

Up until now, all the projects you have created have been simple applications that use a single form. A project, however, can consist of many forms. When projects contain multiple forms, it is important that you know how to pass information from one form to another. One way you can do this is by referencing the controls on another form. To do this, you must first add the name of the unit associated with the other form to your **uses** clause. Afterwards, any controls on that form will be accessible to the current unit. For example, if you want to copy the contents of an edit control from Form2 to Form1, you can create a handler like this:

```
    .    .    .
implementation

uses Unit2;

{$R *.DFM}

procedure TForm1.Button1Click(Sender: TObject);
begin
  Edit1.Text := Form2.Edit1.Text;
end;
```

By specifying the name of the form you wish to reference, Delphi will know that the second edit control (also called Edit1) appears on Form2 and that it should copy the contents of Form2.Edit1.Text to Edit1.Text (on the current form).

There are other ways that you can communicate between forms and units. In Chapter 4 you will learn how to pass parameters to other units without referencing any controls on forms. For now, however, try experimenting by recreating the example above, which copies the contents of an edit control from one form to another form, as follows:

1 Create a new project by choosing File | New Application.

2 On the form, place an edit component and a button component.

3 Double click on the button to open up the Code Editor. Then add the following code to the OnClick event handler of the Button1 control:

```
Edit1.Text := Form2.Edit1.Text;
```

4 Press the Page Up key once and add the following code immediately after the **implementation** reserved word:

```
uses Unit2;
```

5 Use the File | New Form command to add another form to the project.

6 Add an edit component to this form.

7 Set the Text property of the edit component on Form2 to *Test string*.

8 Afterwards, run the program.

You should now be able to click on the button on Form1 to copy the Text property of the edit component on Form2 to the Text property of the edit component on Form1.

Creating a Tabbed Notebook Style Interface

An alternative to placing controls on other forms is to incorporate a TabbedNotebook component or PageControl component in the interface. The TabbedNotebook control is provided mainly for compatibility with Delphi 1.0. For Delphi 3.0, the PageControl component offers greater flexibility and more control. When you run out of room on the screen, you can create new pages for other controls by placing a PageControl component on a form (see Figure 3.5).

To add a PageControl component to a form, choose the PageControl button from the Win95 page of the Component Palette (see Figure 3.6).

You create the pages that the PageControl component displays by right-clicking on the PageControl component and choosing the New Page command from the pop-up menu that appears (see Figure 3.7). Delphi will automatically create a new page called TabSheet1. This page can be renamed by changing the Name property in the Object Inspector. Since the PageControl component can contain multiple pages, you must select the page you wish to edit before its properties will be accessible. To do this, you choose the name of the page you wish to edit by clicking on the down pointing arrow in the upper right corner of the Object Inspector (see Figure 3.8).

Once you select a page for editing, you can change the text on the tab for that page by assigning a new value to the Caption property. Afterwards, components can be added to a page just like you would add controls to a form. When you are done, you can view/edit other pages of the control using the Next Page and Previous Page options by right-clicking on the form.

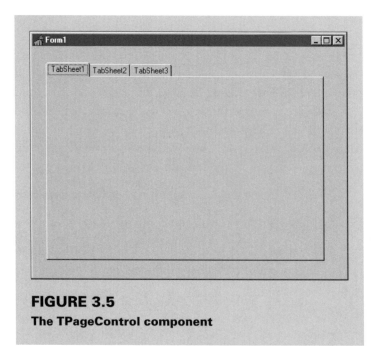

FIGURE 3.5
The TPageControl component

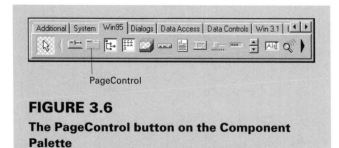

PageControl

FIGURE 3.6
The PageControl button on the Component Palette

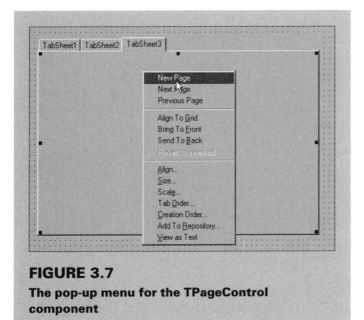

FIGURE 3.7

The pop-up menu for the TPageControl component

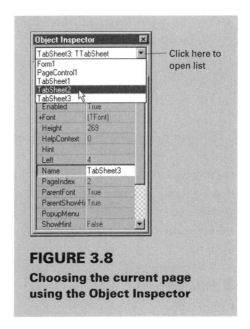

FIGURE 3.8

Choosing the current page using the Object Inspector

The Delphi IDE

The Delphi Integrated Development Environment (IDE) provides many tools that make working with forms easier. With these tools you can speed the development of applications using built-in templates, wizards, and other utilities. In addition, Delphi 3.0 provides added support for customizing the IDE to your own personal needs. In the following section, you will learn how to generate applications that utilize the tools of the IDE.

The Object Repository

The IDE provides a collection of templates known as the Object Repository which you can use to design applications. These pre-defined templates provide time-saving ways to create new projects. To include an item from the Object Repository, from the File menu choose the New... command. The New Items dialog contains tabs for the different categories of templates it contains. By default, the New tab is selected. By clicking on one of the other tabs you can open other pages. The four rightmost tabs of the New Items dialog box provide access to the items in the Object Repository (see Figure 3.9).

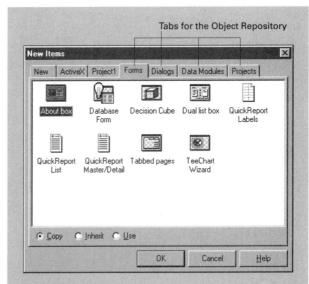

FIGURE 3.9

Object Repository tabs of the New Items dialog box

Selecting Items from the Object Repository

To demonstrate how an item from the Object Repository can be used in an application, choose the About Box option from the Forms page (see Figure 3.10).

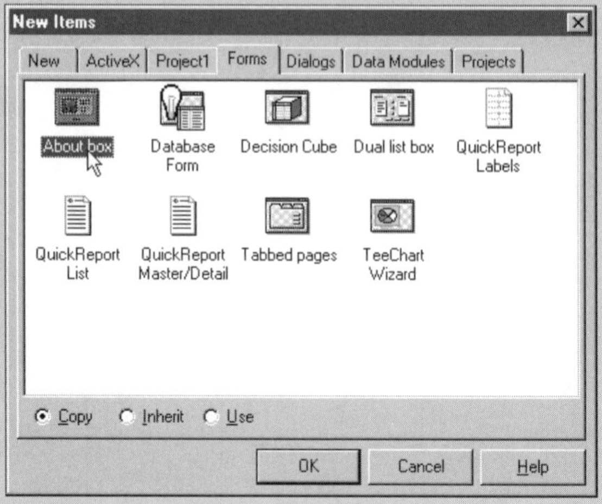

Delphi now displays a new About dialog box on the screen. Figure 3.11 shows how it appears. The About box is a generic dialog box that can be customized for your individual needs. To do this, you use the Object Inspector to set the properties of the components on the form just like you would any other form. Instead of displaying the standard graphic that the dialog box shows, you could set the Picture property of the image control to show your own logo. Similarly, by changing the captions of each label on the form you can also show:

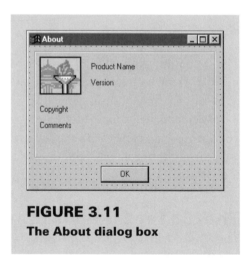

FIGURE 3.10
Choosing the About box from the New Items dialog box

▶ The name of your program

▶ The current version number of the program

▶ A copyright notice

▶ Comments about your program

Once you have set the properties of the controls, you can insert the necessary code for the OnClick event handler of the OK button. To do this, you double click on the OK button to open the Code editor. Since the OnClick event of the OK button should only have to unload the form, the Close method should be placed here.

To display the About dialog box, you use the ShowModal method to make the dialog show modally. Before you can do this, you must add the name of the unit associated with the About dialog to your **uses** clause. The easiest way to do this is to use the File | Use Unit... command and then pick the name of the unit from the list box that appears. The following code demonstrates how to display the About dialog box:

FIGURE 3.11
The About dialog box

```
      .    .    .

implementation


uses Unit2;
```

```
{$R *.DFM}
procedure TForm1.Button1Click(Sender: TObject);
begin
  AboutBox.ShowModal
end;
```

Adding Items to the Object Repository

Whenever you want, you can add your own custom dialog boxes to the Object Repository. You can accomplish this by doing the following:

1 Right-click on the dialog box to show the list of options available to the form object.

2 Choose the Add to Repository command from the pop-up menu that appears.

3 Delphi will display the Add to Repository Dialog box (see Figure 3.12). To add an item to the Object Repository, you must first give it a name (Title).

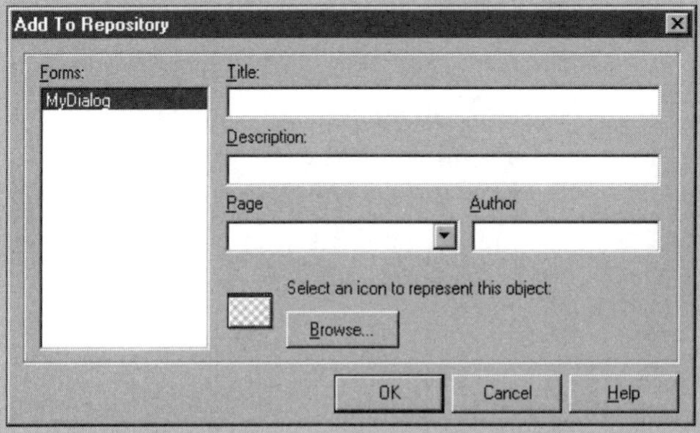

After indicating the name, the following optional items can also be specified:

▶ The item description (such as custom dialog box)

▶ The page of the New Items dialog box that will display your custom dialog box (Forms, Dialogs, Data Modules or Projects)

▶ The author (you)

▶ The icon you wish to associate with the custom dialog box

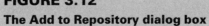

FIGURE 3.12
The Add to Repository dialog box

Once you have added your dialog box to the Object Repository, you can include it as a generic template in all your applications.

Using Component Templates

Another useful tool the IDE supplies is component templates. When working with controls, you may notice certain patterns in the component configurations your applications regularly use. For example, it is standard in many dialog boxes to include an OK and a Cancel button. You may also find yourself repeating much of the same program code sequences. To save time, you can create component templates that automatically add controls to forms. Component templates not only retain the property settings you assign to them but also retain any associated code in their event handlers.

To create a component template:

1 Place the components on a form where you want them to appear in relation to one another, for example, side by side, one control above the other, and so on.

2 Set the properties of each control using the Object Inspector.

3 Create event procedures for each control (optional).

4 Select all the components you wish to add to the template by dragging the mouse cursor around them. Once selected, the components should appear with gray handles around them.

5 From the Component menu, choose the Add Component Template... command.

6 In the Component Template Information dialog, enter the name you wish the template to be saved as, the Component Palette page on which you want it to appear, and the icon that will be used to select the component template from the Component Palette. By default, Delphi uses the icon of the first control in the template. To specify another graphic, choose the Change button. The graphic you indicate must be a bitmap no larger than 24 x 24 pixels.

7 Click on OK to save the new template.

Once saved, you can add the component template to any form by choosing its associated icon from the Component Palette. You can remove a component template from the Component Palette at any time by choosing the Configure Palette command from the Component menu and then selecting the Delete option to remove the component from its associated page.

Configuring Palettes

In Delphi 3.0, you can configure the way the Component Palette appears. For example, you can rename pages, change the order in which controls appear on the Component Palette, and even hide certain components. Although Delphi 3.0 permits you to make these changes, you must be careful since any changes you make will not apply to the standard documentation. However, if at any time you want to restore the defaults, you can do this by clicking on the [All] button in the Pages list box and then choosing the Default Pages button.

Adding ActiveX Components to Forms

Delphi 3.0 also provides support for adding third-party custom controls to the Component Palette. This option is provided through Delphi's new packaging system, discussed in Chapter 12, and through the use of ActiveX components.

Once added to a form, an ActiveX component works basically the same way as any other component. For example, you can view and edit its properties using the Object

Inspector and write event handlers. However, unlike Delphi components, you cannot compile an ActiveX control into a .EXE file. Therefore, you must include the necessary run-time files for the component when you distribute your applications. These files usually include one or more .OCX (ActiveX) and .DLL (Dynamic Link Library) files.

Before an ActiveX component can be used in a project, you must install it. To do this, you use the Import ActiveX Library... command from the Component menu. The top list box shows the list of registered ActiveX components on your system (see Figure 3.13). If the control you need does not appear in this list, click on the Register button to import it into Delphi. Afterwards, by choosing the OK button, Delphi will generate an import unit that contains the necessary class declaration for the component.

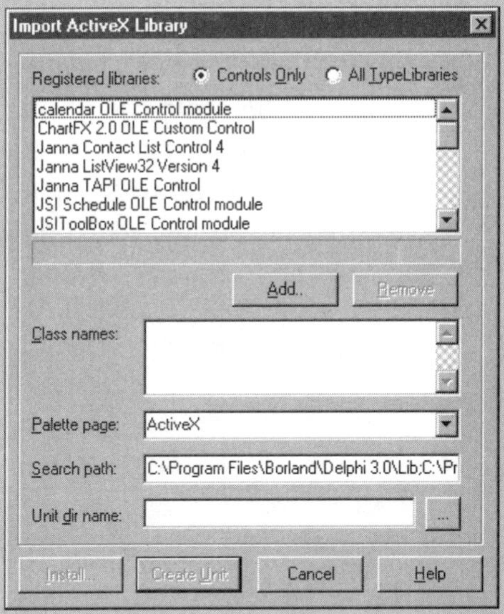

FIGURE 3.13
The Import ActiveX Library dialog

Common Programming Mistakes

Now that you have a working knowledge of the tools you use to create applications, it is important to understand how the logical pieces of the puzzle fit together. Anyone can throw controls on a form. However, in order for a program to be useful, it has to be understood by users. While there is no fixed recipe for what makes a good program design, below is a list of ten common errors beginners usually make. This is not a complete list of common errors, but it will at least give you an idea of some of the kinds of problems you should try to avoid.

Bad or Non-relational Designs

One mistake developers often make is failing to plan ahead before jumping into a project. In many cases, a simple sketch on paper could save weeks of unnecessary coding. Before writing a program, take a minute to think out what you want to do. Often a misunderstanding of the requirements of an application can result in wasted effort that could have been avoided by simply listening to what end-users have to say.

Stacking Controls on Forms

Another common problem beginners often make is stacking controls on forms. If you find that you are running out of space on the screen for new components, the worst thing you can do is to start piling controls on top of one another. This will not only make your programs sloppy, but harder to maintain.

Delphi provides several solutions to this problem. You can easily add more pages when necessary by using a TPageControl component to give you more space on forms.

Delphi also provides another control on the Additional page on the Component Palette called a TScrollBox component (see Figure 3.14). With this control, you can create a scrollable region on a form for other controls. In addition, controls can be dynamically sized and positioned to provide more room on the screen. For example:

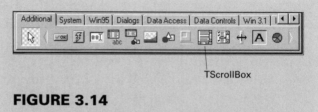

FIGURE 3.14
The TScrollBox icon of the Component Palette

```
procedure TForm1.FormCreate(Sender: TObject);

{ Dynamically size and position image
  component on form }

begin
  Image1.Height := 200;
  Image1.Width := 200;
  Image1.Left := 100;
  Image1.Top := 35;
  Image1.Stretch := True;
  Image1.Picture.LoadFromFile ('seal.bmp');
end;
```

This code will make a small image component larger when it is needed. At design-time, the control only has to be big enough for you to see it. Thus by dynamically sizing components, you can gain the extra space needed for other controls.

Another way you can avoid stacking controls on forms is to dynamically create the components when the program is running. For example, instead of moving the image component on the form, you can create the control at run-time as follows:

```
procedure TForm1.FormCreate(Sender: TObject);

{ Create image control dynamically when
  program starts}

var
  PictImg1: TImage;
begin
  PictImg1 := TImage.Create(Self);
  PictImg1.Height := 200;
  PictImg1.Width := 200;
```

```
    PictImg1.Left := 100;
    PictImg1.Top := 175;
    PictImg1.Stretch := True;
    PictImg1.Parent := Self;
    PictImg1.Picture.LoadFromFile ('Pict1.bmp');
  end;
```

This code will dynamically create an image control and load a bitmap when the form is created. To try this example, the ExtCtrls unit must be added to your **uses** clause and you must also have a bitmap in the current directory called PICT1.BMP.

> **Note** *For a complete discussion on how to create objects in Delphi, see Chapter 12.*

Using Literals Instead of Constants

Another common mistake programmers often make is to use literals instead of constants. A *literal* is a value that appears in the source code of a program. For instance:

```
procedure TForm1.Button1Click(Sender: TObject);

var
  Shelves, Total: Integer;
begin
  Shelves := 5;
  Total := Shelves * 2 + 1;
end;
```

This code is hard to understand because the programmer did not take the time to declare constants. Consider how much easier it would be if the code were rewritten like this:

```
procedure TForm1.btnOKClick(Sender: Tobject);

const SIDES = 2; SPARE_SHELF = 1;

var
  Shelves, Total: Integer;
begin
  Shelves := 5;
  Total := Shelves * SIDES + SPARE_SHELF;
end;
```

By applying constants and standard naming conventions, your programs will not only be easier to read, but also easier to maintain.

Lack of Indentation or Spacing

Although Delphi does not require code to be indented to compile and execute projects, you will find that it is much easier to read a program that incorporates this. For example, the following source code is hard to read because it contains neither indentation nor spacing:

```
procedure SwapBitmaps (imgCtrl, imgCtrl2, imgCtrl3: TImage);
begin
{ Perform animation by swapping two bitmaps in
an image component }
SwapImage := not (SwapImage);
if SwapImage then imgCtrl.picture := imgCtrl2.picture
else imgCtrl.picture := imgCtrl3.picture;
end;
```

Notice how much easier the same procedure is to read now with indented code and spacing included:

```
procedure SwapBitmaps (imgCtrl, imgCtrl2, imgCtrl3: TImage);

begin

  { Perform animation by swapping two bitmaps in
    an image component }

  SwapImage := not (SwapImage);

  if SwapImage then
     imgCtrl.picture := imgCtrl2.picture
  else
     imgCtrl.picture := imgCtrl3.picture;

end;
```

Notice how the executable statements in the event handler are indented after the **begin** and **end** reserved words. In addition, the use of double spacing also makes this code easier to follow.

Hard Coded Paths

Another big mistake beginners often make is to include hard-coded paths in programs. For example:

```
Image1.Picture.LoadFromFile('C:\MyAPP\Graphics\Pict1.Bmp');
```

Since there is no guarantee that end-users will choose to install your program always on drive C:\ or in the default directory, this code will not work on all users' machines. To avoid this problem, it is better to supply the path to the file as an alias (see Chapter 8) or as an option the user can specify in the program. The following code shows how to read the path where bitmaps reside locally on a hard drive from an edit component:

```
procedure TForm1.btnGetPathClick(Sender: TObject);

{ Get path where bitmaps are located on
  hard drive }

var
  PathToBitmaps: String;
begin
  PathToBitmaps := editBitmaps.Text;
end;
```

Using Long Names

A particularly annoying habit that some developers have is to use long names to identify controls and variables. For example, instead of calling the OK button on a form something simple like btnOK they will use a name such as btnOKBrowseFormCustomerApp. Can you understand what this means? This is a prime example of a bad coding style that will only make your programs harder to understand and maintain.

Coding Large Procedures

Another big mistake programmers often make is writing long procedures. Although you have not seen how to create general procedures yet, you know that by entering code in event handlers Delphi will perform the code in those handlers whenever the events for those controls occur at run-time. Ideally, event handlers should be short and contain only the code needed to accomplish a specific task. If a procedure or function starts becoming too big, you can split the code up into different procedures and functions. Failure to do this will make the program harder to understand and will eventually lead to an *out of memory* error.

Repeating or Copying Blocks of Code

A similar problem is unnecessary repetition of code in a program. Sometimes you will find that you need to perform the same operation repeatedly in an application, such as sort a file, create a purchase order, print a report, and so on. In these cases, the worst thing you can do is to copy the same code to another procedure in the program. As you will see in Chapter 4, with a little extra effort, you can create a general handler to accomplish the same thing in a single routine.

Using the GOTO Statement

The GOTO statement branches control unconditionally to another part of the program. Although Delphi provides support for this statement, it is highly recommended that you do not incorporate it in your source code. Programs that use the GOTO statement are hard to read and maintain. Object Pascal provides more structured ways of controlling the flow of code execution in a program and you will probably never need to use the GOTO statement.

Using Non-Standard Fonts

The final issue to be addressed here is the use of non-standard fonts in applications. Windows 95 has added a significant amount of fonts formerly not available in Windows 3.11. However, if your customers choose not to install the complete font set when installing Windows 95, they will not be able to display fancier fonts like Brush Script MT or Colonna MT. As a result, Windows will accommodate for this by applying either the default font or the closest fonts that match the ones your programs use. This often produces odd side effects with differences in text styles and point sizes. To avoid this problem, use standard fonts like Times New Roman or Arial.

Exercise: Building a Multi-page Dialog

1 From the File menu, choose New Application.

2 Choose File | New... to display the New Items dialog.

3 From the New Items dialog, choose the Forms *tab* (not the Form icon).

4 Select the Tabbed pages option by double clicking on this item.

5 From the Object selector drop-down list of the Object Inspector, choose the TabSheet1 page (see Figure 3.15).

FIGURE 3.15

Choosing the TabSheet1 page

6 Set the Caption property of this page's tab to *Test Page1* using the Object Inspector.

7 Place a label and an edit component on this page as they appear in Figure 3.16.

8 From the Object selector of the Object Inspector, choose the TabSheet2 page.

> **Note** *You will have to scroll down in the list to see this option.*

9 Change the Caption property of this page's tab to *Test Page2*.

10 Add a memo component to this page (see Figure 3.17).

11 From the Object selector of the Object Inspector, choose the TabSheet3 page.

12 Change the Caption property of this page's tab to *Test Page3*.

13 From the Win 3.1 page of the Component Palette, choose the DirectoryListBox icon (see Figure 3.18).

14 Choose Project Options....

15 From the Main form drop-down list, choose PagesDlg. Then click on OK.

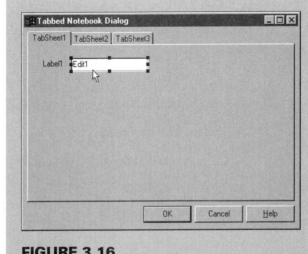

FIGURE 3.16
Positioning the label and edit components on the page

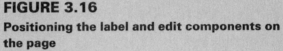

FIGURE 3.17
The memo component icon in the Component Palette

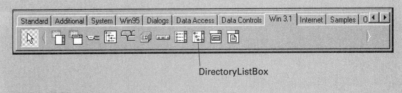

FIGURE 3.18
The DirectoryListBox icon of the Component Palette

16 Run the project. To test the tabbed notebook dialog, click on a tab of the TPageControl component. Notice how the controls you added to that page appear. Similarly, by clicking on other tabs, the controls associated with those pages appear as well.

Summary

In this chapter, you have learned how to build multiform applications. You have also learned to:

- ▶ Change the border style of forms.

- ▶ Display forms modally and nonmodally.

- ▶ Reference controls on other forms.

- ▶ Create a tabbed notebook style interface.

- ▶ Use items from the Object Repository.

- ▶ Add items to the Object Repository.

- ▶ Work with component templates.

- ▶ Incorporate ActiveX controls in applications.

- ▶ Customize the pages of the Component Palette.

- ▶ Size and position controls at run-time.

- ▶ Dynamically create controls when projects are running.

- ▶ Avoid common mistakes often made by programmers.

Writing
Expressions

Using the If
Statement

Using the Case
Statement

Working with Loops

Working with Types

Exercise: Encrypting
a Message

Chapter 4
Programming Standards

In Chapters 1, 2, and 3, you learned how to write simple event handlers
that apply Object Pascal coding. As you will see in this chapter, there is much more to
Delphi than just working with components and forms. Through Object Pascal, Delphi
provides a rich collection of programming capabilities you can use to build applications.
In this chapter, you will learn the Object Pascal language features that permit you to
write expressions, control the flow of code execution, and generate user-defined types.

Writing Expressions

In previous chapters, you have seen examples of how to write expressions in Delphi. An
expression is a statement or part of a statement that calculates or represents a value. For
example:

```
x := 2 + 2;
```

This simple expression will add 2 + 2 and assign the result (4) to variable x. Delphi
can also perform multiplication and division in expressions. To perform multiplication, you use the * operator. For instance:

```
x := 5 * 5;
```

This code will multiply 5 by 5 and store the result (25) in variable x. For division,
Object Pascal uses the **div** operator to divide integers and the / operator for non-integer
division. Object Pascal requires that you use separate operators in integer and non-integer divisions because there is no guarantee that dividing two integers will produce a
whole number (that is, an integer) answer. Delphi therefore restricts these operations.
If you recall that an integer is a whole number that cannot store a decimal, then it follows that this code will produce an error when Delphi tries to compile the program:

```
procedure TForm1.FormCreate(Sender: TObject);
var
  x, y, z: Integer;
begin
  y := 5;
  z := 3;
  x := y / z;
end;
```

Since the variable which will store the answer (x) is declared as an Integer here, you cannot assign the result of this integer division to x since dividing y by z will produce a non-integer answer. To avoid this problem, use the **div** operator like this:

```
procedure TForm1.FormCreate(Sender: TObject);
var
  x, y, z: Integer;
begin
  y := 5;
  z := 3;
  x := y div z;
end;
```

Unlike the / operator, **div** always truncates (removes) the fractional part of the answer before assigning it to the variable that will hold the result. Therefore even if y divided by z produces a non-integer answer in real math, this will not cause an error in the program.

You might wonder if it is possible to find out what the fractional part of the answer is if **div** always truncates the result. The answer to this is that there is another special operator called the **mod** operator. Rather than returning the whole part of the answer like **div**, **mod** returns the fractional part instead. This can be useful in calculations where the whole number part of the answer is not important and you only want to see the fractional remainder.

For example, suppose you are trying to calculate how many backboard panels are needed in a shelving section. Since all cutting will be done on the job, you merely need to know how many whole pieces of plywood should be pulled from stock. Therefore, if the *section length* divided by the *length per section* is not a whole number, one piece should be added to the total to accommodate for the extra short piece needed for the job. The following event handler shows how to write this expression in Delphi:

```
procedure TForm1.FormCreate(Sender: TObject);

const
  LengthPerSection = 5;
var
  TotalPieces, SectionLength: Integer;

begin

  SectionLength := 87; { feet }
  TotalPieces := 0;
```

```
TotalPieces := SectionLength div LengthPerSection;

if SectionLength mod LengthPerSection <> 0 then
    TotalPieces := TotalPieces + 1;

ShowMessage (IntToStr (TotalPieces));

end;
```

The **div** operator is used here to divide *SectionLength* by *LengthPerSection* and store the result in the *TotalPieces* variable. Afterwards, **mod** is applied to see if there is a fractional remainder. If so, an extra piece is added to the answer.

Notice how *TotalPieces* is initially set to 0. Although the division that follows after this line should be adequate for initializing the variable, as a precaution, *TotalPieces* is set to 0 when the program starts. This is important because if you forget to initialize a variable before using it in a program, it is possible that the variable will contain a value that is incorrect when it is used later in an expression.

Real Number Arithmetic

In addition to integer math, you can also write expressions that incorporate real numbers. A *real number* is a number which is represented in floating-point notation, such as 3550.25, 12.5, or 3.74139.

These numbers all share one thing in common. They all contain a decimal point and one or more places of decimal accuracy. Delphi supplies a number of data types suitable for floating-point arithmetic. Table 4.1 summarizes these types.

Which real type you should use depends upon the types of calculations you need to perform and the range of accuracy needed. For example, a scientist might prefer to work with the Extended type but your programs may only require Single precision or Double precision accuracy. The Currency type, as you might expect, is well suited toward monetary calculations. Delphi also supplies an odd type called Comp. Although classified as a real number, Comp does not actually store decimal information. To use

TABLE 4.1   REAL TYPES

Type	Range	Precision	Bytes
Real	2.9×10^{-39} to 1.7×10^{38}	11-12	6
Single	$\pm 1.5 \times 10^{-45}$ to 3.4×10^{38}	7-8	4
Double	5.0×10^{-324} to 1.7×10^{308}	15-16	8
Extended	3.4×10^{-4932} to 1.1×10^{4932}	19-20	10
Currency	-922,337,203,685,477.5808 to 922,337,203,685,477.5807	19-20	8
Comp	-2^{63} to $2^{63}-1$	19-20	8

Comp to express money, you must break the value down to its lowest unit of measure because it holds only integer values. For example, in American currency, a penny is the smallest coin that can be exchanged. To express $1.40 in Comp would be the same thing as saying 140 pennies.

Delphi also supplies one other real type called Real. Not to be confused with the general category of real types themselves (Real, Single, Double, Extended, and so on), the Real type is no longer recommended since it is slower than other comparable types when used in calculations. It is supplied here only for backward compatibility with older versions of Delphi and Borland Pascal.

Order of Precedence

When working with mixed operators, it is important to understand the order in which operators in an expression are evaluated. If an expression contains mixed operators, multiplication and division are performed before addition and subtraction. The logical **not** (discussed later in "Using the If Statement") takes precedence over all operators. Table 4.2 lists the order of operator precedence.

If you are unsure how an expression will be evaluated, you can use parentheses to ensure that a particular part of an expression will be evaluated before another part. For example:

TABLE 4.2   OPERATOR PRECEDENCE

Operator Name	Precedence
@, not	highest
*, /, div, mod,	second highest
as, and, shl, shr, +, -, or, xor	medium
=, <>, <, >, <=, >=, in, is	lowest

```
procedure TForm1.Button1Click(Sender: TObject);

const
  SIDES = 2;
var
  SectionLength, LengthPerShelf: Integer;
  TotalShelves: Single;

begin

  SectionLength := 750; { Inches }
  LengthPerShelf := 60;

  { Compute total shelves needed for two-sided
    shelving section }

  TotalShelves := (SectionLength / LengthPerShelf ) * SIDES;
```

```
    Edit1.Text := FloatToStr (TotalShelves);

end;
```

This event handler will compute the total shelves needed for a shelving section. Notice the use of parentheses in the expression. This example also demonstrates how to promote an integer to a floating-point value. Since the result of the integer division is assigned to a real number (*TotalShelves*), it is permissible to use the / operator in the expression. Also notice the use of the FloatToStr function. This will convert the answer from a floating-point value to a string so it can be assigned to the Text property of the edit control.

Using the If Statement

In previous chapters, you have seen examples of how to apply the **if** statement. The **if** statement allows you to conditionally control the flow of code execution in programs. Until now, all the examples for using the **if** statement have been simple—that is, they all evaluate a single expression and if that condition is met then a line of code is executed. For example:

```
procedure TForm1.Button1Click(Sender: TObject);

var
  x, y: Integer;
begin
  x := 10;
  y := 5;
  if x > y then
     ShowMessage ('Value x is greater than y');
end;
```

In this example, if x is greater than y, a message is shown. However, if y is greater than x, no message is displayed. If you want to report the status in all cases, you can use an **else** clause like this:

```
procedure TForm1.FormCreate(Sender: TObject);
var
  x, y: Integer;
begin
  x := 4;
  y := 8;
```

```
   if x > y then
      ShowMessage ('Value x is greater than y')
   else
      ShowMessage ('Value y is greater than x');
end;
```

The program will now show a message regardless of which variable contains the greater value. Notice that when an **else** clause appears in an **if** statement, you leave off the last semicolon before the **else**.

Complex Conditional Expressions

Sometimes it becomes necessary to perform multiple statements based upon a certain condition in a program. For example:

```
procedure TForm1.FormCloseQuery(Sender: TObject; var CanClose:
         Boolean);

{ Validate input using if statement }

begin

   if CustNumber.Text = '' then begin
      ShowMessage ('Please fill in Customer Number');
      CanClose := False;
      end
   else if CustNumber.Text = '0' then begin
      ShowMessage ('Invalid customer number');
      CanClose := False;
      end
   else
      ShowMessage ('Please remember to backup your work!');

end;
```

If the user tries to close a form without typing a value in the CustNumber edit control, this code will show a message to the user and set the *CanClose* variable to **False**, thus preventing the form from unloading. Notice that when more than one statement is contained in either the **True** or **False** parts of the **if** statement, the code must be contained within a **begin** and **end** block.

An **if** statement can also make use of other operators besides >, <, and =. For example:

```
procedure TForm1.FormCreate(Sender: TObject);

var
  ValidLicense : Boolean;

begin

  ValidLicense := False;

  { Show message if license is no longer valid }

  if not ValidLicense then
    ShowMessage ('Please note your license has expired')

end;
```

Here's another example:

```
procedure TForm1.FormCreate(Sender: TObject);

var
  ItemFound: Boolean;

begin

  ItemFound := True;

  { Show message to report if search item has
    been found }

  if ItemFound <> True then
    ShowMessage ('Search item not found')
  else
    ShowMessage ('Search item has been located!');

end;
```

Both the **not** and <> (inequality) operators return **True** if a condition is **False**. Some developers prefer to use **not** in their expressions. Others feel the inequality operator makes a program easier to read. Delphi often supplies different ways to accomplish the same tasks. Which way is better for you depends on your perspective and unique coding style.

Using the Case Statement

Although the **if** statement is useful, too many **else** clauses in an **if** statement can also make your code harder to read and maintain. An alternative to the **if** statement is the **case** statement. The **case** statement compares an item called a *selector* with a list of items and executes code if a match is found. For example, the following code uses a selector called *ItemPrinted* to show a message:

```
procedure TForm1.FormCreate(Sender: TObject);


var
  ItemPrinted: Integer;
begin

  ItemPrinted := 2;

  { Compare values in case statement }

  case ItemPrinted of
    1: ShowMessage ('First report printed');
    2: ShowMessage ('Second report printed');
    else
      ShowMessage ('No report printed');
    end;

end;
```

Since *ItemPrinted* is initially set to 2, the message *Second report printed* will be shown. Notice that if no match is found, the **else** clause will report this as well. The selector you choose to make the comparison in a **case** statement must evaluate to be an ordinal value. An *ordinal value* is a value that you can count by. These include not only numbers but letters also. For instance:

```
procedure TForm1.FormCreate(Sender: TObject);
```

```
var
  SelectorVar: Char;
begin

  SelectorVar := 'C';

  { Compare values in case statement }

  case SelectorVar of
    'A': ShowMessage ('A selected');
    'B': ShowMessage ('B selected');
    'C': ShowMessage ('C selected');
    'D': ShowMessage ('D selected');
    else
       ShowMessage ('No item selected');
    end;

end;
```

Like the **if** statement, a **begin..end** block with the **case** statement may be used. This technique is useful if you need to perform multiple lines of code when a certain match is found. For example:

```
case SelectorChoice of
   1: ShowMessage ('You chose choice #1');
   2: ShowMessage ('You chose choice #2');
   3: begin
       ShowMessage ('Good-bye!');
       Halt; { End program }
     end;
   else
      ShowMessage ('Can''t you type a number right?');
   end;
```

Notice the use of the double quotes in the string:

```
'Can''t  you type a number right?'
```

Since Object Pascal uses single quotes to indicate a literal string, you must use the second quote to indicate that you want to display the quote in the message. Otherwise, Delphi will interpret this as an unterminated string.

Working with Loops

Another way you can control the flow of execution in programs is by using loops. You use loops to repeatedly perform a block of code while (or until) a certain condition is met. Delphi provides the following looping constructs:

▶ For loop

▶ While..loop

▶ Repeat..until loop

The For Loop

This looping construct is useful when you know *beforehand* exactly how many times the loop will perform. For example, you can use a **for** loop to prompt for a password and terminate the program after three tries if the user fails to enter the correct security code:

```
procedure TForm1.FormCreate(Sender: TObject);

var
  Password: String;
  CountTries, I: Integer;
  PasswordOK: Boolean;

begin

  CountTries := 0;
  PasswordOK := False;

  for I := 1 to 3 do begin

    { Get password from user }

    Password := InputBox('Validate User ID', 'Enter password',
              '');

    if Password <> '2432' then begin
      CountTries := CountTries + 1;
      PasswordOK := False;
      end
    else begin
      PasswordOK := True;
      exit;
```

```
        end;
    end;

    if (CountTries = 3) and (PasswordOK = False) then begin
        ShowMessage ('Strike three, your out! Bye bye!!!');
        Halt;
        end;

end;
```

By convention, the integer variable I is often used as an index (or counter) in a **for** loop. Initially I is set to 1. With each repetition of the loop I is incremented by 1 and the statements within the **begin..end** block are performed. When I reaches 3, the loop terminates.

The While Loop

Like the **for** statement, the **while** looping construct repeats a statement or group of statements until a certain condition is met. You use a **while** loop when you do not know how many times the loop will perform. For example, a **while** loop can be used to read input from a file until the end of the file is reached or to prompt for input until a certain value is entered. Here's an example:

```
procedure TForm1.FormCreate(Sender: TObject);

var
  StrMsg: String;

begin

  { Repeat loop until user types Quit }

  while UpperCase (StrMsg) <> 'QUIT' do begin
      StrMsg := InputBox('Validate User ID', 'Enter password',
                '');
      ShowMessage ('The value you typed was ' + StrMsg);
      end;

end;
```

Since the **while** loop construct evaluates the condition before performing the loop, if the condition is not **True** initially, the statement(s) inside the loop will never be executed.

The Repeat..Until Loop

Delphi also provides a third way of controlling loops. The **repeat..until** loop is similar to the **while** loop. Since the condition for a **repeat..until** loop is always evaluated after the loop is executed, however, the loop will always perform at least once. The following example shows how it can be applied:

```
procedure TForm1.FormCreate(Sender: TObject);


{ Repeat loop until user enters the
  lucky number }


var
  StrMsg, N: String;
begin
  repeat
    N := InputBox('Get Number', 'Please enter a number', '');
  until N = '7';
end;
```

Working with Types

In addition to program control structures, Delphi provides an extensive collection of other language features you can use to develop applications. Among its key strengths is its ability to create user-defined types. In the following section, you will learn how to work with the Object Pascal keywords that permit you to generate user-defined types.

Enumerated Types

This type lets you create an organized list of items. The following example shows how to declare an enumerated type:

```
implementation
{$R *.DFM}


type
  Countries = (England, France, Germany, Italy, USA, Russia);
```

Although the type declaration does not have to be added here, by placing this definition above the procedural blocks, it will be accessible to all the event handlers throughout the unit. Each item contained in the list must be separated by a comma and no blank spaces are permitted in a single element. For example, since *United States* contains a blank space, the preceding example uses *USA* instead.

Once declared, you use an enumerated type in a program by declaring a variable of that type. For example:

```
var
  Market: Countries;
```

After declaring the variable, you can use it in a program by testing its ordinal value. The first item in the list has an ordinal value of 0. Each item thereafter has an ordinal value one greater than the previous. Therefore, since the list begins at 0, England, which is the first item on the list, has an ordinal value of 0, France has an ordinal value of 1, Germany has an ordinal value of 2, and so on. If you were to set Market to Russia, then Market would have an ordinal value of 5. The following example shows how this can be used in a program:

```
procedure TForm1.btnGetPriceClick(Sender: TObject);

var
  Market: Countries;
  ItemPrice: Currency;

begin

  Market := Russia;

  { Get item price according to ordinal
    value of selector }

  case Market of
     England: ItemPrice := 45.00;
     France: ItemPrice := 50.25;
     Germany: ItemPrice := 55.30;
     Italy: ItemPrice := 52.00;
     USA: ItemPrice := 40.50;
     Russia: ItemPrice := 68.50
  else
     ItemPrice := 75.00;
  end;

  { Convert value to string and display answer }

  ShowMessage (FloatToStr (ItemPrice));
```

```
       end;
```

Rather than using undescriptive numbers, the event handler makes use of the Market variable to compare the items in the **case** statement. When a match is found, the program then assigns a price to the item depending on the country status. As you may recall, the **case** statement compares items in its list using the value of its selector. This variable must be an ordinal type. Therefore, no conversion is necessary to use the Market variable as the selector. However, if you want to see the current value of Market, you can get its ordinal value like this:

```
    ShowMessage (IntToStr (Ord (Market)));
```

The Ord function will return the ordinal value of Market (5). Delphi also provides the Succ and Pred functions which return the successor and predecessor of an ordinal expression. For example, if the present value of Market is Italy, then its successor (Succ) is USA and its predecessor (Pred) is Germany.

Subrange Types

Another important language element of Object Pascal is the subrange type. With a subrange, you can define a valid range of answers the user can enter in a program, such as the number of hours in a week, the distance traveled between two locations, the age bracket of a club's members, and so on. A subrange can consist of any of the following types:

▶ Boolean

▶ Char

▶ Integer

▶ Enumerated type

The declaration for a subrange type is similar to that of an enumerated type. However, instead of using a comma separated list to define the items, you specify the list like this:

```
    type
      MySubRange = 1..20;
```

For example, you can use a subrange type to validate the range of numbers input into an edit component. The following code shows how this can be done:

```
    procedure TForm1.Button1Click(Sender: TObject);

    {$R+}
```

```
type
  TBonus = 100..10000;
var
  Answer: TBonus;

begin

  { Demonstrate range checking with
    subrange type }

  Answer := StrToInt(Edit1.Text);

end;
```

The name of the subrange type (TBonus) in this example is preceded by a capital T to indicate that it is a type. Although this is not required, it is strongly recommended that you abide by this convention as it will make the logic in your programs easier to follow. Also notice that Answer is declared as a variable of type TBonus. Therefore, Answer is now restricted by the range specified by the TBonus subrange type (100 to 10,000). When the program runs, if a value is entered inside the edit control that is out of range, the program will generate a run-time error.

> **Note** *To activate range checking, the {$R+} compiler directive must also be included in the program or Delphi will not perform any range tests.*

You can also rewrite the preceding example so that it traps the exception error. For example:

```
procedure TForm1.Button1Click(Sender: TObject);

{$R+}

type
  TBonus = 100..10000;
var
  Answer: TBonus;

begin

  { Demonstrate range checking with
    subrange type }
```

```
try
  Answer := StrToInt(Edit1.Text)
except
  on ERangeError do ShowMessage ('Value out of range');
end;


end;
```

Instead of crashing the program, this code will trap the exception error and display a message to the user. Exception errors are the topic of a later discussion. For more information on how to write exception handlers, see Chapter 7, "Dealing with Errors."

Array Types

An array is an ordered collection of elements of the same data type that makes use of an index to provide access to items in the list. Arrays are useful in many applications. Since the index permits random access of the list's elements, arrays supply a powerful mechanism for organizing data. The following example shows how to declare an array:

```
var
  WeekDays: array [1..7] of String;
```

Like the subrange type, the range of elements that an array will contain is indicated by placing two dots between the minimum and maximum values. The WeekDays array is declared as a string array that has seven elements. This next example shows how to initialize the array:

```
procedure TForm1.Button1Click(Sender: TObject);

{ Declare array }

var
  WeekDays: array [1..7] of String;

var
  DayNo: Integer;
  WeekDay: String;

begin

  { Initialize array with weekday names }
```

```
WeekDays [1] := 'Sunday';
WeekDays [2] := 'Monday';
WeekDays [3] := 'Tuesday';
WeekDays [4] := 'Wednesday';
WeekDays [5] := 'Thursday';
WeekDays [6] := 'Friday';
WeekDays [7] := 'Saturday';
    .    .    .

end;
```

To initialize an element of an array, you assign a value to its associated index. Once you have assigned a value to each element, you can reference the items an array contains by using an index. For example, the following code shows how to get the current day of the week:

```
    .    .    .
DayNo := DayOfWeek (Date);
ShowMessage ('The current day of the week is ' + WeekDays [DayNo]);
```

The Object Pascal function DayOfWeek returns an integer from 1 to 7 that represents the day of the week that a particular date falls on. By passing Date as an argument to DayOfWeek, the function returns the current weekday number. Afterwards, the value assigned to *DayNo* is used as an index to the array to get the current weekday name.

Declaring Multidimensional Arrays

The preceding example demonstrated how to incorporate a one-dimensional array in a program. Object Pascal also permits you to specify multidimensional array types. The following example shows how this can be done:

```
var
   MyArray: array [1..30, 1..30] of Integer;
```

As you can see, the code to declare a two-dimensional array is almost identical to that of a one-dimensional array. Once declared, you can access any item of the array by supplying a second index. The following code shows how to quickly initialize the array with a nested **for** loop:

```
procedure TForm1.btnMultidimClick(Sender: TObject);

var
   MyArray: array [1..30, 1..30] of Integer;
```

```
   Index1, Index2: Integer;

begin

  { Initialize each element in multidimensional array }

  for Index1 := 1 to 30 do
     for Index2 := 1 to 30 do
         MyArray [Index1, Index2] := 0;

end;
```

Record Types

Unlike other types discussed in this chapter, the record type can contain a heterogeneous collection of data types. For instance, you can use a record type to define the structure of an employee record like this:

```
   .   .   .
implementation

{$R *.DFM}

type
  TEmployRec = Record
    LName: String [15];
    FName: String [15];
    HireDate: TDateTime;
    Salary: Currency;
    Department: String;
  end;
```

Notice how the record type is made up of strings, a new type called the TDateTime type and the Currency type. By organizing related groups of items like this, you can better control heterogeneous collections of information.

Before using a record type in an application, it is important to keep in mind that the declaration for the record type defines only the type itself. In order to use that type in a program, you must also declare a variable of that type:

```
var
  EmployeeInfo: TEmployRec;
```

The EmployeeInfo variable is declared of type TEmployRec. Once you have declared this, you can access the individual elements of the record (or what are called *fields*) like this:

```
procedure TForm1.Button1Click(Sender: TObject);

{ Initialize and display employee record }

begin

   EmployeeInfo.LName := 'Smith';
   EmployeeInfo.FName := 'Eric';
   EmployeeInfo.HireDate := Date;
   EmployeeInfo.Salary := 37000;
   EmployeeInfo.Department := 'Development';

   ShowMessage (EmployeeInfo.LName + ' ' + EmployeeInfo.FName +
                ' ' + DateToStr (EmployeeInfo.HireDate));

end;
```

Notice that you use a period to separate the record type variable from the field name it is referencing. Object Pascal also provides an easier way to perform this operation using the **with** statement:

```
procedure TForm1.Button1Click(Sender: TObject);

{ Initialize and display employee record }

begin

   with EmployeeInfo do begin

        LName := 'Smith';
        FName := 'Eric';
        HireDate := Date;
        Salary := 37000;
        Department := 'Development';

        ShowMessage (LName + ' ' + FName + ' ' +
```

```
                        DateToStr (HireDate));


    end; { with }


end;
```

The **with** statement provides shorthand access to a record type's fields. By including the references to the record type within a **begin..end** block, you can specify any fields in the record without having to precede them with the name of the record type variable.

Exercise: Encrypting a Message

In the following exercise, you will learn how to encrypt a message for security purposes using a routine from the developers' library included with this book. After performing this exercise, you should be able to:

▶ Call routines from the Delphi Programmers' Library.

▶ Encode a string using the EncryptMsg function.

▶ Include other units in projects.

> **Note** *For more information on using library routines, see Chapter 5, "Working with Procedures and Functions."*

1 Start a new project by choosing File | New Application.

2 From the Standard page of the Component Palette, add a button component, a label component, and an edit component to the form.

3 Set the properties of each control as follows:

Component	Property	Value
Label1	Caption	Message to encrypt:
	Left	37
	Top	32
Edit1	Text	(null string)
	Left	145
	Top	30
Button1	Caption	OK
	Left	40
	Top	60
	Name	btnEncrypt

4 From the File menu, choose the Add to Project... command.

5 Add the LMString unit to the project by typing **C:\DLIB\LMSTRING.PAS**.

Note *This step assumes you installed the example files included on the CD in the C:\DLIB path. If these files are located in another drive or directory, be sure to specify the correct path.*

6 Click on Open to add the unit to the project.

7 Double click on the btnEncrypt button and add the following code to the OnClick event handler of the control:

```
ShowMessage ('The message encrypted is ' +
             EncryptMsg (Edit1.Text, 5));
```

When the program runs, this code will encrypt a message for security purposes.

8 Choose the File | Use Unit command.

9 Select the LMString unit from the Use Unit dialog and then click on OK.

10 Run the program by choosing the F9 fast key.

11 Type **test message** in the Edit1 text box.

12 To demonstrate how the EncryptMsg library routine works, click on the OK (btnEncrypt) button. The program will now encrypt the message for security purposes. Figure 4.1 shows how the output appears.

FIGURE 4.1
Output for the chapter exercise

Summary

In this chapter, you have learned how to work with user-defined types and other control structures. Specifically you have learned how to:

▶ Work with different data types.

▶ Write expressions.

▶ Use the **if** and **case** statements.

▶ Apply looping constructs in programs.

▶ Utilize enumerated, subrange, array, and record types.

▶ Use the **with** reserved word.

▶ Encrypt/decrypt messages.

Placement of
Procedures and
Functions

Accessing the
Delphi
Programmers'
Library

Commonly Used
Delphi Procedures
and Functions

Exercise: Defining
Hotspots on a Form

Chapter 5
Working with Procedures and Functions

In preceding chapters, you learned how to create event handlers for controls. When you create an event handler, Delphi automatically adds the reserved word **procedure** to the declaration. As this would imply, the building blocks of event handlers are made from procedures. You have already seen some examples of procedures, most notably, the ShowMessage procedure which permits you to display a message in a simple modal dialog box.

This book has also demonstrated how to incorporate a similar language element, called a **function,** in programs. Examples of this include InputBox, StrToInt, IntToStr, StrToFloat, FloatToStr, and more. In this chapter, we will take a closer look at Delphi's pre-defined subroutines and discuss the rules for creating user-defined procedures and functions.

A procedure is a subprogram that can be called from another part of the program to perform a particular task. The difference between a procedure and a function is that a function returns a value and a procedure does not. For instance:

```
procedure TForm1.Button1Click(Sender: TObject);

{ Repeat loop until user enters the
  lucky number }

var
  StrMsg, N: String;

begin

  StrMsg := 'Please enter a number from 1 to 10:';

  repeat
    N := InputBox('Get Number', StrMsg, '');
  until N = '7';

  ShowMessage ('You guessed the lucky number ' + N);

end;
```

Notice how InputBox returns a value and ShowMessage does not. However, both the function and the procedure can accept one or more parameters to produce the necessary results. In the case of the ShowMessage procedure, a string is passed to the procedure so it can be displayed. InputBox is similar, only the function has been written to accept multiple parameters. Both a procedure and a function can be supplied with zero or more parameters. In order to understand how to declare procedures and functions, it is necessary to understand syntax.

Object Pascal Syntax

The syntax of a computer statement is a schematic representation of how code should look and work. For example, the syntax of the ShowMessage procedure is:

```
procedure ShowMessage (const MessageToShow: String);
```

The **const** reserved word indicates that *MessageToShow* will be treated as a constant value by the procedure—that is, ShowMessage will not try to modify the string. When calling ShowMessage, you do not actually have to type the word **const**. The **const** reserved word is already defined in the procedure heading for this procedure (declared in the Dialogs unit). After the *MessageToShow* parameter, a colon is used to separate the parameter from its data type (String). Again, this syntax is only for reference and for Delphi's internal purposes when it compiles and runs a program.

When calling procedures and functions, you never have to actually type the colon in the parameter list. The only time that this is required is when you define your own procedures and functions (discussed later in this chapter). You can also pass multiple parameters to a procedure or function by separating them with commas. For instance:

```
function InputBox (const DialogCaption, DialogPrompt, DialogDefault:
                   String): String;
```

In addition to the comma-separated parameter list, the InputBox function also has a return value of type String. When calling a function, it is important to remember that the return value must be assigned to a variable of the same type. For example:

```
procedure TForm1.Button1Click(Sender: TObject);

{ Convert floating-point value to
  formatted string }

var
  N: Extended;
  Precision, Decimals: Integer;
```

```
begin
  N := 525.50;
  Precision := 7;
  Decimals := 2;
  Edit1.Text := FloatToStrF (N, ffCurrency, Precision, Decimals);
end;
```

The FloatToStrF function converts a floating-point value to a formatted string. Here it is used to format a real-type value for currency and convert it to a string (see Figure 5.1). Notice how the string is assigned to an edit component. Since the Text property of an edit control is of type String, this assignment is perfectly valid.

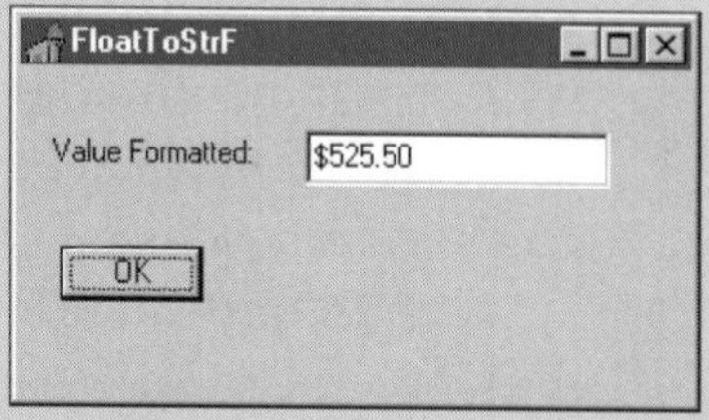

FIGURE 5.1
Formatting a value for currency

User-Defined Procedures and Functions

Throughout this book, you have seen examples of how to work with event handlers. Since Delphi automatically creates event handlers for its components, you may wonder why it is necessary to write procedures and functions. Often when coding applications, you may find yourself coding the same routines over and over again. For example, a purchasing program may have several places in the code where a purchase order can be created. Rather than repeating the same statements in several event handlers, you can create a procedure or function to handle this task whenever you request it. By writing your own procedures and functions, your applications will also have the following advantages:

▶ The code will be reusable.

▶ Less code will have to be written.

▶ Changes can be made centrally in a procedure/function without having to repeat the same changes throughout the program.

Imagine how much harder it would be to write a program if you could not use Delphi's pre-defined routines like ShowMessage, InputBox, IntToStr, StrToInt, FloatToStrF, and so on. Not only would you have to write these same routines yourself, but without procedures and functions, you would also have to repeat the same code over and over again every time you had to show a modal dialog box, convert an integer to a string, or format a value. Thus Delphi's pre-defined procedures and functions are an invaluable tool to you as a developer. Moreover, by writing your own procedures and functions, you can define reusable blocks of code that can be used in all your applications.

Coding Procedures and Functions

To define a procedure or function in a unit, you must first declare the procedure or function header. For example:

```
procedure ShowStr (MessageOption: Integer; lblCtrl: TLabel);
```

The header begins with the reserved word **procedure**. Afterwards, the name of the sub-routine (ShowStr) appears, followed by the parameter list enclosed in parentheses. *MessageOption* is passed to the procedure as type Integer. Notice the colon before the type specification and the semicolon that appears after the Integer type. This semicolon must appear here to separate it from the next parameter in the list. The second parameter (lblCtrl) is of type TLabel. Like variables, components can also be passed to procedures and functions as parameters.

After the procedure header, you can place any necessary variable declarations that the procedure will use. By declaring a variable inside a procedure, it becomes local within that procedure. What this means is that the variable only exists in memory while the code in the procedure is being performed. For instance, the ShowStr procedure defines two variables:

```
var
   Str1, Str2: String;
```

Str1 and Str2 are used by the procedure to build a message (see example below). Afterwards, Delphi automatically frees the memory allocated to these strings and makes that memory available again for use in other parts of the program.

The Body of a Subroutine

Inside a procedure or function, any code you place in a subroutine will execute when that routine is called. However, unlike event handlers, if you wish to reference a component inside a subroutine, you must pass it to the procedure/function for it to be accessible:

```
procedure ShowStr (MessageOption: Integer; lblCtrl: TLabel);

{ Create message and display it }

var
   Str1, Str2: String;

Begin

   if MessageOption = 1 then begin
      Str1 := 'Please remember to backup your work before posting ';
      Str2 := 'changes to the History file.';
```

```
      end
  else begin
    Str1 := 'Warning, you have not backed up your work. ';
    Str2 := 'Are you sure you want to continue?';
  end;


  lblCtrl.Caption := Str1 + Str2;


End;
```

Once declared in a unit, the following code shows how to call the ShowStr procedure:

```
procedure TForm1.Button1Click(Sender: TObject);


{ Call procedure to display message }


Const
 Show_BackupMessage = 1;


begin
  ShowStr (Show_BackupMessage, Label1);
end;
```

This code will invoke the ShowStr procedure and pass two parameters to the sub-routine. Notice that the names of the parameters passed to the procedure are not the same as the names it accepts. By permitting you to rename parameters passed to sub-routines, Delphi gives you the flexibility to call a procedure or function and pass it different variables and objects. For example:

```
procedure TForm1.Button1Click(Sender: TObject);


{ Call procedure to display message }


Const
  Show_BackupMessage = 1;
  Show_WarningMessage = 2;
begin
  ShowStr (Show_BackupMessage, Label1);
  ShowStr (Show_WarningMessage, Label2);
end;
```

Notice that ShowStr is called twice now from the event handler. Each time ShowStr is called, it is passed a different set of parameters. Although these parameters have different names, they are compatible to the extent that both the Show_BackupMessage and Show_WarningMessage constants store integer values and both the Label1 and Label2 components are of type TLabel. Going back to our original procedure header, notice how this matches the expected parameter list:

```
procedure ShowStr (MessageOption: Integer; lblCtrl: TLabel);
```

With the ability to accept different variables and objects as parameters, a subroutine can be reused in many ways. The first time the ShowStr procedure is called, for example, the following message is assigned to the Caption property of Label1:

```
Please remember to backup your work before posting
            changes to the History file.
```

By assigning a new value to the *MessageOption* parameter and passing Label2 instead of Label1 upon the second call to the procedure, a different message is now displayed in Label2:

```
Warning, you have not backed up your work. Are you
            sure you want to continue?
```

This flexibility makes it possible for you to code a single subroutine that can be used as a generic handler for different objects and variables. In Part II of this book, you will see many examples of how this can be useful to you as a developer.

Coding User-Defined Functions

The code to declare a function in a unit is similar to a procedure definition. However, unlike a procedure, a function can return a value. Therefore the header for a function must include the return type.

Syntax

```
function IdentifierName [(Parameter List)]: ReturnType;
```

This book uses square brackets ([]) to include optional items in syntax specifications. Here they imply that the parameter list is optional and that it can be omitted if the function does not require any parameters.

Example

```
function SquareVal (NumberToSquare: Integer): Integer;
```

The body of a function is also similar to a procedure. It begins with an optional variable declaration section and is followed by the executable statements you insert between the **begin** and **end** reserved words. To return a value from the function, you assign a value to the name of the function. For example:

```
function SquareVal (NumberToSquare: Integer): Integer;

{ Square value and return answer }

begin
  SquareVal := NumberToSquare * NumberToSquare;
end;
```

This function computes the square of a number and returns the value back to the calling routine to a variable of the same type (ReturnValue):

```
procedure TForm1.btnOKClick(Sender: TObject);

{ Call function to square number }

var
  NumberToSquare, ReturnValue: Integer;
begin
  NumberToSquare := 5;
  ReturnValue := SquareVal (NumberToSquare);
  Label1.Caption := IntToStr (ReturnValue);
end;
```

Passing Parameters

When working with subroutines, it is important to understand the way parameters are passed in programs. Earlier, you saw two examples of constant parameters. Delphi also supports other types of parameters as well. The most common types of parameters a program typically uses are the following:

▶ Value parameters

▶ Variable parameters

▶ Constant parameters

Value Parameters versus Variable Parameters

When you code the header for a procedure or function, if you do not specify the parameter type, Delphi will pass the parameter as a value parameter. A *value parameter* is a copy of the original parameter passed from the calling routine. When called from an event handler or other subroutine, the original variable/object is known as the *actual parameter*. The parameter read in by the subroutine is called a *formal parameter*.

Since the value parameter is only a copy of the original parameter, if you assign a new value to the parameter in the subroutine, the actual parameter will still retain its original value after the procedure/function has been called. If you need to pass a parameter to a subroutine and have it retain its value after the procedure/function has processed it, you can pass the parameter as a *variable parameter*. To do this, you use the **var** reserved word in the procedure/function heading:

```
procedure MyProc (var X: Integer);

{ Get variable parameter and change
  its value}

begin
  X := X + 1;
end;


procedure TForm1.Button1Click(Sender: TObject);

{ Call test subroutine }

var
  X: Integer;
begin
  X := 2;
  MyProc (X);
  ShowMessage (IntToStr (X));
end;
```

Now instead of just passing a copy of the original value, the variable parameter can directly reference the actual parameter and change its value. Since a variable parameter is a reference to the original memory address of the actual parameter, any change made to the parameter in the subroutine will be reflected in the calling routine.

Constant Parameters

As mentioned before, Delphi also provides the ability to pass a value as a constant parameter to a subroutine. By including the **const** reserved word before a parameter in a procedure or function header, Delphi will restrict you from inadvertently assigning a new value to the parameter. By using this technique, you are assured that the formal parameter will never accidentally be assigned a new value in the subroutine. Although you are already protected from inadvertently changing the original value of the parameter in the calling procedure when you pass the parameter as a value parameter (default), there is no restriction within the subroutine itself to prevent you from inadvertently modifying the copy of the original value and then processing it within the subroutine. To avoid this problem, use the **const** reserved word in the header declaration of the procedure:

```
procedure MyProc (const X: Integer);
      .     .     .
```

Placement of Procedures and Functions

Like event handlers, the code for a procedure or function must be entered into the **implementation** section of the unit. By default, subroutines are only made available within the current unit. To make a procedure/function accessible to other units, you must add the header for the subroutine also to the **interface** section of the unit. For example, the boldfaced lines below show how to add the SquareVal function to a unit and make it available to other units:

```
unit Unit1;

interface

uses
  Windows, Messages, SysUtils, Classes, Graphics, Controls, Forms,
  Dialogs;

type
  TForm1 = class(TForm)
  private
    { Private declarations }
  public
    { Public declarations }
  end;

var
  Form1: TForm1;

function SquareVal (NumberToSquare: Integer): Integer;
```

```
implementation

{$R *.DFM}

function SquareVal (NumberToSquare: Integer): Integer;

{ Square value and return answer }

begin
  SquareVal := NumberToSquare * NumberToSquare;
end;

end.
```

Once this declaration is made, the function can be called by adding the name of that unit to the **uses** clause in either the **implementation** or **interface** section. However, if the unit is not available in the current search path, you will have to either add the unit to the project or save the project source code in the directory where the include unit resides on disk.

Positioning Subroutines

If a procedure or function is to be called within the same unit in which it is defined, the subroutine must be placed above the event handler or other subroutine that calls it. For example:

```
function Valid_UserPassword: Boolean;

{ Validate user password }

var
  P : String;

begin

  P := InputBox ('Password', 'Enter password','');

  if P = '64325' then
    Valid_UserPassword := True
  else
    Valid_UserPassword := False;
```

```
end;


procedure TForm1.FormCreate(Sender: TObject);


{ Call function }


begin
  If not Valid_UserPassword then
     Halt;
end;
```

Since the call to the Valid_UserPassword function is made from the OnCreate event handler of the form, the code for the Valid_UserPassword function must be placed above this call. The one exception to this rule is with forward declarations. By adding the **forward** directive to a procedure or function heading, the implementation of the subroutine can be placed before or after the calling routine.

```
  .    .    .
implementation


{$R *.DFM}


function Valid_UserPassword: Boolean; forward;


procedure TForm1.FormCreate(Sender: TObject);


{ Call function }


begin
  If not Valid_UserPassword then
     Halt;
end;


function Valid_UserPassword: Boolean;


{ Validate user password }


var
```

```
    P : String;

begin

  P := InputBox ('Password', 'Enter password','');

  if P = '64325' then
    Valid_UserPassword := True
  else
    Valid_UserPassword := False;

end;

end.
```

This technique is useful for applications that require mutual recursive calls to sub-routines. *Recursion* is a process in which a subroutine repeatedly calls itself. Thus *mutual recursion* is when two subroutines call each other. This technique is advanced and not recommended since it can lead to infinite loops if care is not taken to ensure that there is always a way of exiting from the chained procedure or function calls.

Accessing the Delphi Programmers' Library

This book comes with a developers' library that contains many reusable routines. The Delphi Programmers' Library consists of 13 reusable code modules which you can use for the development of applications, provided you agree to the terms in the licensing agreement and do not use the library routines to develop a competing reusable code system.

The library modules are separated by subroutine purpose. For example, database routines are contained in the LMDB unit (see Chapter 14), multimedia routines are contained in the LMMedia unit (see Chapter 15), rich text format routines are contained in LMREdit (see Chapter 16), and so on.

To include a routine from the developers' library in a project, add the name of the unit to the **uses** clause of the unit which will call the library routine and choose the File | Add to Project... command to include the unit in the project. Once you have included the unit name in the **uses** clause and added the library module to the project, you can call any routine in that module using the same techniques described earlier in this chapter.

Unless otherwise noted, the procedures and functions of the library all accept value parameters. Part II of this book discusses the developers' library. At the end of this chapter, you will have a chance to use a routine from the LMScr32 unit in an exercise. For more information on how to use the Delphi Programmers' Library, see Part II— The Library.

> **Important** *Due to the method used to compile/link Delphi applications, if you add a* **uses** *clause to the* **implementation** *section of a unit, the name of the unit that you reference must be added to the project first (using the File | Add to Project... command) or else Delphi will remove the* **uses** *clause from the project's source code the first time you compile the program! This bug/feature has been reported.*

Commonly Used Delphi Procedures and Functions

In addition to the original routines included with this book, Delphi supplies a wide range of procedures and functions that you can use to build applications. You have already seen several examples of Delphi subroutines. In this next section, you will learn how to incorporate other common Delphi procedures and functions in applications.

The Abs Function

The Abs function returns the absolute value of an expression. The *absolute value* of a number is a number with its sign information removed. For example, the absolute value of -654 is 654. The syntax of the Abs function is as follows:

```
function Abs(N);
```

N can be an integer-type or any real-type value (Single, Double, Extended, Currency, and so on). For example, you can use the Abs function to determine the relative number of pixels that the mouse has moved in a screen saver application:

```
procedure TForm1.FormMouseMove(Sender: TObject; Shift: TShiftState; X,
  Y: Integer);

begin

  { Terminate screen saver if mouse has moved
    since screen saver kicked in }

  if Abs (X) - Abs (StartPos_X) > 5 then begin
    Close;
  end;
```

```
    if Abs (Y) - Abs (StartPos_Y) > 5 then begin
        Close;
    end;

  end;
```

The code inside the OnMouseMove event of the form determines whether the mouse has moved since the screen saver was started. If so, the screen saver automatically stops running. To determine whether the mouse position has changed, the Abs function is applied to get the relative number of pixels the mouse has moved since the screen saver started. If this number is greater than five pixels, the program ends.

The Copy Function

The ability to manipulate strings is an important skill that all programmers must learn. The Copy function provides an easy way of working with strings. Copy returns a substring from a string. The syntax is as follows:

```
function Copy(S: String; Start, Size: Integer): String;
```

The parameters are:

S: String to copy characters from

Start: Starting position in string to copy from

Size: Size of string to copy

> **Note** *If Size is greater than the number of characters available, the Copy function returns all the characters from Start to the end of the string.*

The StrExtractCmd function of the library uses the Copy function to return a substring from a string. The string that will be searched is:

```
GraphicsPath = C:\ProgImg
```

To determine the path where graphics are stored on the local hard drive, the Pos function is first applied to get the position where the equal sign appears in the string. Afterwards, 1 position is added to this answer to determine the *Start* position. Then to calculate the size of the substring that should be copied, the original starting position (P) is subtracted from the length of the string:

```
    .      .      .
P := Pos('=', CommandStr);
Temp := Copy(CommandStr, P + 1, Length (CommandStr) - P);
```

The ExtractFileName Function

When working with files, sometimes it becomes necessary to extract a file name from a path. For example, if the path is C:\MyApp\Data1.txt, then the program must somehow extract the name of the file from that string. As the preceding example has demonstrated, this can involve tedious programming that requires analyzing the string and breaking it down into its essential parts. Fortunately, Delphi provides a function that does this already. The ExtractFileName function returns the name of a file from a path. The syntax is as follows:

```
function ExtractFileName(const Path: String): String;
```

The following example shows how to use the ExtractFileName function to extract the file name returned from the Open common dialog:

```
procedure TForm1.btnOpenClick(Sender: TObject);

var FileName, FullPath: String;

begin

  { Extract file name from path returned from
    Open common dialog }

  if OpenDialog1.Execute then begin
     FullPath := OpenDialog1.FileName;
     FileName := ExtractFileName (FullPath);
     end;

end;
```

Note *The TOpenDialog control is discussed in Chapter 16, "Rich Edit Routines."*

The ExtractFilePath Function

In addition to ExtractFileName, Delphi also supplies the ExtractFilePath function to report a path name without the file specification. For instance, if the path is C:\PathToBitmaps\Demo1.bmp then ExtractFilePath returns C:\PathToBitmaps\.

Syntax

```
function ExtractFilePath(const FileName: String): String;
```

The following example shows how to remove a file specification from a path so the program can change directories:

```
procedure TForm1.btnChangePathClick(Sender: TObject);

{ Change directory by extracting path
  from string }

var
  FilePath, NewPath: String;
begin
  FilePath := 'C:\Videos\Demo1.avi';
  NewPath := ExtractFilePath(FilePath);
  ChDir(NewPath);
end;
```

The FileGetDate Function

This function permits you to determine how old a file is. FileGetDate accepts as an argument a handle to the file. To get this value, you can open the file using the FileOpen function. For example:

```
var
  Handle1, Temp: Integer;
  DateVal: TDateTime;

begin

  { Get file handle by opening it }

  Handle1 := FileOpen (FileListBox1.FileName, 0);
  Temp := FileGetDate(Handle1);
     .    .    .
```

FileGetDate returns a file's date-and-time stamp as an integer. To convert this to a TDateTime value, you use the FileDateToDateTime function:

```
var
  Handle1, Temp: Integer;
  DateVal: TDateTime;
```

```
begin
    .    .    .
DateVal := FileDateToDateTime(Temp);
```

Afterwards, if you need to display the value you can use the DateTimeToStr function to convert the value of TDateTime to a string:

```
Label1.Caption := DateTimeToStr(DateVal);
```

The Sleep Function

Occasionally when programming, you may find a need to delay an operation. For example:

```
procedure TForm1.FormCreate(Sender: TObject);

{ Show Message when program loads }

begin
  Form1.Show;
  Label1.Caption := 'ABC Company Presents...';
  Application.ProcessMessages;
  Sleep (2000);
  Label2.Caption := 'Semi-Painless Accounting';
end;
```

When the program runs, this code will show two messages on the form. The Sleep procedure accepts as an argument the number of milliseconds to pause between operations. Since a second is equal to 1,000 milliseconds, this example will delay the showing of the second message for approximately 2 seconds.

Notice the use of the line that reads:

```
Application.ProcessMessages;
```

The ProcessMessages method of the Application class (included by default in every application) will cause the program to respond to pending events. Without this line, neither message would appear until after the delay is completed!

Another important line in the preceding example is the use of the Show method. You might wonder why it is necessary to use this method when the main form for an application is automatically loaded. The show method will make the form visible so that you can see the output being displayed in the labels while the form is loading. Otherwise the messages won't appear until after the form has been loaded and the delay has been completed!

The UpperCase Function

Another important function that Delphi provides is the UpperCase function. When comparing strings, Delphi considers "abc" to be different than "ABC". Therefore, your programs must either explicitly test for both uppercase and lowercase strings or convert everything to the same case. For example, the following code contains an anomaly because it only checks for one case:

```
procedure TForm1.brnGetInputClick(Sender: TObject);

{ Read string from edit control }

begin
  if Edit1.Text = 'programmer' then
     ShowMessage ('Salary = 30K+');
end;
```

This handler will only show a message if the user types *programmer* in all lowercase letters. Although you could explicitly test for both uppercase and lowercase matches in the **if** statement, this technique will not work if the user enters an unexpected combination of uppercase and lowercase letters, such as PRogrammer. To avoid this problem, use the UpperCase function to convert the string to all caps.

Example

```
procedure TForm1.brnGetInputClick(Sender: TObject);

{ Read string from edit control and convert
  it to uppercase }

begin
  if UpperCase (Edit1.Text) = 'PROGRAMMER' then
     ShowMessage ('Salary = 30K+');
end;
```

In addition to uppercase conversions, you can also change a string to all lowercase letters using the LowerCase function. Moreover, Delphi supplies the StrUpper and StrLower functions when working with the PChar data type. This type is useful for operations that require external language support. For example, when trying to access code written in another programming language that does not support the String type, you need to use the PChar type to pass parameters to the .DLL (dynamic link library). The PChar type is discussed in Chapter 9. For more information on using PChar, see Chapter 9.

The TrimLeft and TrimRight Functions

Often when working with strings, you will find that it is necessary to remove leading and trailing spaces from a string. Since extra spaces in a string can cause a string comparison to fail, the TrimLeft and TrimRight functions are among two of the most important functions you will ever use. The following example shows how to remove trailing spaces from a string:

```
procedure TForm1.Button1Click(Sender: TObject);

{ Remove trailing spaces from string }

var
  S: String;
begin
  S := TrimRight (Edit1.Text);
  Edit1.Text := S;
end;
```

Sometimes it becomes necessary to remove both leading and trailing spaces from a string. Rather than calling both TrimLeft and TrimRight, you can use the Trim function to perform both operations at the same time:

```
procedure TForm1.Button1Click(Sender: TObject);

{ Remove both leading and trailing spaces
  from a string }

var
  S: String;
begin
  S := Trim (Edit1.Text);
  Edit1.Text := S;
end;
```

The ParamStr Function

Another really useful function Delphi provides is the ParamStr function. Some applications require that they be passed certain parameters when they are started. This advanced technique permits you to initialize the program differently, depending on what values the application starts with. For example, you can make it a requirement that the user enter a certain code in order to gain access to administrator features within the program. The ParamStr function reads in these values when a program is launched.

Since some programs require multiple parameters to run, ParamStr stores each value entered in an array. To determine what values a program is started with, you can use a loop like this:

```
procedure TForm1.FormCreate(Sender: TObject);

{ Fill list box with parameters read in as
  program runs }

var
  I: Integer;
begin
  for I := 1 to ParamCount do
      ListBox1.Items.Add (ParamStr (I))
end;
```

Here's another example:

```
procedure TForm1.FormCreate(Sender: TObject);
var
  I: Integer;
begin

  { Run program minimized if Minimized is typed
    at the command line when starting application }

  for I := 0 to ParamCount do begin
      ListBox1.Items.Add (ParamStr (I));
      if ParamStr (I) = 'Minimized' then
          Form1.WindowState := wsMinimized;
  end;
end;
```

ParamCount defines the maximum number of parameters the user has supplied. If ParamStr(0) is specified, Delphi will report the path where the program is running from. To specify the parameters you wish to read in when a program starts, use the Run | Parameters... command in Delphi to call up the Run parameters dialog box (see Figure 5.2). This will produce the same results as running your program with the Start | Run command in Windows 95 and passing it the parameters. For example:

```
C:\MyApp\MyProg.Exe SupervisorRights Minimized
```

Other Delphi Procedures and Functions

The Delphi subroutines discussed in this chapter are only a small taste of the complete language reference. The Borland documentation you received with Delphi contains a complete listing of all its routines. It is strongly recommended that you familiarize yourself as much as possible with these routines. By knowing ahead of time what procedures and functions Object Pascal provides, you can save yourself unnecessary effort trying to program routines already included in the language. In addition, later chapters in this book discuss many of these routines. Any time you want additional information on a feature discussed in this book you can quickly find topics using the online Help Search command in Delphi. Help is also context-sensitive so if you want information on any Delphi object, reserved word, property, method, and so on, you can place the cursor over the word in the Code editor and press F1 to call up Help for that topic.

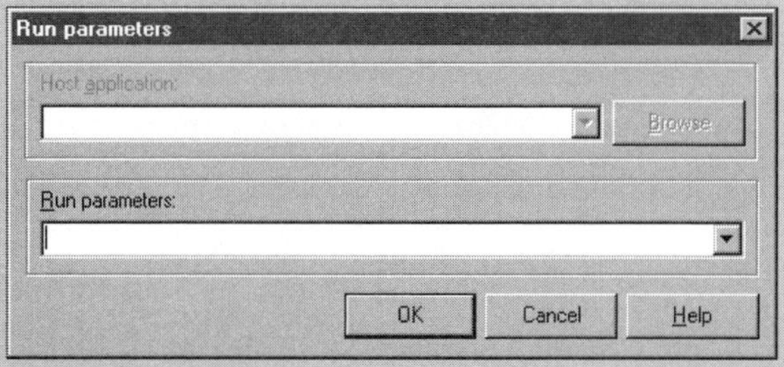

FIGURE 5.2
The Run Parameters dialog box

Exercise: Defining Hotspots on a Form

The following exercise will give you a better idea of what you can achieve by writing reusable code modules. In the following exercise, you will create a simple program that displays three hotspots on a form using a routine from the developers' library. After this exercise, you should be able to:

▶ Define hotspots on a form or image control.

▶ Change the shape of the mouse cursor when it is positioned over a hotspot.

▶ Display a help hint next to each hotspot.

1 From the File menu, choose New Application.

2 Add the following controls to the form from the Standard and Additional pages of the Component Palette.

Component	Property	Value
Label1	Left	61
	Top	48
Label2	Left	101
	Top	184

Label3	Left	261
	Top	80
Image1	Left	241
	Top	44
	Stretch	True

3 Double click on the image control to call up the Picture Editor. Use the Load option to pick a graphic from the \Windows directory or any other directory where you have bitmaps saved. Be sure to pick a graphic that is not too dark, because the caption color of Label3 (which will appear above the bitmap at run-time) is set to its default color clBlack.

4 Double click on the *form* to enter the Code editor. Be sure to double click the form and not a component on the form.

5 You should now be inside the OnCreate event handler of Form1. Add the following code between the **begin** and **end** reserved words:

```
Form1.ShowHint := True;
Label1.Hint := 'This is a hotspot with a hint';
Label2.Hint := 'This is another hotspot with a hint';
Label3.Hint := 'This is a third hotspot with a hint';
Label3.Transparent := True;
Label3.BringToFront;
ShowHotSpot (Label1);
ShowHotSpot (Label2);
ShowHotSpot (Label3);
```

6 In the **interface** section of the unit, add the *LMScr32* unit to the **uses** clause.

7 From the File menu, choose the Add to Project... command.

8 In the File Name edit box, type **c:\dlib\lmscr32.pas** and then click on Open.

Note *This assumes that you installed the library modules in c:\dlib. If this is not the case, be sure to specify the correct path.*

9 Run the project. To test the program, move the mouse cursor over a hotspot. You should see the mouse cursor change from the standard pointer shape to a hand pointer. At the same time, you should also see the help hint for the hotspot appear.

10 Move the mouse cursor away from the hotspot. Notice how the hint disappears and the mouse cursor shape is restored back to its original pointer shape. Now move the mouse cursor to another hotspot on the form. The mouse cursor turns back into a hand pointer and the hint for the associated hotspot appears.

Summary

In this chapter, you have learned how to work with procedures and functions. Specifically, you have learned how to:

▶ Call procedures and functions.

▶ Format real-type values for currency.

▶ Create user-defined subroutines.

▶ Work with value parameters, variable parameters, and constant parameters.

▶ Use the **forward** directive.

▶ Access routines from the Delphi Programmers' Library.

▶ Manipulate strings.

▶ Extract file names and paths from strings.

▶ Determine when a file was last modified.

▶ Convert strings to uppercase.

▶ Trim strings.

▶ Incorporate delays in programs.

▶ Use the ProcessMessages method of the Application class.

▶ Make a form visible while it is loading using the Show method.

▶ Read parameters into a program at startup.

▶ Display hotspots on a form or image control.

Using the Menu
Designer

Controlling Menu
Items at Run-time

Creating Pop-Up
Menus

Exercise: Creating
a Drop-Down Menu
System

Chapter 6
Creating Menus

One of the great advantages of using Delphi to create applications is its easy-to-use and powerful Menu Designer. With the Menu Designer, you can quickly add drop-down style menus to a program by simply defining the names of the items you want to appear on a menu. Alternately, you can make use of Delphi's pre-defined menu templates to create menus faster. In this chapter, you will learn how to build menus both from scratch and by using menu templates. In addition, you will learn how to add short-cut keys and accelerator keys to menus and to create nested menus and pop-up menus.

Using the Menu Designer

In Chapter 3, you learned how to save room on forms by dynamically creating, placing, and sizing controls and by using components like the TPageControl and TScrollBox control. Delphi also permits you to conserve space on forms by adding program commands to menus. For example, instead of placing three buttons on a form, you can add the same functionality that they provide to a menu. Since the items in a drop-down menu only appear when you open the menu, you can save a considerable amount of space on forms by making use of drop-menus (see Figure 6.1).

Another advantage of using menus is that you can make commands more descriptive. Rather than placing a button on a form with a caption that reads **Purge,** you can use the Menu Designer to define a menu item called **Remove Items from History File**. To do this, add a TMainMenu component to a form (see Figure 6.2). Afterwards, to call up the Menu Designer, double click on the component.

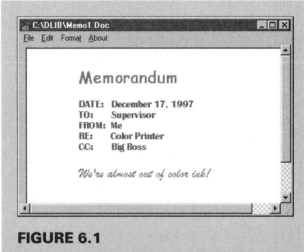

FIGURE 6.1

A sample program with drop-down menus

FIGURE 6.2

The TMainMenu component

Creating Menu Items

When you call up the Menu Designer for a new menu, an empty window appears with a place-holder for the first menu item (see Figure 6.3).

By convention, many Windows applications first display a File menu in what is called the *menu bar* (see Figure 6.4). To define this item, type the word *File* and press Enter. Delphi will use this label to identify the caption that will appear in the menu bar. Like other components, Delphi automatically defines a name for each menu item you define. You can, of course, set the menu items to more descriptive names by setting the Name property of each item via the Object Inspector. However, Delphi will only assign a name to a menu item if you define the caption for the item first.

When you type a name in the Menu Designer, Delphi assigns by default the string to the Caption property of the current menu item. You can override this default by first using the Object Inspector to define the Name property of the menu item. If you define your menu items this way, no caption will appear for a menu item until you define the Caption property of that menu item.

Adding Separator Bars to a Menu

With separator bars, you can logically divide groups of menu items within menus. A *separator bar* is a horizontal divider that appears between menu items. Figure 6.5 shows an example of a menu that contains two separator bars.

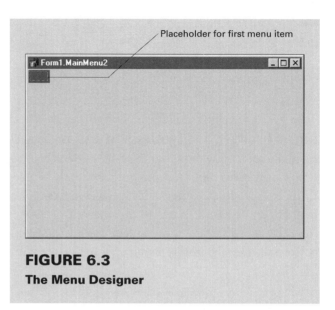

FIGURE 6.3
The Menu Designer

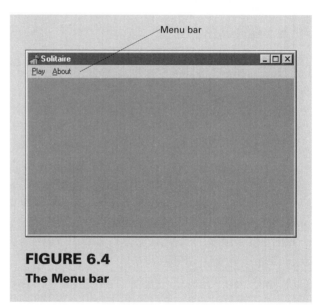

FIGURE 6.4
The Menu bar

To add a separator bar to a menu, you use a hyphen (-) to specify the Caption property of the menu item. If you want to insert a separator bar in an existing menu, press the Insert key where you want the separator bar to appear. This will insert a blank menu item in the list. Afterwards, by typing a hyphen, a new separator bar will appear in the menu.

Defining Accelerator Keys on a Menu

In addition to separator bars, a menu can contain accelerator keys so the user can quickly choose items from a menu at run-time. An accelerator key allows you to type the first letter of a menu item to make a selection from an open menu. To define an accelerator key in a menu:

1 Move the cursor to the menu item you wish to associate with the accelerator key.

2 Use the Object Inspector to edit the Caption property of the menu item. Type an ampersand (&) before the key you wish to use as the accelerator key. For example, to make the *O* in *Open* an accelerator key, you would type &Open.

You can also define accelerator keys at the same time you define the menu items by specifying the ampersand within the caption of the menu item. Once defined, the accelerator key will appear underlined within the menu. Figure 6.6 shows an example of a menu with accelerator keys.

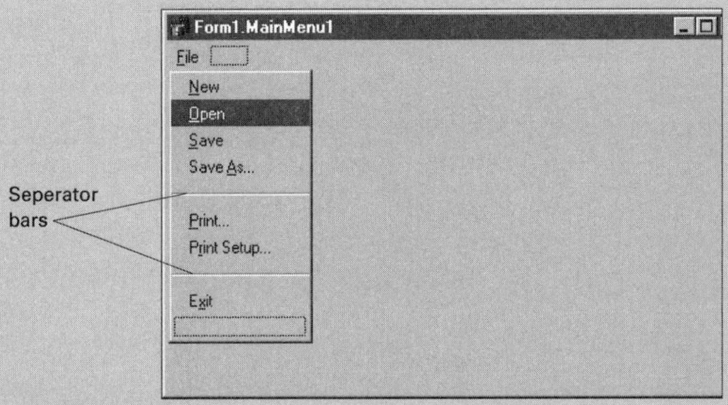

Adding Shortcut Keys to a Menu

FIGURE 6.5
Separator bars on a menu

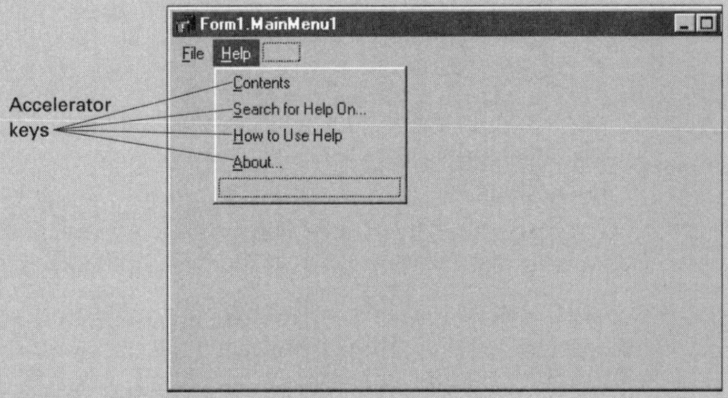

FIGURE 6.6
Accelerator keys

Like accelerator keys, *shortcut keys* provide quick access to a menu's commands. Unlike accelerator keys, however, shortcut keys let you access commands within menus that are not open. For example, you can define a menu command to quickly exit an application when the user presses the Ctrl+X keys together.

To define a shortcut key for a menu item, use the Object Inspector to set the ShortCut property (see Figure 6.7). After choosing the shortcut, the keys you choose will appear in the menu next to the associated menu item. Figure 6.8 shows an example of a menu that contains shortcut keys.

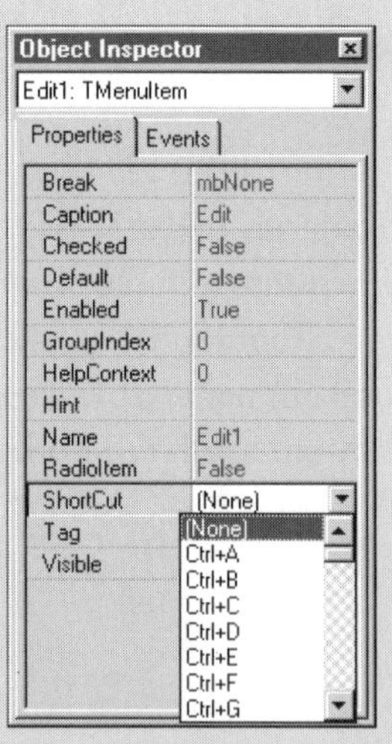

FIGURE 6.7

Defining shortcuts for menu items

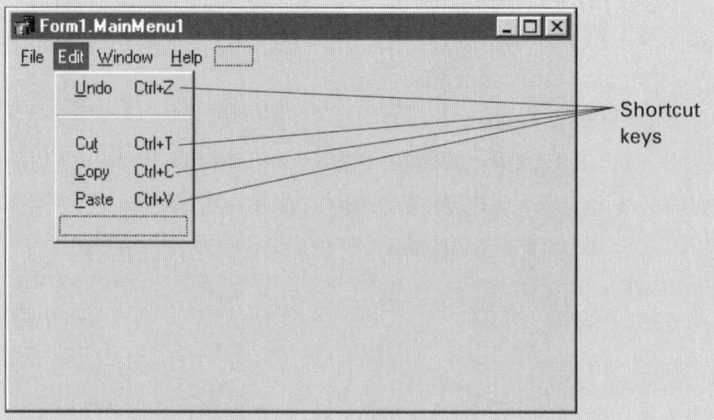

FIGURE 6.8

A sample menu with shortcut keys

Creating Submenus

Submenus, also known as nested menus, appear next to a parent menu to provide additional information for a particular menu command. For example, you can show a list of reports that can be printed when the user moves the mouse pointer over the Print... menu command. To create a submenu, in the Menu Designer, press the Ctrl+Right keys together to associate the current menu item with a submenu. Alternately, you can accomplish the same thing by pressing the right mouse button on the item in the Menu Designer. This will call up the Menu Designer SpeedMenu (see Figure 6.9).

As its name implies, the SpeedMenu provides quick access to often-used commands within the Menu Designer. By choosing the Create Submenu option, a new placeholder box will appear for you to define the first item that will appear in the nested menu (see Figure 6.10). You define the items for a submenu the same way you would define a first-level menu—that is, you type the caption of the first menu item for the submenu and then press Enter to define the next menu item.

Although submenus are useful, too many in an application can make a program harder to use because the

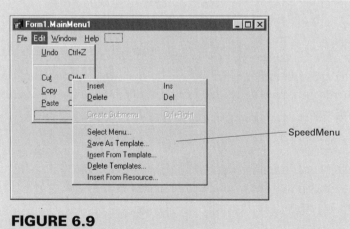

FIGURE 6.9

The SpeedMenu of the Menu Designer

cursor can move while trying to make a selection. To avoid this, you may wish to display modal dialog boxes when certain menu commands are selected in your programs. Unlike nested menus, modal dialog boxes stay on the screen once they are opened even if the user accidentally moves the cursor to another window. Because of this, many applications today (including Delphi), rely less on the traditional nested menu scheme.

Editing Menu Items

Once an item in a menu or nested menu is defined, you can very easily redefine that item by typing a new value in the Caption property and changing its Name property via the Object Inspector. If you wish to remove a menu item, simply press the Delete key on that item, or choose the Delete command from the SpeedMenu. Likewise, to add a new item to a menu, press the Insert key in the Menu Designer. The new menu item will appear directly above wherever you pressed the Insert key. If you need to reposition a menu item, you can use the mouse to drag the item to a new area within the menu.

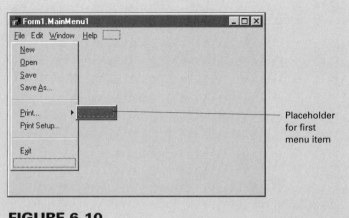
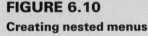

FIGURE 6.10
Creating nested menus

Programming Menu Controls

Once you have defined the structure of a menu, the next step is to write the short blocks of coding instructions that tell the program what to do when a menu item is selected. As with other components, you enter the code for menu items into event handlers. For example, to program the event handler for a program that contains a Help | About menu item, at design-time you would open the Help menu by either clicking on Help or by pressing Alt+H and then choosing the About... menu item. Alternately, you can create an event handler for the menu item by double clicking on that item in the Menu Designer or by choosing the OnClick event from the Events page of the Object Inspector.

Inside the event handler, you can place any code you wish to perform when the Help | About... command is selected. The following code uses the MessageDlg function to display the credits for a program when the Help | About... menu item is selected:

```
procedure TForm1.About1Click(Sender: TObject);

const NewLine = Char (13) + Chr (10);

begin

  { Show program credits with the Windows Information
```

```
      icon in a modal dialog box }

   MessageDlg('My Application' + NewLine + NewLine +
            'By Me, Myself and I', mtInformation,
            [mbOk], 0);
   end;
```

This example uses the Object Pascal Chr function to define the NewLine constant (Char (13) + Chr (10)). At run-time, this code will show a message formatted on two lines. The mtInformation constant, defined in the Dialogs unit, will display an Information icon in the dialog box. Figure 6.11 shows how the output appears.

FIGURE 6.11
The About dialog box

Using Menu Templates

Although the process for creating menus is fairly straightforward, Delphi provides time-saving templates that make creating menus even easier. To use one of these templates, right-click in the Menu Designer to call up the SpeedMenu and select the Insert From Template... command. Delphi will show a list of menu templates for you to choose from (see Figure 6.12). To use one of these templates, click on a menu template name and then choose OK. Delphi will then insert the new menu at the current position in the menu bar.

> **Note** *If the menu appears in the wrong place, you can drag the caption of the menu item to a new position in the menu bar.*

Saving Menu Templates

Delphi also permits you to create and save your own menu templates. If you find yourself constantly using the same types of menus in your programs, you can save yourself time by adding the menu name to the list of templates. In addition, this ability lets you establish a consistency between your applications. To save a menu template:

FIGURE 6.12
Choosing a menu template

1 Right-click in the Menu Designer to call up the SpeedMenu.

2 Choose the Save As Template... command.

3 In the Template Description box, type a description for the template.

4 Click on OK to save the template.

The menu template will now be available to all your programs whenever you call up the SpeedMenu of the Menu Designer.

Controlling Menu Items at Run-time

At design-time, you use the Menu Designer to add items to a menu. At run-time, you can also define new menu items as well. Some applications use this technique to show or to collapse menus items. For example, suppose the menu bar contains a drop-down menu called Options and in that menu is a menu item called Full Menus. At run-time, when the user clicks on the Full Menus command of the Options menu, you can show an expanded list of menu commands. One way this can be done is by setting the Visible property of the menu items initially to **False** and then unhiding them at run-time by changing the Visible property of each item to **True**.

Example

```
procedure TForm1.mnuFullMenusClick(Sender: TObject);

{ Unhide menu items when Full Menus
  are selected }

var
    I: Integer;
begin
    File1.Items[5].Visible := True;
    Edit1.Items[9].Visible := True;
    Edit1.Items[10].Visible := True;
    Window1.Items[10].Visible := True;
    Help1.Items[2].Visible := True;
end;
```

This code will unhide one item from the File menu, two items from the Edit menu, one item from the Window menu, and one item from the Help menu. The Items property of a menu specifies the index of each menu item. As with Delphi components, the index of a menu item starts at 0. Another way you can add items to a menu is by dynamically inserting them into the menu. For example:

```
procedure TForm1.mnuFullMenusClick(Sender: TObject);

var
  NewMenuItem: TMenuItem;

begin

  { Generate a new menu item }
```

```
NewMenuItem := TMenuItem.Create(mnuOption);

{ Define caption for the new menu item}

NewMenuItem.Caption := 'Set Program Colors...';

{ Insert menu item at position 3 in menu }

mnuOption.Insert(3, NewMenuItem);

end;
```

Although this technique involves more work than un-hiding menu items, the program can now add menu selections without knowing ahead of time what all of the menu choices will be. A good example of this is the File | Reopen command in Delphi (see Figure 6.13). Since there is no way you can anticipate what files the user will open during a session, you cannot simply hide a list of file names at design-time and unhide them at run-time. Therefore, the names of the files are populated in the list *dynamically* as the program runs.

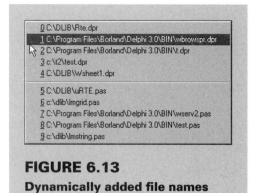

FIGURE 6.13
Dynamically added file names

Enabling and Disabling Menu Items

In addition to showing and hiding menu items, Delphi permits you to enable and disable the commands that appear on a menu at run-time. When the Enabled property of a menu item is set to **False**, the menu item appears grayed-out at run-time (see Figure 6.14). You can use this technique to restrict users from performing certain menu options until those options become valid selections. For example, when the user chooses the File | Open command, the program can enable the editing commands in the Edit menu.

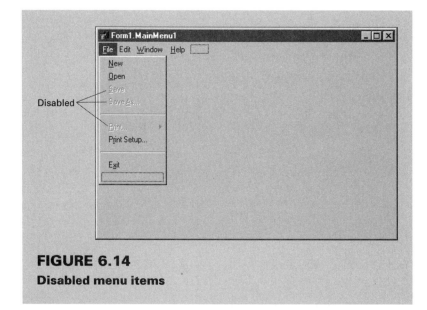

FIGURE 6.14
Disabled menu items

Example

```
mnuUndo.Enabled := True;
mnuCut.Enabled := True;
mnuCopy.Enabled := True;
mnuPaste.Enabled := True;
```

Displaying Check Marks and Bullets in Menus

Another way you can validate the choices that appear on a menu is through check marks. When the Checked property of a menu item is set to **True**, a check mark will appear by the associated menu item at run-time (see Figure 6.15). Using this technique, the user can toggle on and off certain menu selections. For example, the following code shows how to turn on/off a menu item called mnuQuickSave:

```
procedure TForm1.mnuQuickSaveClick(Sender: TObject);

{ Toggle ON/OFF menu item }

begin
  mnuQuickSave.Checked := not mnuQuickSave.Checked
end;
```

At run-time, when the user clicks on the Quick Save menu items, this code will toggle the display of the check mark on or off. Later, the program can check the value of the Checked property to determine whether the Quick Save option is currently enabled:

```
if mnuQuickSave.Checked then
      .    .    .
```

Note *In Delphi 3.0, you can change the mark that appears by a menu item from a check mark to a bullet by setting both the Checked property and the RadioItem property to* **True.**

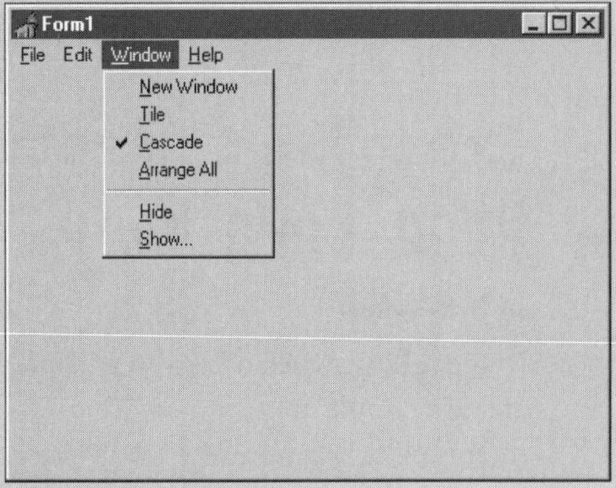

Creating Pop-Up Menus

In addition to drop-down menus, Delphi also supports another kind of menu called a pop-up menu. Unlike drop-down menus, pop-up menus do not appear until you invoke the **Popup** method. They are also different from

FIGURE 6.15
Displaying check marks by menu items

drop-down menus in that you can display a pop-up menu virtually anywhere on a form. Moreover, pop-up menus can be linked to any Delphi component that has a PopupMenu property. Using this technique, you can show context-sensitive menu options for any component that supports the PopupMenu property.

In order to display a pop-up menu, you must set the PopupMenu property of the object that will show the menu to the name of the pop-up menu (for example, PopupMenu1). To define the menu choices, double click on the TPopupMenu component to define the menu choices using the Menu Designer. Afterwards, you can display the menu using the Popup method. The following code shows how to display a pop-up menu at the current mouse coordinates when the user clicks the right mouse button on the form:

```
procedure TForm1.FormMouseDown(Sender: TObject; Button:
        TMouseButton; Shift: TShiftState; X, Y: Integer);

{ Show pop-up menu at current mouse coordinates
  when right mouse button is clicked }

begin
  if Button = mbRight then
      PopupMenu1.Popup (X, Y);
end;
```

The FormMouseDown event handler returns the position of the current mouse coordinates (in the X and Y arguments). These coordinates are then supplied to the PopupMenu method to display the menu. Figure 6.16 shows how the pop-up menu appears.

Exercise: Creating a Drop-Down Menu System

In the following exercise, you will learn how to create a simple application with drop-down menus. After performing this exercise, you should be able to:

▶ Create a drop-down menu system.

▶ Validate menu choices at run-time.

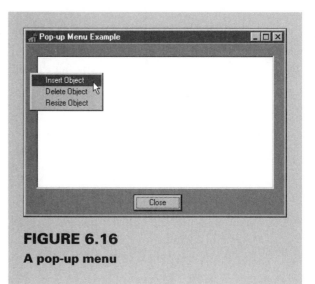

FIGURE 6.16

A pop-up menu

▶ Use the TStringGrid component to show/schedule appointments on a grid.

▶ Save and retrieve appointments using the string grid routines of the library.

1 From the Standard Page of the Component Palette, choose the TMainMenu component. If you do not remember what this component looks like, use the View I Component List command to find it in the Component List.

2 Double click on the TMainMenu component to open the Menu Designer.

3 At the top of the screen, a placeholder appears for you to enter the first menu definition (see Figure 6.17). Type **&File**.

4 Press Enter to save this item and advance to the next menu position.

5 Type **&Open** and press Enter.

6 Type **&Save** and press Enter.

7 Type - (a hyphen) and press Enter. This will create a separator between the Save and Exit menu items.

8 Type **&Exit** and press Enter.

9 Click on the Save menu item.

10 Using the Object Inspector, set the Enabled property of this menu item to **False**.

11 Click on the dotted input box (that is, the placeholder) that appears in the menu bar to the right of the File menu (see Figure 6.18).

> **Note** *If the Object Inspector is in your way, you can drag it to another part of the screen by clicking on the title bar and holding the left mouse button down as you move it.*

12 Type **&About**.

13 Click on the File menu item to open the File menu.

14 Double click on the Open menu item.

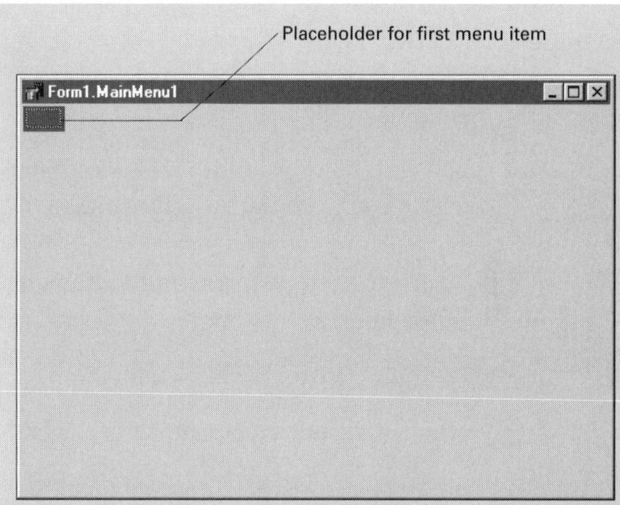

FIGURE 6.17
Defining a menu item

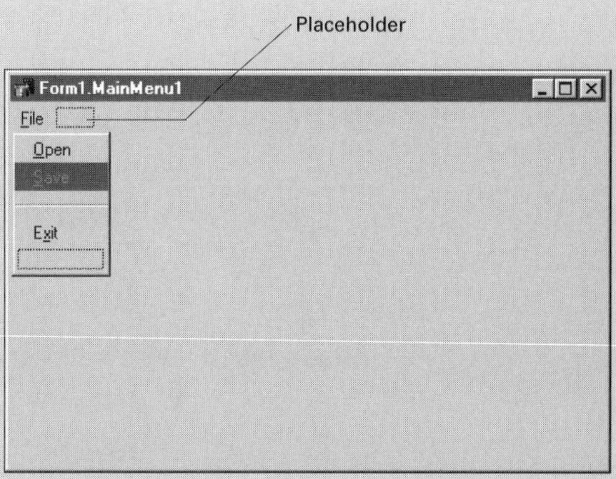

FIGURE 6.18
Placeholder for next menu item

15 In the OnClick event handler of the Open menu item, type:

```
{ Get weekly appointments }

OpenStringGrid (StringGrid1, 'StrGrid.Txt');
Save1.Enabled := True;
StringGrid1.Enabled := True;
```

16 Using the **Toggle Form/Unit** button on the toolbar, switch back to the Menu Designer.

17 Double click on the Save menu item.

18 In the OnClick event handler of the Save menu item, type:

```
SaveStringGrid (StringGrid1, 'StrGrid.Txt');
```

19 Using the **Toggle Form/Unit** button on the toolbar, switch back to the Menu Designer.

20 Double click on the Exit menu item.

21 In the OnClick event handler of the Exit menu item, type:

```
Close;
```

22 Using the **Toggle Form/Unit** button on the toolbar, switch back to the Menu Designer.

23 Double click on the About menu item.

24 In the OnClick event handler of the About menu item, add the lines below appearing in boldface:

```
procedure TForm1.About1Click(Sender: TObject);

const NewLine = Chr(13) + Chr (10);

begin
  MessageDlg('Appointment Scheduling Application' + NewLine +
            NewLine + 'By (your name here)',
            mtInformation, [mbOk], 0);
end;
```

25 Using the **Toggle Form/Unit** button on the toolbar, switch back to the form.

26 Click on the Menu Designer once to give it focus.

27 Close the Menu Designer by clicking on the X that appears in the upper right corner of the *Menu Designer* (Not Delphi!).

28 Using the Object Inspector, set the properties of the form as follows:

Width = 568

Height = 350

Position = PoScreenCenter

29 Using the View | Component List command, choose the TStringGrid control (see Figure 6.19).

30 Double click on the *form* (not the TStringGrid control).

31 Add the boldfaced lines below to the OnCreate event handler of the form:

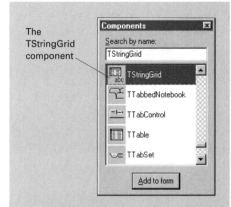

The TStringGrid component

FIGURE 6.19

Choosing the TStringGrid component from the Component list

```
procedure TForm1.FormCreate(Sender: TObject);


{ Initialize string grid using the library }


var
  TotalCols, TotalRows, ColPixels: Integer;


begin

  TotalCols := 8; TotalRows := 25;
  ColPixels := 90;


  InitStringGrid (StringGrid1, TotalCols, TotalRows,
               ColPixels);
  WeeklySchedule (StringGrid1);


  StringGrid1.Width := Form1.Width;
  StringGrid1.Height := Form1.Height;
  StringGrid1.Left := 0;
  StringGrid1.Top := 0;


end;
```

32 Choose File | Add to Project.

33 Type **c:\dlib\lmgrid.pas** in the File name box.

> **Note** *This assumes that you installed the library modules in c:\dlib. If this is not the case, be sure to specify the correct path here.*

34 Click on Open to add the file to the project.

35 Switch back to the Unit1 unit by clicking on the **Unit1** tab.

36 Add *LMGrid* to the project's **uses** clause in the **interface** section.

37 Using the **Toggle Form/Unit** button on the toolbar, switch back to the form.

38 Click on the grid once to give it focus.

39 Set the Enabled property of the string grid to **False** using the Object Inspector.

> **Note** *If the Object Inspector is not visible, you can use the View | Object Inspector (F11) command to open it or bring it back into view.*

40 Click on the **Events** tab of the Object Inspector.

41 Use the vertical scroll bar in the Object Inspector to scroll down until you see the OnMouseDown event.

42 Double click on the OnMouseDown event to open the Code Editor.

43 Place the missing boldfaced lines into this handler:

```
procedure TForm1.StringGrid1MouseDown(Sender: TObject;
Button: TMouseButton; Shift: TShiftState; X, Y: Integer);

{ Create and display test appointment on grid }

var
  ColPos, RowPos: Integer;
begin
  StringGrid1.MouseToCell(X, Y, ColPos, RowPos);
  StringGrid1.Cells[ColPos, RowPos] := 'John Smith';
end;
```

44 To test the program, run the project and choose the File | Open command from the menu. Since the grid maintains a perpetual calendar, you will most likely not see any appointments for the current week unless you have run the GRIDPRJ.DPR project recently. Figure 6.20 shows how the menu and grid should appear.

45 Click on the grid to schedule an appointment. The program will automatically display *John Smith* in this cell.

46 From the File menu, choose the Save command. The new appointment will now be saved to the file.

47 Click on the About menu option to see the program credits. You should now see your name in this box.

48 Choose the File | Exit command to end the session.

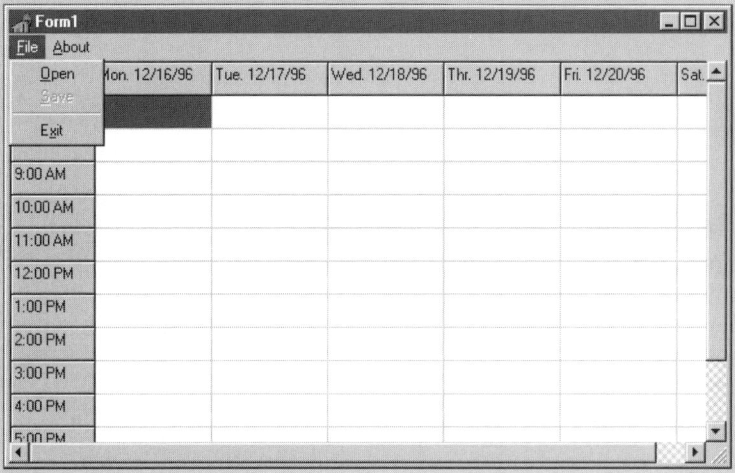

FIGURE 6.20
Output for sample exercise

Summary

In this chapter, you have learned how to create both drop-down and pop-up style menus. Specifically, you have learned how to:

▶ Use the Menu Designer to define menu items.

▶ Create nested menus.

▶ Use menu templates.

▶ Code event handlers for menu items.

▶ Add shortcut and accelerator keys to menus.

▶ Display check marks and bullets by menu items.

▶ Dynamically add menus items at run-time.

▶ Enabled/disable menu items.

▶ Display pop-up menus in applications.

▶ Create a drop-down menu system.

Overview of the
Debugger

Debugging
Techniques

Debugging
Applications in
Delphi 3.0

Viewing Calls to
Subroutines

Resource Protection
and Error Handling

Exercise: Using
Exception Handlers

Chapter 7
Dealing with Errors

Regardless of how well you plan your applications, inevitably all programs end up with errors. Locating and resolving *bugs* (that is, errors) in a program can take time and patience. In some traditional development environments, programmers are provided only limited ways to debug applications. The Delphi IDE, however, provides many tools to help you resolve errors quickly and easily. In this chapter, you will learn how to handle errors both before and after they occur.

Overview of the Debugger

A *debugger* is a program that provides tools that permit you to find erroneous source code in a program. Delphi's built-in debugger permits you to debug an application without having to leave the integrated development environment. With the debugger, you can step through a program's source code as it runs, observe how it behaves and even monitor the values of variables and properties.

Types of Errors

Fundamentally, there are three kinds of errors that can occur in a program:

▶ Compile errors

▶ Run-time errors

▶ Logic errors

A *compile* or *syntax error* occurs when the code in an application is improperly constructed. For example, if you forget to add a semicolon after an Object Pascal statement, Delphi will trap this type of error and report an error message to you. Once an application has been compiled successfully, it is still possible the program can contain run-time and logic errors.

A *run-time* error occurs when a program is coded correctly but still causes an invalid operation when it is executed. Some common examples of this include:

▶ Dividing a value by zero

▶ Trying to open a file that does not exist

▶ Assigning a value to a variable or property that is beyond the minimum or maximum value it can hold

▶ Trying to remove a record from a file that is empty

In addition to run-time errors, a program can also contain logic errors. A *logic error* occurs when the code in a program is correct in terms of syntax and does not produce a run-time error but still yields invalid results. For example, a report that shows incorrect answers to calculations or the wrong grand totals is an example of an application with logic errors.

Errors the Debugger Can Help With

The integrated debugger can be used to locate both run-time errors and logic errors. Note, however, that although the debugger can assist you in locating erroneous code, it cannot resolve bugs in a program. Since only the programmer knows the internal logic of an application, ultimately it is up to you to interpret what the debugger finds and to determine what actions need to be taken.

Using the Debugger

Before you can actually use the debugger, you must make sure that debugging information is available to the application. Although Delphi generates this information for you by default, you can also manually enable or disable this option. To compile a project with debugging information:

1 Choose Project | Options... and then click on the **Compiler** tab.

2 Click on the **Debugging information** check box and then choose OK to save the new configuration.

> **Note** *Although you need to enable integrated debugging in an application in order to get debugging information from the compiler, this option will also result in a larger executable size for the program. Therefore, you should disable debugging information before distributing the final .EXE file for the project.*

The debugger provides more than one way to choose a certain debugging option. In addition to the Run menu, you can often use the Code Editor SpeedMenu or toolbar to select debugging commands. Figure 7.1 shows the debugging options of the toolbar.

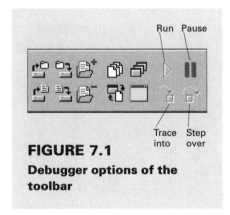

FIGURE 7.1
Debugger options of the toolbar

Debugging Techniques

Once debugging information is available, the next step to debugging a program is to plan a debugging strategy. Delphi provides several ways you can find bugs in projects. In the following section, you will see how to debug applications using these techniques.

Running to the Cursor

One of the easiest ways to debug a project is to use the Run to Cursor option. When a program is run this way, the debugger will pause the run of the program at the cursor location. At this point, you can use some of the other tools the debugger provides to step through the project's source code, monitor its values, and observe how it behaves. To run to the cursor position:

▶ Press the F4 fast key.

Or

▶ From the Run menu, choose Run to Cursor.

Or

▶ Click the right mouse button in the Code editor to call up the Code Editor SpeedMenu (see Figure 7.2) and then choose the Run to Cursor command.

After choosing the Run to Cursor option, Delphi will highlight the next line of source code it will execute. This line is known as the *execution point*. From here you typically would use either the trace or step options to execute the next line or subroutine. Alternately, you could use the Run | Evaluate/Modify... command or Run | Add Watch command to examine the value of a variable or property setting.

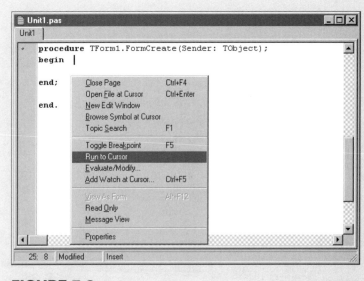

FIGURE 7.2
The Code Editor SpeedMenu

Tracing and Stepping over Code in a Project

The Run | Trace Into (F7) command permits you to slowly trace through the source code of a program and observe which lines of code are executing. When tracing a program, the debugger will also branch into procedures and functions so you can see whether the code is operating the way that you expect. For example, if the project contains a procedure with a loop inside it, you can see if the loop inside the subroutine is being performed using this option.

Although tracing can be useful, sometimes you do not want to execute a subroutine when debugging an application. For example, if you know that a certain function is already returning the correct value, you can use the Run | Step Over (F8) command to skip over the subroutine and execute the next line of code. Technically speaking, the

Step Over command does not actually skip over the subroutine. Instead, the debugger simply executes it faster so you do not have to be bothered by the details of the operation.

Controlling the Flow of Execution

After tracing/stepping through a program, if you wish to resume the normal run, you can press F9 to continue where you left off or you can choose the Run command from the toolbar or Run menu. If you want to start over, you can also choose the Run | Program Reset (Ctrl+F2) option to restart the program. When this option is selected, Delphi will close all open files and release all variables in memory but still retain the settings of the debugger for the next run.

Using Breakpoints

Like the Run to Cursor command, *breakpoints* pause the execution of a program. However, breakpoints are more flexible in that you can define more than one place in the code where program execution will pause. When a breakpoint is defined, the current line is highlighted with a red bar (see Figure 7.3).

Breakpoints are especially useful when you cannot find a logic error in your program by simply poring over the code. For instance, say you have written a business program that contains numerous calculations on a given set of data, determined by specific accounting criteria. The program executes to the end, but the output is wrong in only a couple of the resulting numbers. Instead of stepping through the program, you can add breakpoints in your code to determine at what point the calculation error takes place. This can help you determine where you coded a logic error.

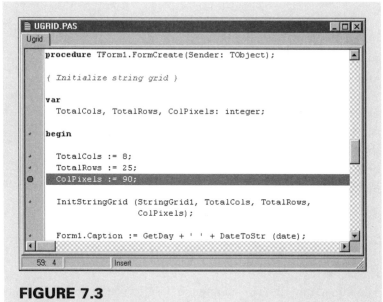

FIGURE 7.3
A sample breakpoint

Setting a Breakpoint

In order to set a breakpoint:

▶ Choose Toggle Breakpoint (F5) from the Code Editor SpeedMenu to set a breakpoint at the cursor position.

Or

▶ Choose Run | Add Breakpoint... to set a breakpoint at the cursor position.

Or

▶ Click the left margin on the line where you wish to set the breakpoint.

Breakpoints are also different than running to the cursor in that they remain enabled until you either toggle them off or close the project. Therefore, if you do not want the program to pause anymore, you must delete or at least disable the breakpoint.

Removing a Breakpoint

In order to remove a breakpoint that you have set:

▶ Press F5 on the line that contains the breakpoint.

Or

▶ Choose Toggle Breakpoint from the Code Editor SpeedMenu to delete a breakpoint at the cursor position.

Or

▶ Click the left margin to toggle off a breakpoint for that line.

Or

▶ Choose View | Breakpoints and then right-click on the breakpoint you wish to remove in the Breakpoints list (Figure 7.4) and choose the Delete command (Ctrl+D).

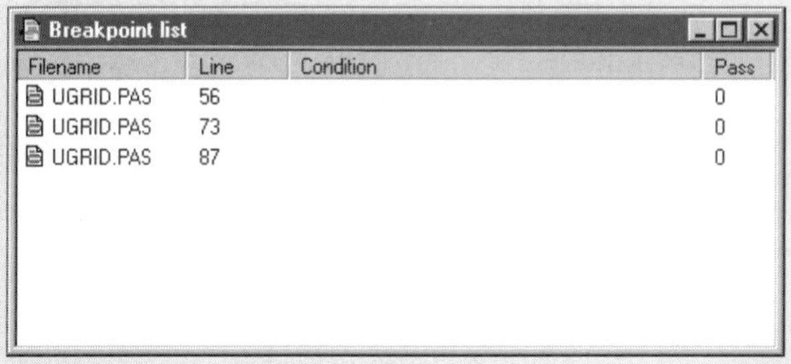

When setting breakpoints, it is important to keep in mind that the debugger will not be able to make use of the breakpoint if you set it on a non-executable line of code (such as a comment, declaration, or blank line). Although the IDE will ignore the invalid breakpoint if you choose the Yes (continue) option, you will receive this same error every time you run the project until you either remove the invalid breakpoint or close the project.

🖹 Breakpoint list			_□×
Filename	Line	Condition	Pass
🖹 UGRID.PAS	56		0
🖹 UGRID.PAS	73		0
🖹 UGRID.PAS	87		0

FIGURE 7.4
The breakpoint list

Setting Conditional Breakpoints

Delphi's integrated debugger also supports breakpoints that activate upon certain conditions. This option is particularly useful when you know that the bug only occurs when a certain condition is true. For example, if you suspect the problem only happens when a flag has been set or after a counter in a loop reaches a certain value, you can set a conditional breakpoint to pause the program at that condition. To create or modify a conditional breakpoint:

> ▶ Choose Run | Add Breakpoint... to call up the Edit breakpoint window and then type the breakpoint condition in the Condition edit box. Afterwards, click on New to create the breakpoint.

Or

> ▶ Choose View | Breakpoints and then right-click on the breakpoint you wish to modify and choose the Properties command to call up the Edit breakpoint window. Then enter the breakpoint condition in the Condition edit box and click on Modify when you are done.

The integrated debugger also permits you to specify that a breakpoint can be executed after a certain condition has occurred. This option, called a *pass count breakpoint,* is useful when you know already that the error only occurs in certain instances, such as after the routine has executed *x* number of times. To define a pass count breakpoint, from the Edit breakpoint window, type the number of times the code should be executed before the breakpoint should be activated (see Figure 7.5).

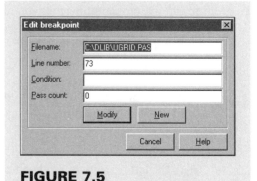

FIGURE 7.5
The Edit breakpoint window

Monitoring Values of Expressions

Although tracing, stepping, and setting breakpoints are invaluable debugging tools, often it becomes necessary to do more to find errors in a program. By monitoring the values of expressions, you can easily see how program variables and property settings are being initialized at run-time. To create a watch expression, use any of the following methods:

> ▶ Choose Add Watch at Cursor (Ctrl+F5) in the Code Editor.

> ▶ Choose Run | Add Watch.

> ▶ Press Ctrl+F5.

> ▶ Double click in the Watch window to call up the Watch Properties List.

Watch expressions are useful when you need to continuously monitor the values of program elements. For example, you can define a watch expression to evaluate the values of an index in a **for** loop. Each time the value of the **for** loop counter changes, the new value will appear in the Watch List (see Figure 7.6).

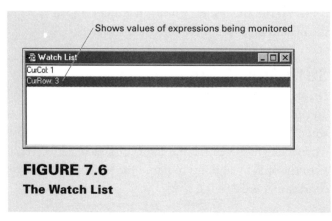

FIGURE 7.6
The Watch List

If a variable is not accessible when a particular routine is being evaluated, the debugger will inform you that its value is unavailable due to optimization. For instance, if a variable is defined locally within a procedure or function and the debugger is evaluating a code block outside that routine, the value of the variable will be unavailable until program control returns to the subroutine.

Removing or Disabling Watch Expressions

To remove a watch expression, right-click on a watch in the Watch List window to call up the SpeedMenu. Then choose either Delete Watch (Ctrl+D) to remove the current watch or Delete All Watches to remove all watches defined.

If you prefer, the debugger permits you to disable watch expressions instead of deleting them. This option is useful when you are not sure that you want to remove the watch expression yet, but do not wish to monitor its value at the current time. When a watch expression is disabled, the debugger will operate faster since it does not have to evaluate the values of each expression as the program runs. To disable a watch expression:

▶ Double click on the Watch List window to call up the Watch Properties dialog box and then click on the **Enabled** check box to remove the check mark from the control. Afterwards, click on OK to save the change.

Or

▶ Choose the watch you wish to remove from the Watch List box and right-click to call up the SpeedMenu. Afterwards, use the Disable Watch command to deactivate the watch.

Setting Test Values

Perhaps the most valuable feature of the integrated debugger is its ability to test possible solutions to bugs without having to modify the program until you are sure a particular solution will work. The Evaluate/Modify... dialog box allows you to perform these tests. To indicate the expression you wish to evaluate or modify:

▶ Choose the Evaluate/Modify command from the Run menu. Then type the item you wish to evaluate in the Expression edit box and click on Evaluate to see its value. To test how the program is affected when the value of the expression is changed, type a value in the New Value edit box and click on Modify.

> **Note** *You can also access the Evaluate/Modify dialog box by choosing the Evaluate/Modify command from the Code Editor SpeedMenu.*

The Evaluate/Modify option is also particularly useful when you want to see the value of an expression but do not want to define a watch expression. For example, if you only want to see whether a Boolean flag is set to **True**, the Evaluate/Modify option can save you the trouble of having to delete the watch expression after it has been evaluated.

Debugging Applications in Delphi 3.0

In Delphi 3.0, the debugger automatically displays the values of expressions in help hints when you move the mouse cursor over items you wish to evaluate. By combining this technique with other tools the debugger provides, you can quickly find and resolve bugs in many cases without even having to define watch expressions.

Viewing Calls to Subroutines

The Call Stack window command permits you to find out the order in which subroutines were called to reach the current program location (see Figure 7.7). The topmost name in the list is the current subroutine or event handler. To access the Call Stack window, from the View menu, choose the Call Stack command.

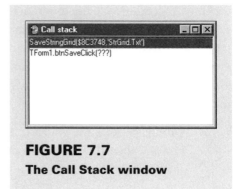

FIGURE 7.7
The Call Stack window

Alternately, you can use this option to switch from one subroutine to another by clicking on a subroutine name in the list. The Call Stack window command is useful when you accidentally traced a subroutine into a procedure/function instead of stepping over it. By choosing a routine to resume at, you can continue debugging from that handler/subroutine.

Resource Protection and Error Handling

Until now, this chapter has focused on how to deal with errors after they have occurred in a program. Delphi also permits you to safeguard your code before errors occur by writing resource protection handlers and exception handlers. In the following sections, you will learn how to create these handlers and also how to override Delphi's default exception handling.

Resource Protection Handlers

By writing resource protection handlers, you can ensure that allocated resources are freed after a code block has executed. Examples of common resources that should be released include files, memory, objects, and Windows resources. To ensure a resource is properly released after it is used, you place the code you wish to protect in a **try..finally** block. An example of this is as follows:

```
    .    .    .
Screen.Cursor := crHourGlass;


try
```

```
      SMTP1.Connect(GetNoParam, GetNoParam);
    finally
      Screen.Cursor := crDefault;
    end;
```

This example uses a **try..finally** block to ensure that the mouse cursor is restored to its default shape after trying to connect to an SMTP (Simple Mail Transfer Protocol) mail server. (For a complete discussion on how to connect to an SMTP mail server, see Chapter 13, "Delphi and the Internet.") If an exception error occurs when the line in the **try** part of the block is executing, program execution immediately jumps to the clean-up code in the **finally** part of the block. Any statements that appear here will always execute regardless of whether an exception error has occurred or not. Therefore, setting the mouse cursor to its default shape in the termination routine (that is, the clean-up block) will ensure that the mouse cursor will be restored back to crDefault.

Writing Exception Handlers

Although the **try..finally** construct is helpful for protecting resources, it does not actually handle the error. A protected block is not given information regarding the type of error that has been raised or that an error has even occurred. By using a **try..except** block, you can better determine what action needs to be taken when an exception error occurs. For example:

```
    .    .    .
    try
      FormulaCtrl.FilePrint (True)
    except
      on EOleError do
        Application.MessageBox('Cannot print empty worksheet',
        'Print Error', MB_ICONEXCLAMATION + MB_OK);
      end;
```

This example shows how to recover from an exception error when the Cancel button is selected while printing a Formula One worksheet. If an exception error occurs, a message is shown with an exclamation point icon and the operation continues without having to restart the program (see Figure 7.8).

You may wonder where the EOleError constant came from. This constant is defined in the OLEAuto unit. When an exception error occurs in a program, Delphi returns the name of the constant you need to use in order to safeguard the code against a recurrence of the same exception error. Figure 7.9 shows the error that is returned when the Cancel button is selected while trying to print a Formula One worksheet.

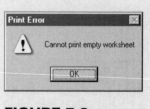

FIGURE 7.8
The message box

By noting the name of the constant returned, you can easily create handlers to deal with exception errors. A few special points must be noted here. Notice for example that the OLEAuto unit is not one of the standard units that Delphi automatically adds to a unit when it creates a project:

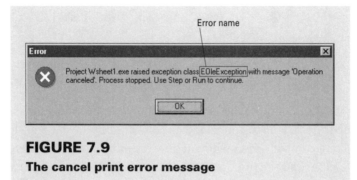

FIGURE 7.9
The cancel print error message

```
unit Unit1;


interface
uses
   Windows, Messages, SysUtils, Classes, Graphics, Controls, Forms,
   Dialogs;
```

Since the OLEAuto unit is not included automatically, you must add this unit reference to the **uses** clause. How do you determine what unit defines the constant name of the error returned? The easiest way to find out is to search Help on the error name.

After determining the error constant and what unit (if any) needs to be added to the **uses** clause, it is important to keep in mind that, by default, projects running in the Delphi environment break upon exceptions even if you have defined an exception handler. Although this may be useful in that you will always know when exception errors occur while you are designing the program, you may find this feature annoying. If so, you can disable it by choosing the Tools | Options... command and then clicking on the **Break on exception** check box to toggle off the check mark that appears (see Figure 7.10).

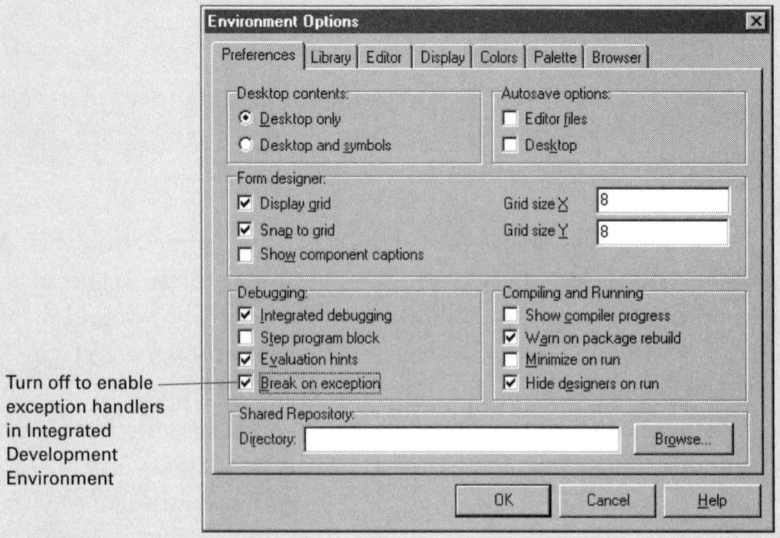

It is important to keep in mind that when you add

FIGURE 7.10
The Break on exception check box

code to the **try** part of the exception handler, the **except** part of the handler will take care of exception errors that occur in subroutines that are called in the **try** part, if no exception handler is provided within those subroutines. For example, the **try** part of the exception handler can call a procedure to divide numbers and safeguard against the EDivByZero error or other invalid calculating mistakes, all in the same routine.

Reraising Exceptions

Delphi supplies exception error information to its applications by generating an object that represents the exception. When an exception error is trapped by a **try..except** block, this effectively destroys the exception object, meaning that it is no longer available to the program. Thus if a subroutine handles the exception locally, a main handler that calls that subroutine may never get a chance to respond to the error. If you want the main handler also to handle the error, the local handler must *reraise* the exception. To do this, you use the **raise** reserved word. An example is as follows:

```
procedure GetPartyList;

{ Retrieve party list if available. Only
  show message if error arises locally }

begin
  try
    { Search routine goes here }
  except
    MessageDlg('Unable to retrieve party list', mtWarning, [mbOk], 0);
    raise;
  end;
end;

procedure TForm1.btnSearchListClick(Sender: TObject);

{ Try getting party list by calling procedure. Handle
  main error response here if list is inaccessible }

begin

  try
    GetPartyList;
  except
    SavePartyListStatus;
```

```
      CreateNewPartyList;
   end;


 end;
```

This example uses the **raise** reserved word to reraise the exception after displaying an error message in the local handler (GetPartyList). Afterwards, when control returns back to the calling routine, the main error handling is performed. By reraising the exception with the **raise** keyword, both the subroutine and the calling routine get a chance to handle the error.

Note that whether you are working with components or simply calling a routine from the Delphi RTL (Delphi Run Time Library), you can handle both types of exceptions using **try..except** to trap and recover from errors. You can also write your exception handlers to handle errors silently without showing a status message. Instead of notifying the user that an exception error has occurred, you exclude the status message and simply set a flag to indicate the operation failed. You may wish to use this technique when you want to rerun automatically an operation a certain number of times. Alternately, you can use this technique to handle non-crucial errors that would not interfere with the normal performance of the program. For instance, you can use a **try..except** block to open a text file and read records onto a string grid at the start of a session when the data file has already been created:

```
 .    .    .

AssignFile(FileStrGrid, FileToOpen);

{ Try to read records from file }

try
   Reset (FileStrGrid);
except
   OpenFailed := True;
   Exit;
end;
```

If the grid has not been saved at least once, the text file will not be available to restore the grid. In this case, the program sets a flag to indicate the status and resumes without an error.

> **Note** *On a more advanced level, Delphi permits you to create your own exception objects. Because it is not crucial to handling exceptions and because of its advanced nature, this procedure is not covered in this book. For information on how to create exception objects, search Delphi Help under exceptions.*

Exercise: Using Exception Handlers

To demonstrate how you can safegaurd your code, try the following exercise to create a simple program that uses an exception handler. After performing this exercise, you should be able to:

▶ Write exception handlers.

▶ Safeguard programs against list range errors.

▶ Change IDE environment options.

1 From the File menu, choose New Application.

2 Add a ListBox, button, and label component to the form.

3 In the OnCreate event handler of the form, add the following code:

```
ListBox1.Items.Add ('List Item 1');
ListBox1.Items.Add ('List Item 2');
ListBox1.Items.Add ('List Item 3');
ListBox1.Items.Add ('List Item 4');
ListBox1.Items.Add ('List Item 5');
```

4 In the OnClick event handler of the button, type:

```
try
   Label1.Caption := ListBox1.Items [7];
except
   Application.MessageBox ('List index out of bounds',
   'List Error', MB_ICONEXCLAMATION + MB_OK);
end;
```

5 Choose Tools | Environmental Options... to open the Environment Options dialog box.

6 Click on the **Break on exception** check box to toggle off this option.

7 Choose OK to save the new environment configuration.

8 Run the program and click on the button. Since the list only contains five items, trying to reference item 7 (a nonexistent item) raises an exception error. Instead of crashing the program, however, the exception handler traps the error and displays a message.

Summary

In this chapter, you have learned how to use the debugger and how to write resource protection and exception handlers. Specifically, you have learned how to:

▶ Run to the cursor position.

▶ Trace/step code in programs.

▶ Monitor the values of expressions.

▶ Modify and test expressions.

▶ View subroutine calls.

▶ Write resource protection and exception handlers.

▶ Change environment options.

▶ Reraise exceptions.

▶ Create silent exception handlers.

Building Database
Applications in
Delphi

Using the
DBRichEdit
Component

Using Data Modules

Writing Code to
Maintain Databases

Exercise: Creating
a Table

Chapter 8
Working with Databases

In previous chapters, you learned how to create simple applications by placing controls on forms, setting properties, and writing event handlers. Already you have gained a strong knowledge of the program development process in Delphi and of the advantages of its object-oriented model. In this chapter, you will learn how to create even more robust applications that make use of Delphi's powerful data access features.

Building Database Applications in Delphi

To achieve database access, Delphi makes use of the BDE (Borland Database Engine), which seamlessly integrates data from different database formats into your programs. With the BDE, your programs can take advantage of desktop databases like dBASE, Paradox, Access, and also control data from a variety of other sources. Best of all, Delphi's high-level data access objects provide the ability to automate many tasks that in the past would require a significant amount of programming. For example, in a matter of minutes, you can create a data entry or database maintenance screen to manipulate database records without writing a single line of code! Moreover, your programs can incorporate graphics, lookup lists, formatted memos, and more.

Before you can create database applications in Delphi, there are a few basic terms you should be familiar with. Table 8.1 summarizes these terms. In this chapter, we will cheat a little by first showing how to display and work with records from an existing database table. Afterwards, we will come back to the issue of database design and how tables can be created in Delphi.

Quick Start

In the following exercise, you will create a simple program to display and edit information from a database. After this exercise, you should be able to:

▶ Bind a table to data components on a form to display and manipulate database records.

▶ Display information from a table on an editable grid.

▶ Work with graphics stored in a database table.

▶ Show/edit memos from a table.

TABLE 8.1   KEY DATABASE TERMS

Term	Definition
Field	An individual data item (or column) of a table.
Record	A group of related fields.
Table	A structure based upon rows and columns of data.
Database	An organized collection of tables.
Index	An identifier linked to one or more fields in a table that maintains a logical order within the table and is used to quickly locate records.
Key	A primary index where duplicate records are prohibited.

▶   Use a data-bound combo box to facilitate data entry in a program.

1 Choose File | New Application to start a new project.

2 Using the Object Inspector, set the properties of the form as follows:

Left = 9

Top = 34

Height = 405

Width = 623

Position = poScreenCenter

3 From the Data Access page of the Component Palette, add a DataSource component and a Table component to the form (see Figure 8.1).

> **Note** *To see the Component Palette, you can drag the form out of your way for now by left-clicking on the title bar and holding this button down as you move the mouse.*

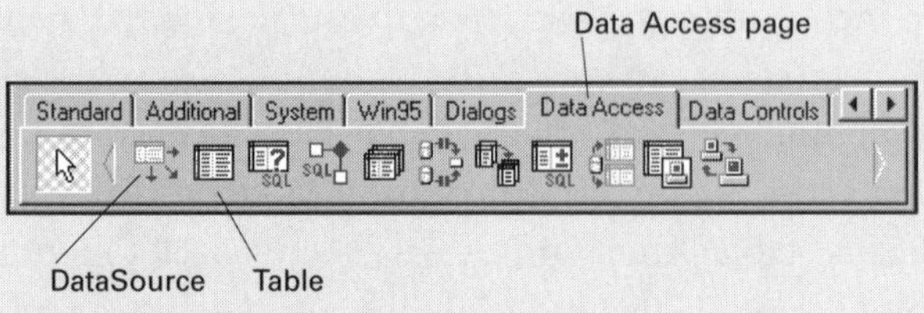

FIGURE 8.1
Data Access components for the sample exercise

4 Set the properties of these components as indicated below:

Component	Property	Value
Table1	DatabaseName	DBDEMOS
	TableName	EVENTS.DB
DataSource1	DataSet	Table1

DBDEMOS is an alias supplied by Borland which contains several example tables. Delphi uses aliases to indicate the location of database tables and to specify connect parameters for database servers. In the "Creating a Table" exercise later in this chapter, you will learn how to define an alias.

5 From the Data Controls page of the Component Palette, add a DBGRID component and a DBNavigator component to the form. Use the help hints to find these components. Set their properties as follows:

Component	Property	Value
DBGrid	DataSource	DataSource1
	Left	8
	Top	172
	Height	190
	Width	601
DBNavigator	DataSource	DataSource1
	Left	368
	Top	137

6 Add a DBImage control to the form. Set its properties as follows:

Property	Value
Left	448
Top	8
Height	113
Width	161
DataSource	DataSource1
DataField	Event_Photo

7 Add the following components to the form. Place and size each control roughly as it appears in Figure 8.2.

Component	Page on Component Palette
DBMemo1	Data Controls
DBText1	Data Controls
DBEdit1	Data Controls
DBComboBox1	Data Controls
Label1	Standard
Label2	Standard
Label3	Standard

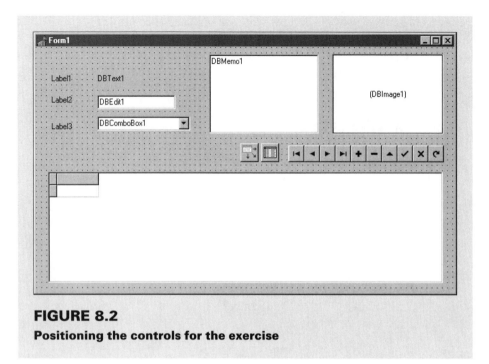

FIGURE 8.2

Positioning the controls for the exercise

8 Set the properties of each control listed below as follows:

Component	Property	Value
DBMemo1	DataSource	DataSource1
	DataField	Event_Description
DBText1	DataSource	DataSource1
	DataField	Event_Date
DBEdit1	DataSource	DataSource1
	DataSource	Event_Name
DBComboBox1	DataSource	DataSource1
	DataSource	Ticket_Price
Label1	Caption	Event Date:
Label2	Caption	Event Name:
Label3	Caption	Ticket Price:

9 Double click on the *form* and add the following code to the OnCreate event handler:

```
DBComboBox1.Items.Add('5.00');
DBComboBox1.Items.Add('7.50');
DBComboBox1.Items.Add('10.00');
DBComboBox1.Items.Add('12.50');
```

10 Set the Active property of the Table component to **True**.

Since the data controls on the form are bound to the table component, the records from the table should now appear on the screen.

To test the project, press F9 or choose the Run command from the toolbar or Run menu. To move from record to record, use the buttons on the DBNavigator component (see Figure 8.3). Note that each time you click on the Next or Prior button, a different record will appear—that is, the number and name of the event will appear in the DBEdit controls along with a description that will show up in the DBMemo component, the picture of the event in the DBImage control, and so on. Also note that since these controls are *data aware*, if you change a value in the DBGrid or modify the name, description, event price, or other item, Delphi will automatically save that change when you move to another record in the table. Alternately, you can update the record using the Post button of the DBNavigator component or use the Cancel button to disregard a change.

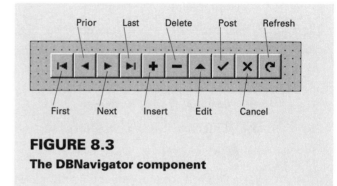

FIGURE 8.3
The DBNavigator component

A Closer Look

In the preceding exercise, you created a program to display records from a dataset and to edit its records, using Delphi's data-aware components that permit you to interface with the BDE. The two most important components in accomplishing this are the TTable and TDataSource components. To specify a data source, the DatabaseName property of the Table component (TTable) is set to an alias that represents the database. This alias (DBDEMOS), supplied by Borland, is a collection of tables which contain sample data you can use. By supplying an alias name for the database and the name of the table within the database to draw records from, the necessary link to the file is established. In order to interface with the visual data controls that appear on the form (DBGrid, DBEdit, DBImage, and so on), the program uses the TDataSource component to create the link to Table1.

To sum things up, to create a link to a dataset, the following properties must be set:

Component	Property	Example
Table	DatabaseName	DBDEMOS
	TableName	EVENTS.DB
DataSource	DataSet	Table1

After specifying these properties, you bind a component from the Data Controls page of the Component Palette to a dataset by setting its DataSource property to the name of the DataSource component and its DataField property to the name of the field that it will draw information from. For example, to bind DBEdit1 to the Event_Name field in the EVENTS.DB table, you'd set these properties as:

Component	Property	Value
DBEdit1	DataSource	DataSource1
DBEdit1	DataField	Event_Name

Using the same logic, to bind the Event_Photo field to the dataset, the DataSource and DataField properties must be set to:

Component	Property	Value
DBImage1	DataSource	DataSource1
DBImage1	DataField	Event_Photo

Likewise, to bind the DBMemo component to the dataset, you would indicate this as:

Component	Property	Value
DBMemo1	DataSource	DataSource1
DBMemo1	DataField	Event_Description

For a DBGrid component, you do not have to specify a field to bind to. Since the DBGrid control does not have a DataField property, you cannot specify this property setting anyway. By default, when you specify the DataSource property of the DBGrid component, all the fields from the dataset are automatically linked to the control. However, before the data will appear on the grid, you must set the Active property of the TTable component to **True**. The same principle holds true for other data-bound components as well. Before any data will appear in the controls, you must activate the link by setting Active to **True**. For example:

Component	Property	Value
DBGrid1	DataSource	DataSource1
Table1	Active	True

Note *Although the DBGrid component does not have a DataField property, it does have a Columns property that you can use to add/remove the columns that appear on the grid.*

Using the DBRichEdit Component

Delphi 3 provides a new development tool called the DBRichEdit component. With DBRichEdit, you can display/edit rich text memos stored in a database. Rich text is a format that enables you to display enhanced memos that contain multiple fonts, styles, alignments, point sizes, colors, and more. Although the control permits you to edit these documents, it does not provide any interface to facilitate the formatting of memos. This book, however, comes with a sample rich text editor (RTE.DPR) which permits you to create rich text memos using a menu-driven interface. To get a memo, use the Edit | Copy command in RTE.DPR to copy a selected block and then Shift+Insert to paste the text into a DBRichEdit memo. Figure 8.4 shows an example of a document created with the sample editor. The following example shows how to bind a dataset to the DBRichEdit control:

Component	Property	Example
Table1	DatabaseName	MYALIAS
	TableName	MYTABLE.DB
DataSource1	DataSet	Table1
DBRichEdit1	DataSource	DataSource1
	DataField	MyField
DBNavigator1	DataSource	DataSource1
Table1	Active	True

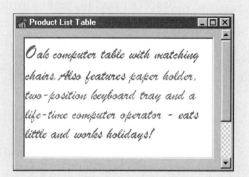

FIGURE 8.4
A sample rich text memo

This example uses the DBNavigator component to move the record pointer in the table to update a rich text memo. Since the current version of the DBRichEdit control provides no interface to facilitate rich text formatting, you may wish to set the ReadOnly property of the DBNavigator component to **True** and use it only to display formatted memos.

When binding a DBRichEdit component to a field in a table, you must bind the control to a field that is capable of displaying rich edit text. DBRichEdit memos are typically bound to Paradox *formatted memo* fields. The Database Desktop utility permits you to create and restructure Paradox tables. In the exercise that follows later in this chapter, you will see how to create tables that can incorporate rich text memo fields.

> **Note** *If your applications do not require saving memos to a dataset, you can save a significant amount of resources by using the Rich Edit control instead. For a complete discussion of the TRichEdit component, see Chapter 16.*

Using Data Modules

Although it may seem odd at first, the components Delphi uses to access or manipulate datasets appear on two different pages of the Component Palette. The Data Access page, as its name implies, provides access to datasets. Since these components are used only to manipulate data and are not actually visible at run-time, they are kept separate from the components that appear on the Data Controls page of the Component Palette.

To facilitate the development of projects, Delphi provides a method of collecting all the data access components you use in a single application where they can easily be referenced from any part of the program. All the data access components you use are placed in a *data module* where every form that uses the module has access to these components. For instance, instead of placing the TDataSource and TTable components on a form, you can add or move these to a data module so that every form in the project can use them.

To add a data module to a project, you use the File | New Data Module command in Delphi. Data modules look like forms, only their background color is set to white and at run-time the modules are invisible (see Figure 8.5).

Like components, you can change the Name property of a data module by setting its Name property via the Object Inspector. As with forms, each data module is associated with a unit. To change the unit name, use the File | Save As... command.

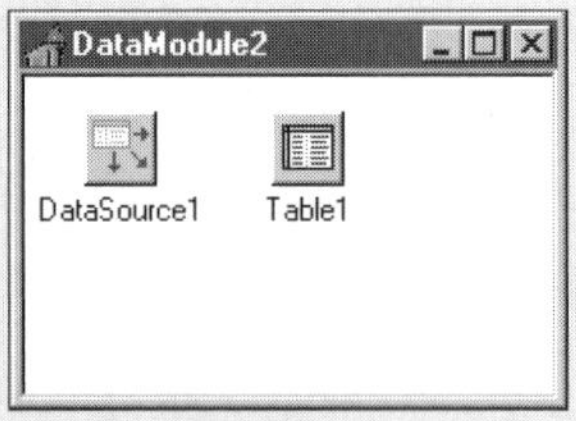

To use a data module in a project, follow these two steps:

1 From the File menu, choose the Use Unit... command.

2 Pick the name of the unit from the Use Unit list and then click on OK.

FIGURE 8.5
A sample data module

Alternately, you can link a data module to a form by right-clicking on the TTable component and choosing the Fields Editor... option from the SpeedMenu. A new window will appear with the name of the Data Module and four dots after it in the title bar. Right-click this window and choose the Add field option (Ctrl+A). Delphi will show you a list of fields in the dataset. Choose any (or all) of the fields and click on OK.

Afterwards, by dragging one of the field names onto the form, Delphi will automatically create the link to the data module (upon request) and even generate a data-bound control for that field! For example, if you drag a text field onto the form, Delphi will create a DBEdit control, set the appropriate properties to bind it to the dataset, and add a label above the control to show the name of the field. By selecting all the fields at once and dragging them, you can create a data-bound table maintenance form in a single drag (see Figure 8.6).

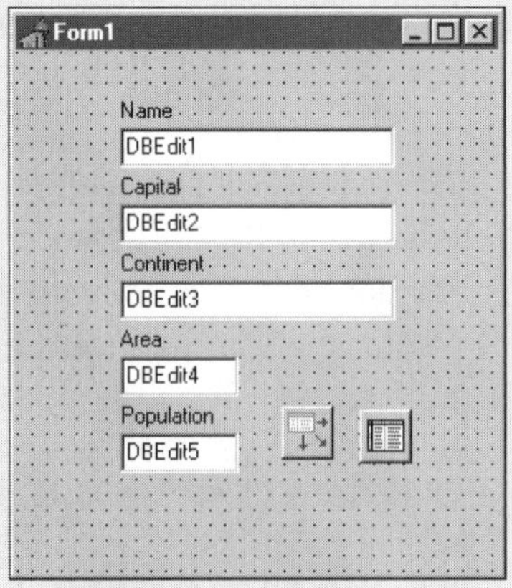

To select all the fields:

1 Click on the first field name in the fields list.

2 Hold the Shift key down and click on the last field name in the list to select all the fields.

FIGURE 8.6
Data-bound controls created by dragging fields

After selecting the fields, drag them onto the form by clicking on the data module and holding the left mouse button down. The mouse pointer shape will change to a drag cursor. Without letting up on the mouse button, move to the form window and then click on it. Delphi will generate a complete data-bound collection of controls for the dataset.

> **Tip** *You can also select a non-continuous group of fields in the fields list by pressing Ctrl+Left Click on each field name you wish to add.*

Writing Code to Maintain Databases

Although Delphi provides a rich collection of data access components and controls, it is necessary to write code in order to fully take advantage of the Borland Database Engine. If you are new to Delphi, you will appreciate its easy-to-use data manipulation tools. Unlike other development environments, such as Visual Basic, Delphi does not require you to **Dim** or **Set** a Database or Recordset object before you can take advantage of its professional features. Moreover, Delphi offers greater consistency between its Desktop, Developer, and Client-Server editions than Visual Basic does with its Standard, Professional, and Enterprise editions. For example, the following three lines of code can be used to open a dataset in Delphi's Client-Server edition as well as its Developer and Desktop editions:

```
procedure TForm1.FormCreate(Sender: TObject);


{ Initialize dataset }


begin


Table1.DatabaseName := 'DBDEMOS';
Table1.TableName := 'ANIMALS.DBF';
Table1.Open;


end;
```

By providing a more uniform set of commands to manipulate datasets, Delphi narrows the learning curve between its editions. Whether you plan to write full-blown client-server applications or just simple desktop database programs, Delphi provides a smooth transition from one edition to the next.

Working with Datasets

In the previous section, you learned how to open a table when a form is loaded. Once you have specified a dataset to work with, you can easily reference any field in the table by naming the field like this:

```
ShowMessage (Table1['Name']);
```

This code will display the value of the *Name* field from the ANIMALS.DBF table in a modal dialog box. When you first open a dataset, Delphi positions the file pointer at the first record within the dataset. The following code shows how to move to the next record in the table:

```
Table1.Next;
```

Using a similar technique, you can move to a previous record like this:

```
Table1.Prior;
```

Using the MoveBy Method

The **MoveBy** method allows you to move directly to a database record. For example, to position the file pointer on the fifth record in the table, the following code can be used:

```
Table1.MoveBy(5);
```

By specifying a negative index, you can also move backward in the dataset:

```
Table1.MoveBy(-2);    { Move back 2 records }
```

Table 8.2 summarizes the database methods you use to move around in a dataset.

TABLE 8.2   DATASET MOVEMENT METHODS

Method	Description
First	Moves to first record in dataset.
Last	Moves to last record in dataset.
Prior	Moves to previous record in dataset.
MoveBy	Moves forward or backwards the specified number of records.
Next	Moves forward one record.

Finding Information in Tables

When you use the DBNavigator component to scroll through records in a dataset, Delphi automatically moves the file pointer from record to record. You can also write a loop to browse records in a table. The following code shows how to loop through a dataset until the end of the file is reached or until a certain condition is met:

```
{ Read each record in loop until either pattern is found or
  EOF returns True }

Table1.DatabaseName := 'DBDEMOS';
Table1.TableName := 'ANIMALS.DBF';
Table1.Open;

While Not Table1.EOF do

  begin
```

```
    if TrimRight (Table1['Name']) = 'Boa' then
      begin
        ShowMessage (Table1['Name']);
        Exit;
      end;

    Table1.Next;

  end;
```

The **EOF** property determines the status of the record pointer. If **EOF** returns **True**, the record pointer has reached the end of the table. Notice, too, that the program also uses an **If then** block and **exit** procedure to conditionally break from the loop. If the *Name* field in any record is equal to "Boa", the loop terminates and program execution continues at the next executable line in the program.

For sake of simplicity, the examples in this chapter make use of the default names given to Delphi's data access components and controls. You can, of course, set these components to more meaningful names, such as tblClients, tblOrders, or tblInventory.

Notice the use of the *tbl* prefix. All the examples in the remainder of this chapter will use this prefix to indicate the TTable component. By applying the same naming conventions in your programs, the code you write will be easier to read and maintain.

Performing Faster Searches

The sequential searching method previously demonstrated works fine for small databases. For large tables, however, it could take a considerable amount of time to locate records. With the **GotoKey** and **GotoNearest** methods, you can quickly locate records using indexes. The **GotoKey** method returns the first exact match of a search criteria. The **GotoNearest** method seeks the first partial match of a search criteria. For example, the following code opens the ANIMALS.DBF table from the DBDEMOS database and finds the first animal with a name similar to *Par* (parrot, in this case):

```
procedure TForm1.FormCreate(Sender: TObject);

{ Open dBASE table from DBDEMOS alias }

begin
  tblAnimals.DatabaseName := 'DBDEMOS';
  tblAnimals.TableName := 'ANIMALS.DBF';
end;

procedure TForm1.btnSeekClick(Sender: TObject);
```

```
begin

{ Close table if open before setting
  new index }

if tblAnimals.State <> dsInactive then
   tblAnimals.Close;

tblAnimals.IndexName := 'Name';
tblAnimals.Open;
tblAnimals.SetKey;
tblAnimals['Name'] := 'Par';
tblAnimals.GotoNearest;

MessageDlg(tblAnimals['Name'], mtInformation,
   [mbOk], 0)

end;
```

This example assumes that the table is indexed by the *Name* field. Notice that you must first close the table before setting the index. Afterwards, the **SetKey** method must also be applied to initialize the new key.

Although the ability to find records based on partial matches is often sufficient, there are instances in which it is necessary to find an exact match. For example, you may wish to search by a product number or by an employee's ID. In such cases, you could use **GotoKey** to seek the first exact match. For example:

```
procedure TForm1.FormCreate(Sender: TObject);

{ Open Paradox table from DBDEMOS alias }

begin
  tblReservat.DatabaseName := 'DBDEMOS';
  tblReservat.TableName := 'RESERVAT.DB';
end;

procedure TForm1.btnSeekClick(Sender: TObject);
```

```
begin

{ Close table if open before setting
  new index }

if tblReservat.State <> dsInactive then
   tblReservat.Close;

tblReservat.DataBaseName := 'DBDEMOS';
tblReservat.TableName := 'Reservat';
tblReservat.IndexName := 'CustNo';
tblReservat.Open;
tblReservat.SetKey;
tblReservat ['CustNo'] := 22;
tblReservat.GotoKey;

if not tblReservat.GotoKey then
   MessageDlg('Customer not found', mtInformation, [mbOk], 0)
else
   MessageDlg(tblReservat ['Pay_Method'], mtInformation, [mbOk], 0);

end;
```

This example uses the **GotoKey** method to find a customer number equal to 22. If a match is found, **GotoKey** returns **True** and the value of the *Pay_Method* field is displayed.

Adding Records to a Table

The **Insert** and **AppendRecord** methods allow you to add new records to tables. The difference between the two is that **Insert** adds a new record at the current record position, whereas **AppendRecord** always adds new records to the end of the table.

AppendRecord provides an easy way of saving new records. By specifying a comma-separated field list, you can easily add new records to a table. Each field must supply a value that is appropriate for the given field. For example, a string must be enclosed in quotes and a date field must be set to a valid date value. To add a field without initializing it, you can also use the **Nil** reserved word. The following code is an example of adding a new record without supplying a default value for the third field in the record:

```
    .          .          .
tblHoldings.Open;
tblHoldings.AppendRecord ([2353, 'NJ', Nil, 12, '10/11/1998']);
```

The **AppendRecord** method has one drawback. If the structure of the table is redefined, the wrong values may be plugged into the record when it is added, thereby causing the append to fail. With the **Insert** method, you can add a record and be sure the initialization parameters will correspond to the correct fields. For example:

```
procedure TForm1.btnAddRecClick(Sender: TObject);

begin

  { Add new record using Insert method }

  tblHoldings.DatabaseName := 'DBDEMOS';
  tblHoldings.TableName := 'HOLDINGS.DBF';
  tblHoldings.Open;

  Application.ProcessMessages;

  tblHoldings.Insert;

  tblHoldings['ACCT_NBR'] := 123;
  tblHoldings['SYMBOL'] := 'ABC';
  tblHoldings['SHARES'] := 354.30;
  tblHoldings['PUR_PRICE'] := 434.33;
  tblHoldings['PUR_DATE'] := Date;

  tblHoldings.Post;

end;
```

Since it is rare that you will assign a literal value to a field, you will most likely find it necessary to use controls on the form to get input from users. For instance:

```
procedure TForm1.btnAddRecClick(Sender: TObject);

begin

  { Add new record using Insert method }

  tblHoldings.DatabaseName := 'DBDEMOS';
  tblHoldings.TableName := 'HOLDINGS.DBF';
```

```
tblHoldings.Open;

Application.ProcessMessages;
tblHoldings.Insert;

tblHoldings['ACCT_NBR'] := editAccNumber.Text;
tblHoldings['SYMBOL'] := editSymbol.Text;
tblHoldings['SHARES'] := editShares.Text;
tblHoldings['PUR_PRICE'] := editPurPrice.Text;
tblHoldings['PUR_DATE'] := editDate.Text;

tblHoldings.Post;

end;
```

Notice that Delphi automatically converts the strings read in from the edit controls to the appropriate types. This example uses the default dataset method FieldValues to assign the new record to the table. As with the record type introduced in Chapter 4, this example can also be coded more easily using the **with** statement. For instance:

```
with tblHoldings do begin

    DatabaseName := 'DBDEMOS';
    TableName := 'HOLDINGS.DBF';
    Open;

    Insert;
    FieldValues ['ACCT_NBR'] := editAccNumber.Text;
    FieldValues ['SYMBOL'] := editSymbol.Text;
    FieldValues ['SHARES'] := editShares.Text;
    FieldValues ['PUR_PRICE'] := editPurPrice.Text;
    FieldValues ['PUR_DATE'] := editDate.Text;
    Post;

end;
```

The **with** statement provides shorthand access to a record type's fields and to an object's properties and methods. Once a record is added to a dataset, the transaction must be saved using the **Post** method, or else the changes will automatically *rollback* after the transaction. To prevent the possibility of data loss, you should always close the table when it is not in use. For example:

```
tblHoldings.Close;
```

Editing Table Records

After adding records to a dataset, you can easily go back to a record and change the value of one of its fields with a minimal amount of coding. For example:

```
with tblAnimals do begin

  DatabaseName := 'DBDEMOS';
  TableName := 'ANIMALS.DBF';
  Open;

  Edit;
  FieldValues ['Name'] := 'Unicorn';
  Post;
  Close

end;
```

To modify a field, you use the **Edit** method to place the TTable control in edit mode. Afterwards, a value of the appropriate type can be assigned to any field of the record. Once a field has been changed, you must be sure to **Post** the changes to make the edits permanent.

The preceding example shows how to edit a string field. It is also possible to modify other types of fields as well. For instance:

```
procedure TForm1.FormCreate(Sender: TObject);

{ Open Paradox table from DBDEMOS alias }

begin
  tblReservat.DatabaseName := 'DBDEMOS';
  tblReservat.TableName := 'RESERVAT.DB';
end;

procedure TForm1.btnGetCustClick(Sender: TObject);

{ Find customer and change payment information }
```

```
begin

  with tblReservat do begin

    if State <> dsInactive then
      Close;

    IndexName := 'CustNo';
    Open;
    SetKey;
    FieldValues ['CustNo'] := 19;
    GotoKey;

    if not GotoKey then
      MessageDlg('Customer not found', mtInformation, [mbOk], 0)
    else begin
      Edit;
      FieldValues ['NumTickets'] := 12;
      FieldValues ['Amt_Paid'] := 97.44;
      FieldValues ['Paid'] := True;
      Post;
      end;

  end;

end;
```

Using the SetFields Method to Update Records

As with **Insert**, the **SetFields** method allows you to manipulate an entire record in a single operation. Also like **Insert**, you must be careful when using SetFields because Delphi will not be able to accommodate for any structure changes you make to the table, and your application will crash if you attempt to supply a value of the wrong data type to a field.

Example

```
tblHoldings.DatabaseName := 'DBDEMOS';
tblHoldings.TableName := 'HOLDINGS.DBF';
tblHoldings.Open;

{ Modify record }
```

```
with tblHoldings do

  begin
    Edit;
    SetFields ([802, 'AB', nil, nil, '07/05/1998']);
    Post;
  end;
```

Deleting Table Records

The **Delete** method lets you remove unwanted records from tables. Unlike the DBNavigator component, the **Delete** method does not prompt you before removing the record. It is your responsibility to provide a warning to your users when using **Delete**.

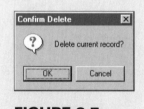

FIGURE 8.7
The message box

This next example shows how to apply the **Delete** method and prompt the user to confirm the operation before it is executed. The **MessageBox** function uses the MB_ICONQUESTION constant (defined in the Windows unit) to show a question mark icon in a modal dialog box (see Figure 8.7). If the user clicks on the OK button, the operation is then carried out:

```
{ Show model dialog to confirm delete }

tblHoldings.DatabaseName := 'DBDEMOS';
tblHoldings.TableName := 'HOLDINGS.DBF';
tblHoldings.Open;

tblHoldings.Next;

if Application.MessageBox('Delete current record?', 'Confirm Delete',
   mb_OKCancel + MB_ICONQUESTION) = IDOK then
   begin
     tblHoldings.Delete;
     ShowMessage ('1 record deleted.');
   end;
```

Checking for Empty Datasets

Before attempting to edit or delete a record in a table, you should always check for an empty dataset. If the table contains no data, an exception error will result if you attempt to edit or remove a record that is not there. If the record pointer appears at both the be-

ginning and end of the file, it means the dataset is empty. To test for this, you simply
check the BOF (Beginning of File) and EOF (End of File) properties. For example:

```
with tblParts do begin

   DatabaseName := 'DBDEMOS';
   TableName := 'PARTS.DB';
   Open;

   if EOF and BOF then
      MessageDlg('Table is empty.', mtInformation, [mbOk], 0)
   else
      MessageDlg('Table is not empty.', mtInformation, [mbOk], 0);

   end;
```

Using Bookmarks

A *bookmark* is a placeholder in a file that lets you return to a previous position.
Bookmarks are useful in a variety of applications. For example, you can record a history of transactions by saving bookmarks to an array. The following code demonstrates
how to record a bookmark:

```
var
  Form1: TForm1;
  LastPos: TBookmark;
  .     .     .
  .     .     .

procedure TForm1.btnRecordBookmarkClick(Sender: TObject);

begin

  { Record bookmark }

  LastPos := tblAnimals.GetBookmark;

  { Move down two records }

  tblAnimals.Next;
```

```
    tblAnimals.Next;

  end;
```

The *LastPos* variable is declared as type **TBookmark**. Since the variable is declared outside of any event handler or subroutine, it is made available throughout the unit. To return to a bookmark, you use the **GoToBookmark** method of the TTable component. Afterwards, when the bookmark is no longer needed, you can use the **FreeBookmark** method to release the variable from memory:

```
procedure TForm1.btnGoBookMarkClick(Sender: TObject);

{ Return to bookmark }

begin
  tblAnimals.GoToBookmark(LastPos);
  tblAnimals.FreeBookmark(LastPos);
end;
```

Exercise: Creating a Table

In the following exercise, you will create a new Paradox 7 table. After performing this exercise, you should be able to:

▶ Create an alias.

▶ Use the Database Desktop to generate a new table.

▶ Work with Formatted Memo fields and other field types.

▶ Define a key field for a table.

1 Choose File | New Application to start a new project.

2 Choose Tools | Database Desktop to load the Database Desktop utility.

3 Once the program is loaded, from the Tools menu of the *DataBase Desktop* choose the Alias Manager command.

4 Click on the New button in the Alias Manager dialog box to create a new alias.

5 In the Database alias combo box, type **PROD**.

6 In the Path box, type **C:\DLIB**.

Note *This step assumes that you installed the example files for this book in C:\DLIB path. If this is not the case, be sure to specify the correct file location.*

7 Click on OK to create the alias.

8 Delphi will inform you that the public aliases have changed and ask if you want to update the IDAPI.CFG file (that is, the configuration file for BDE settings). Click on Yes.

9 From the File menu of the Database Desktop program, choose New and then select the Table... option.

10 Click on the OK button in the Create Table dialog box to generate a new Paradox 7 table.

11 A new dialog box will appear where you define the structure of the table. Use the following table to indicate the structure of the table:

Field Name	Type	Size	Key
Item Number	N (Numeric)	N/A	*
Item Name	A (Alphanumeric)	20	
Item Description	F (Formatted Memo)		100
Item Price	$ (Money)	N/A	

Note *You can get a list of Paradox field types by right-clicking on the Type column.*

12 Choose the Save As option.

13 In the File name box, type **PRODLIST.DB**.

14 In the Alias box, choose the PROD alias.

15 Choose the Save option to add the new table to the PROD alias.

16 To test the new table, close the Database Desktop utility by choosing the File | Exit command and then add the following controls to the form. Place and size each component as it appears in Figure 8.8.

Component	Page on Component Palette
Table1	Data Access
DataSource1	Data Access
DBEdit1	Data Controls
DBEdit2	Data Controls
DBEdit3	Data Controls
DBRichEdit1	Data Controls
DBNavigator1	Data Controls

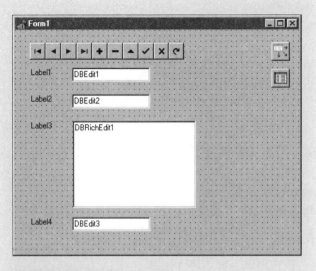

FIGURE 8.8
Positioning and sizing the components

Label1	Standard
Label2	Standard
Label3	Standard
Label4	Standard

17 Set the properties of each component as follows:

Component	Property	Example
Table1	DatabaseName	PROD
	TableName	PRODLIST.DB
DataSource1	DataSet	Table1
DBEdit1	DataSource	DataSource1
	DataField	Item Number
DBEdit2	DataSource	DataSource1
	DataField	Item Name
DBRichEdit1	DataSource	DataSource1
	DataField	Item Description
DBEdit3	DataSource	DataSource1
	DataField	Item Price
DBNavigator1	DataSource	DataSource1
Table1	Active	True
Label1	Caption	Item Number:

Label2	Caption	Item Name:
Label3	Caption	Item Description:
Label4	Caption	Item Price:
Form1	Position	PoScreenCenter
	Width	367
	Caption	Product List Table

18 Click on the *form* and add the following code to the OnCreate event handler:

```
DBRichEdit1.Font.Color := clBlue;
```

19 Run the project and enter the following information. Use the DBNavigator component to save the records and advance the record pointer to the next record in the dataset.

Item Number	Item Name	Item Description	Item Price
123	Watch	Backward running	43.21
343	Computer	Broken	211.23
879	Desk	Genuine pine!	50.00

Summary

In this chapter, you have learned how to work with the data manipulation components of Delphi. In addition, you have learned how to:

▶ Display rich text memos.

▶ Work with data modules.

▶ Automatically generate data-aware controls on forms.

▶ Create database tables and aliases.

▶ Write code to interface with the BDE.

▶ Find records in tables.

▶ Use bookmarks.

**Fundamentals of
SQL**

**Starting InterBase
Windows
Interactive SQL**

**Using the Query
Component**

**Exercise: Running
Queries from
Delphi**

Chapter 9

Using Structured Query Language

Fundamentals of SQL

Structured Query Language (SQL) is a data manipulation language and a data definition language that allows you to perform various operations on datasets. Commonly known for its powerful searching capabilities, SQL is more than just a querying language. With SQL, you can modify database structures, merge tables, maintain records, perform group updates, generate statistics, and more.

SQL, most often pronounced "es cue el" or "sequel," is an industry standard that spans many development platforms. Thus by learning the Delphi syntax, you will find that you can easily apply the same commands to other programming environments.

Delphi provides two ways of incorporating SQL into projects:

▶ Using the integrated SQL engine

▶ Using an external server

With the InterBase Windows Interactive SQL utility (included with Delphi as part of the Local InterBase Server), you can build queries in an interactive environment. This special utility allows you to create and run queries by selecting options from menus. It also lets you define new databases, change table structures, rerun queries, and look up SQL commands using an online Help reference. Best of all, Windows ISQL is especially useful for learning SQL.

In essence, SQL's commands can be divided into two major categories:

▶ *Data Definition Language (DDL)* maintains database structures. Examples include CREATE TABLE, ALTER TABLE, CREATE INDEX, DROP INDEX, and more.

▶ *Data Manipulation Language (DML)* allows you to retrieve subsets of records from datasets and manipulate table records. Examples include SELECT, INSERT, DELETE, UPDATE, and so on.

As a Data Definition Language (DDL), SQL lets you create and maintain database structures. For instance, you can define tables, insert fields, generate indexes, and even modify table structures. As a Data Manipulation Language (DML), SQL provides the ability to find records, change their contents, insert and delete records, sort columns, and so on.

Many of the examples in this chapter incorporate the sample databases included with Delphi. Therefore, you may wish to follow along at the computer and run the examples from the InterBase interactive environment and from Delphi.

Starting InterBase Windows Interactive SQL

Since SQL enables you to define as well as maintain database tables, the best way to learn how to use SQL is to create a database. To do this, from the Interbase 4.2 program group, choose the InterBase Windows ISQL program item[1]. When the program loads, from the File menu, choose Create Database. Afterwards, enter the Database Name, User Name, and Password information as follows:

> Database Name: MYSQLDB
>
> User Name: (null)
>
> Password: (null)

If you receive an error message at this point, it is probably because you need to create a user-ID before proceeding (depending on what version of Windows ISQL you are using). To establish a new user-ID, in the InterBase Server Manager, you login as *SYSDBA* with the password *masterkey*. Afterwards, you can generate a new user-ID by choosing the Tasks | User Security... option and then selecting the Add User... command. Alternately, you can login for now as the System Database Administrator by typing:

> User Name: SYSDBA
>
> Password: masterkey

Adding a Table to the Database

The **CREATE TABLE** command defines a new table in a database. **CREATE TABLE** has the following syntax:

```
CREATE TABLE TableName
    (Column1 ColumnType [NOT NULL UNIQUE],
     Column_x ColumnType [NOT NULL]);
```

TableName is one of the most powerful and versatile commands of SQL. Note that this syntax does not take into account all the far-reaching options of **CREATE TABLE** as documented in the online Help. Since the full syntax spans more than a single printed page, only the most common features are provided here.

To create the table, enter the following commands into the SQL Statement window (see Figure 9.1). The semicolon at the end of the commands is optional. SQL is not case-sensitive. Therefore, the **CREATE** command can be entered in all caps, with an initial capital letter, or in lowercase.

---

[1] This assumes you have already installed Interbase Windows ISQL. Although included with Delphi 3.0, InterBase Windows ISQL is not automatically installed by the Delphi setup program.

```
CREATE TABLE CDROM_TITLES
    (CDName CHAR(20) NOT NULL UNIQUE,
     Manufacturer CHAR(30) NOT NULL);
```

This statement will create a new table called CDROM_TITLES. The table contains two fields: CDName and Manufacturer. Both fields are declared using the **CHAR** function. CDName is a 20-character string and Manufacturer is a 30-character string. Table 9.1 shows a list of other field types you can use.

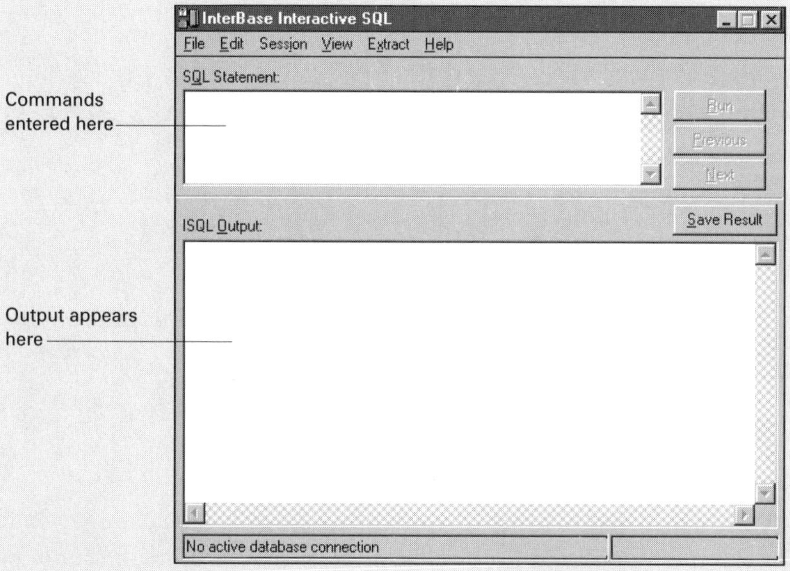

After creating the table, you can check it by selecting View and then MetaData Information from the interactive environment. When you are done, select Index from

FIGURE 9.1
InterBase Interactive SQL

TABLE 9.1   SUPPORTED INTERBASE DATA TYPES

Data Type	Description	Range	Storage
BLOB	Binary Large Object (graphics, digitized voice, or text)	N/A	variable
CHAR(n)	character string	1 to 32,767 bytes	n characters
DATE	date and time information	01/01/100 to 01/11/5941	64 bits
DECIMAL	(precision, decimal)	precision: 1..15; decimal: 1 to 15	variable
DOUBLE PRECISION	15-digit precision	1.7×10^{-308} to 1.7×10^{308}	64 bits
FLOAT	single precision, that is, 7 digits of precision	3.4×10^{-38} to 3.4×10^{38}	32 bits
INTEGER	signed long	-2,147,483,648 to 2,147,483,648	32 bits
NUMERIC	(precision, decimal)	precision: 1..15; decimal: 1 to 15	variable
SMALLINT	Signed short	-32,768 to 32,767	16 bits
VARCHAR	variable length character string	1 to 32,767 bytes	n characters

the View Information On drop-down list. This will show all the indexes that exist in the table:

```
SHOW INDEX
RDB$1 UNIQUE INDEX ON CDROM_TITLES(CDName)
```

Inserting Records into a Table

The **INSERT** command allows you to add new records into a table. **INSERT** has the following syntax:

```
INSERT INTO TableName VALUES (field1 value,
    field2 value, fieldn value);
```

For testing purposes, you will need to add a few records into the table. Add the first record by typing:

```
INSERT INTO CDROM_TITLES VALUES ("World Encyclopedia",
    "Software Developer Associates");
```

Afterwards, add two more records using the following commands. Be sure to run each statement separately because the interactive environment cannot process both statements together.

```
INSERT INTO CDROM_TITLES VALUES ("Dinosaurs",
    "X Conglomerates");
```

Here is the second statement:

```
INSERT INTO CDROM_TITLES VALUES ("Paleolithic Man",
    "Some Big Company");
```

Now that you have some test data, you can view the contents of the table using the **SELECT** command. To do this, type:

```
SELECT * FROM CDROM_TITLES
```

The asterisk after **SELECT** specifies that all fields from the CDROM_TITLES table be included in the query. Note that you could also limit the scope of fields to be displayed by replacing the asterisk with a comma-separated field list. For example, the following query will create a list that shows just the names of the CD-ROM manufacturers:

```
SELECT Manufacturer FROM CDROM_TITLES
```

Since the table contains only two columns (CDName and Manufacturer), the following queries will yield identical results:

```
SELECT CDName, Manufacturer FROM CDROM_TITLES
```

and

```
SELECT * FROM CDROM_TITLES
```

The output from the queries will look like this:

```
SELECT * FROM CDROM_TITLES

CDNAME                   MANUFACTURER
====================     ==============================


World Encyclopedia       Software Developer Associates
Dinosaurs                X Conglomerates
Paleolithic Man          Some Big Company
```

Performing Queries

The **SELECT** statement is one of the most useful and important commands in SQL. You can use **SELECT** to seek both partial and exact matches of search patterns. To see how it works, try entering the following statement and running it:

```
SELECT * FROM CDROM_TITLES WHERE
    CDName = "Dinosaurs"
```

This query returns the CD named *Dinosaurs*. Since no duplicates are allowed, only one record appears in the ISQL Output window.

SQL also provides an easy way of locating information based on partial matches of search criteria. For example, the following statement returns all manufacturers in the table with names that begin with the letters "So".

```
SELECT * FROM CDROM_TITLES WHERE
Manufacturer LIKE "So%"
```

When you run this statement, the ISQL Output window shows the following results:

```
SELECT * FROM CDROM_TITLES WHERE
Manufacturer LIKE "So%"


CDNAME                   MANUFACTURER
====================     ==============================
```

```
World Encyclopedia    Software Developer Associates
Paleolithic Man       Some Big Company
```

The % symbol returns zero or more characters. Thus it is possible to locate quickly table information without knowing the exact spelling of an item. Note that you could also use an underscore to seek any single character. For example, assuming you had a table called TstTbl, the following query returns *dog, fog, hog,* and *log* from *fieldn.*

```
SELECT * FROM TstTbl WHERE Fieldn LIKE "_og%"
```

Updating Records and Table Definitions

InterBase SQL also permits you to update records in tables. This extremely powerful feature allows you to perform multiple changes in a column using a single statement. The **UPDATE** command has the following syntax:

```
UPDATE TableName SET condition1 WHERE condition2
```

For example, the following statement changes the manufacturer *Some Big Company* to *Even Bigger Conglomerate:*

```
UPDATE CDROM_TITLES
    SET
        Manufacturer = "Even Bigger Conglomerate"
    WHERE
        Manufacturer = "Some Big Company"
```

It is even possible to perform group updates using mathematical expressions. Since the sample database contains no numeric fields, you will need to modify the structure of the table to perform this test. Use the following statement to make the change:

```
ALTER TABLE CDROM_TITLES ADD ListPrice NUMERIC (10, 2);
```

The **ALTER TABLE** statement lets you change a table's structure. In the preceding example, **ALTER TABLE** is used to add a new column called *ListPrice* which is defined as a ten-digit, two-decimal place field.

Now that you have created the new column, use the following statements to add three more records to the table. Note that each **INSERT** must be entered and run separately.

```
INSERT INTO CDROM_TITLES VALUES ("New Title 1", "Company 1", 0);


INSERT INTO CDROM_TITLES VALUES ("New Title 2", "Company 2", 0);


INSERT INTO CDROM_TITLES VALUES ("New Title 3", "Company 3", 0);
```

Before you can run a query using mathematical expressions, the *ListPrice* column must be initialized for each record in the table. Do this the following way:

```
UPDATE CDROM_TITLES
    SET
       ListPrice = 40.00
    WHERE
       ListPrice = 0
```

This statement will initialize each field in the table where *ListPrice* has not already been given a value. After initializing the records, you can use the following assignment to increase the *ListPrice* of the Paleolithic Man CD-ROM by five percent:

```
UPDATE CDROM_TITLES
   SET
      ListPrice = (ListPrice * .05) + ListPrice
   WHERE
      CDNAME = "Paleolithic Man"
```

Removing Table Records

InterBase SQL provides a quick way of removing records from tables. For example, to delete the manufacturer named *Software Developer Associates*, you could type:

```
DELETE FROM CDROM_TITLES WHERE
      Manufacturer = "Software Developer Associates"
```

Caution *If you forget to include the WHERE clause in an SQL DELETE, all the records in the table will be removed. Before experimenting with the DELETE command, be sure to backup your work.*

Specifying Ranges

The **BETWEEN** operator determines the range of values that will be returned by a query. For example, you can use the **BETWEEN** operator to find all records in the table with a *ListPrice* greater than or equal to $41.95 *and* less than or equal to $50.00.

```
SELECT CDName, ListPrice FROM CDROM_TITLES
      WHERE ListPrice BETWEEN 41.95 AND 50.00
```

Note *Before changes will take effect, you must save your work by choosing File | Commit Work or use File | Rollback Work to reverse the edits.*

Using the Query Component

With the Query component, you can perform queries using the integrated SQL engine provided as part of the Delphi environment. The Query component works in combination with other components. Typically, you bind TQuery to a TDataSource and use a grid to display or edit the results. In the following exercise, you will create and bind a Query component and use it to supply a SQL string at run-time.

Exercise: Running Queries from Delphi

For this exercise, you will need the following components:

Component	Page on Component Palette
Query	Data Access
DataSource	Data Access
DBGrid	Data Controls

1   Place the objects on the forms as they appear in Figure 9.2.

2   Set their properties as:

Component	Property	Value
Query	DatabaseName	DBDEMOS
DataSource	DataSet	Query1
DBGrid	DataSource	DataSource1
Query	SQL	SELECT * FROM BioLife
Query	Active	True

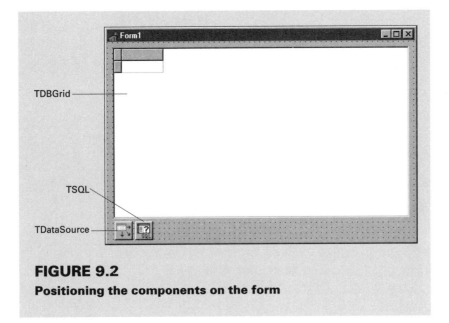

FIGURE 9.2
Positioning the components on the form

3 Once you set the Active property of TQuery, Delphi automatically displays the results of the query. Note that if you edit the command string specified by the SQL property, you will have to set the Active property to **True** again before the new query will take effect.

Writing Code to Execute Queries

Setting queries at design-time is fine, but to fully control a dataset, you need to write code. To specify a query, you use the **Add** method to execute the text in the SQL property of the Query component. For example, the following procedure shows all columns in the BioLife table where Category = "Shark":

```
procedure TForm1.Button1Click(Sender: TObject);

begin

  { Close table if open before setting query }

  if Query1.State <> dsInactive then
     Query1.Close;

  Query1.SQL.Clear;
  Query1.SQL.Add ('SELECT * FROM BioLife WHERE Category = "Shark"');
  Query1.Open;

end;
```

To initiate a query at run-time, you use the **Close** method to close the dataset before setting the query and **Clear** method to refresh the SQL property. Afterwards, you set the new SQL text and use **Open** to execute the **SELECT**. On operations where a *result set* (or dataset) is not returned, you use the **ExecSQL** method to perform the operation. These statements include **INSERT, UPDATE, DELETE,** and any Data Definition Language statements (such as **CREATE TABLE, ALTER TABLE, DROP TABLE,** and so on). For example, the AddField function of the LMDB unit uses **ExecSQL** to dynamically insert a new field into a table. Since this function is already included in the developers' library distributed with this book, you do not have to enter this code yourself. Just add the LMDB.PAS unit to your project, include it in your **uses** clause, and you can directly call any routine in the unit using standard Object Pascal syntax. For more information on how to use the AddField function, see Chapter 14, "Database Routines."

```
function AddField (Query: TQuery; tblName: String; FieldName,
                   FieldType, FieldSize, FieldDec: String): Integer;
```

```
var
  SQLTblDef: String;
  AddStatus: Integer;

begin

  { Try adding a new field to table structure }

  Query.Close;
  Query.SQL.Clear;

  AddStatus := 0;

  if UpperCase (FieldType) = 'NUMERIC' then
    SQLTblDef := 'ALTER TABLE ' + tblName + ' ADD ' + FieldName + ' '
    + FieldType + ' (' + FieldSize + ', ' + FieldDec + ')'
  else
    SQLTblDef := 'ALTER TABLE ' + tblName + ' ADD ' + FieldName + ' '
    + FieldType + ' (' + FieldSize + ')';

  Query.SQL.Add (SQLTblDef);

  try
    Query.ExecSQL;
  except
    on EDBEngineError do AddStatus := 1;
  end;

  AddField := AddStatus;

end;
```

Sorting a Dataset

The procedure to sort a dataset is basically the same as issuing a **SELECT**. To sort a dataset, you use the **ORDER BY** clause. For example:

```
procedure TForm1.Button1Click(Sender: TObject);
```

```
begin

  if Query1.State <> dsInactive then
    Query1.Close;

  Query1.SQL.Clear;

  { Sort by Category }

  Query1.SQL.Add ('SELECT * FROM BioLife ORDER BY Category');
  Query1.Open;

end;
```

Here the dataset is sorted by Category name. By default, the sort is performed in ascending order. To sort in descending order, you use the **DESC** keyword after the **ORDER BY** clause:

```
if Query1.State <> dsInactive then
  Query1.Close;

Query1.SQL.Clear;

{ Sort by Category field in descending order }

Query1.SQL.Add ('SELECT * FROM BioLife ORDER BY Category DESC');
Query1.Open;
```

The Query component also permits sorting by multiple columns. For example, you could sort the BioLife table by category and then by species length within each category:

```
if Query1.State <> dsInactive then
  Query1.Close;

Query1.SQL.Clear;

{ Sort by Category and Length_In and show only these columns in grid }

Query1.SQL.Add ('SELECT Category, Length_In FROM BioLife ORDER BY ¬
              Category, Length_In');
Query1.Open;
```

Checking for Null and Inequality

The inequality operator (<>) lets you check whether two values are not equal to one another. This operator is particularly important in table lookups and key verification. For example, you can use the inequality operator to see whether a product exists in a table before saving it. In this next example, it is used to return all records from the Country table where Continent is *not* equal to "South America":

```
procedure TForm1.Button1Click(Sender: TObject);

var

  Temp: String;

begin

  if Query1.State <> dsInactive then
     Query1.Close;

  Query1.SQL.Clear;

  { Show selected fields from Country table that
    do not equal pattern }

  Temp := 'SELECT Continent, Population FROM Country ';
  Temp := Temp + 'WHERE Continent <> "South America"';

  Query1.SQL.Add (Temp);
  Query1.Open;

end;
```

Since the Continent and Population columns are the only columns contained in the scope, the dataset returned does not reflect the other columns—that is, only the Continent and Population columns appear in the result set (see Figure 9.3).

With numeric columns, you cannot use a null string to test for fields that have not been initialized. Instead, you use the **IS NULL** operator to determine whether a field contains a value.

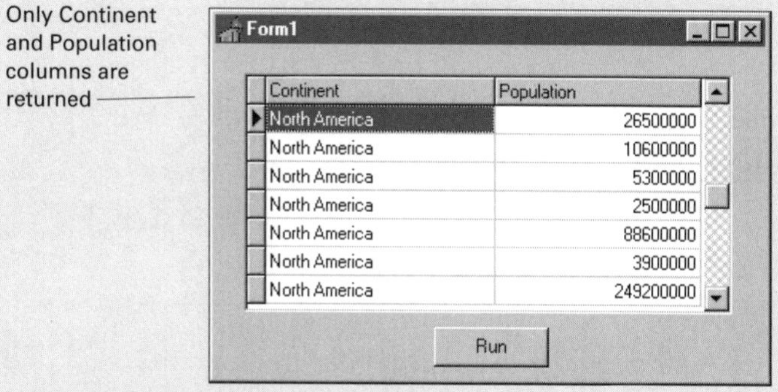

Only Continent and Population columns are returned —

FIGURE 9.3
Limiting columns in a result set

Performing Interactive Queries

In real-world applications, it is often necessary to plug in values at run-time. This kind of query is known as a *parameter query*. The following SQL statement dynamically links a query parameter by reading it from an edit control:

```
procedure TForm1.Button1Click(Sender: TObject);

var
  SQL_Pattern, Temp: String;

begin

  { Read parameter for query during run }

  if Query1.State <> dsInactive then
    Query1.Close;

  Query1.SQL.Clear;

  if Edit1.Text <> '' then begin
    SQL_Pattern := Edit1.Text;
    Temp := 'SELECT * FROM Orders WHERE OrderNo = ';
    Temp := Temp + SQL_Pattern;
    Query1.SQL.Add (Temp);
    Query1.Open;
    end;
```

```
end;
```

Notice that the Text property of Edit1 is tested before the query is executed. If Edit1 has not been initialized, the query is simply not performed.

Database Manipulation Routines of the Library

The developers' library included with this book provides five special routines for handling datasets. These routines allow you to modify database structures, load and execute saved queries, bind tables to grids, and more. Table 9.2 summarizes the database handling procedures of the library. For more information on the database manipulation routines of the library, see Chapter 14, "Database Routines."

TABLE 9.2 DATABASE HANDLING ROUTINES OF THE LIBRARY

Routine	Description
AddField	Adds a new field to a table structure.
DisplayQueryRecs	Displays the results of a query on a grid.
IsEmpty	Returns True if a table is empty.
LoadQuery	Loads and executes a saved query.
SortTable	Sorts records in a table.

Summary

In this chapter, you have learned how to use SQL to query datasets and manipulate table structures. Specifically, you have learned how to:

▶ Define database structures.

▶ Return subsets of records from a dataset.

▶ Restrict the number of columns returned from a query.

▶ Seek partial matches of patterns.

▶ Add, change, and delete records.

▶ Sort datasets.

▶ Execute parameter queries.

▶ Check for null fields.

▶ Perform range tests.

▶ Display the results of a query on grid.

Creating a Simple Report

Printing Reports from Delphi

Chapter 10
Building Reports

The ReportSmith report generator (included with the Developer and Client/ Server Suite editions of Delphi) lets you create professional reports quickly and easily. This full-featured report editor can be used to build columnar, form, label, and crosstab style reports. It also supports dBASE, Paradox, Local InterBase, and ODBC-type databases. In this chapter, you will learn how to design formatted reports that incorporate calculated fields, database filters, table links, record sorting, and summary fields.

Creating a Simple Report

The best way to learn how to design a report is to create one. To start the report generator, from the Delphi 3.0 program group, double click on the ReportSmith icon. Once loaded, the Open Report screen appears (see Figure 10.1). Click on Cancel to close this dialog. Then select File New to build a new report.

Afterwards, select the type of report you wish to create. For this exercise, you will create a columnar style report. Then click on OK to begin creating the report. Next, choose Add table... and pick the MASTER.DBF file from the table list. Once you are done, click on OK to return to the Report Query—Tables dialog. Then choose Table columns... to define the columns that will appear in the report.

Columns can be inserted into a report in any of the following ways:

▶ By choosing the Select All (columns) button.

▶ By pressing Shift+Left mouse button to select a continuous range of columns in the Files list.

▶ By pressing Ctrl+Left mouse button to select a non-continuous range of columns in the Files list.

▶ By entering an alias name to refer to the field and then clicking on the Assign new alias button.

For the purposes of this exercise, you can select all the columns by choosing the Select All button. When

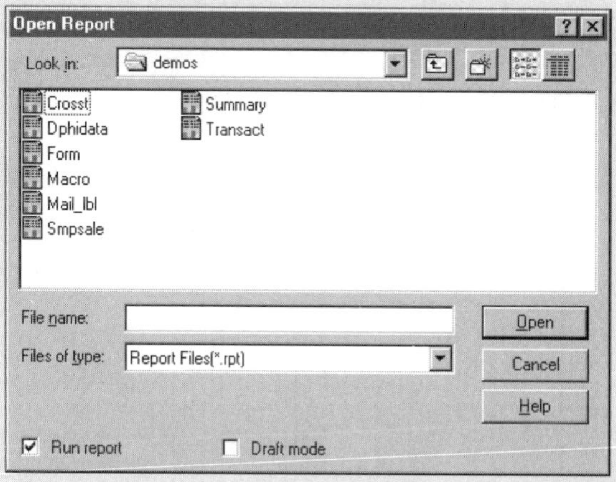

FIGURE 10.1
The Open Report screen

you are finished, click on OK to return to the Report Query—Tables dialog. Then click on Done to create the new report.

Formatting Reports

By default, ReportSmith imports data records into reports to help you visualize how the report will look while you are working with it. You may wish to change the column headings, report title, and other formatting before printing it. The toolbar in ReportSmith provides quick access to various formatting commands. As you move the mouse pointer over the toolbar, a description of what each button does appears at the bottom of the screen (in the status bar). Figure 10.2 shows what the toolbar looks like and what each of its buttons does.

In addition to the toolbar, ReportSmith lets you select from a pop-up menu of options when you right-click on a report item. The exact options that appear in the menu depend on what item you click on. For example, if you right-click on a record in the *detail* section of the report (that is, where the data records appear), a list of options like those in Figure 10.3 are shown.

FIGURE 10.3
The popup speed menu

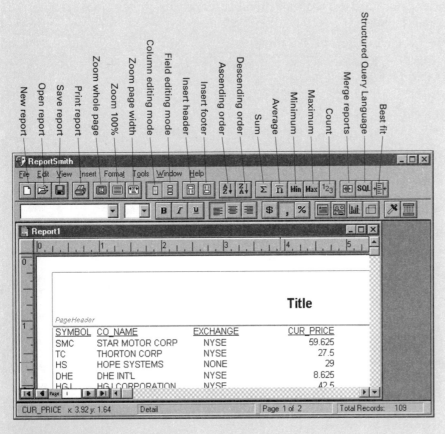

FIGURE 10.2
The toolbar

Most of the options in the pop-up menu are fairly straightforward and easy to understand. One option of particular interest is the Borders... command. With this option, you can add single line, double line, and even drop shadow borders to emphasize important text. For example, you can add a drop shadow to highlight a summary field or the report title.

Editing Report Headings and Columns

When you create a new report, ReportSmith automatically adds an identifying label at the top of the report that shows where the title should appear. You can change this label by double clicking on the field. Once you select a report item for editing, the cursor remains in the field until you click on another part of the report. The following editing keys are used to change text in field editing mode:

Delete	Deletes current character.
Backspace	Deletes previous character.
Left, Right, Up, Down arrows	Move cursor.
Ctrl+Home	Moves cursor to beginning of line.
Ctrl+End	Moves cursor to end of line.
Ctrl+Left	Moves cursor to previous word.
Ctrl+Right	Moves cursor to next word.

Changing Columns

ReportSmith also provides shorthand access to many often used commands. To remove a column, for example, you can use either the Edit | Cut command or simply press Ctrl+X. Alternately, pressing the Delete key on a column will achieve the same end. To bring back deleted items, use the Undo command from the Edit menu or press Alt+Backspace.

ReportSmith also lets you use the mouse to control various column attributes. For instance, you can resize a column by stretching it or even reorder columns by dragging them across the report.

Inserting Fields

The Field... command from the Insert menu allows you to add new fields to a report. By default, ReportSmith displays a list of data fields from each table in the report. You can also specify a different field type by choosing another option from the drop-down list of field types. The following options are available:

▶ Data fields

▶ Report fields

▶ Report variables

- ▶ System fields

- ▶ Summary fields

For instance, to add the current date into the report, choose the System field type from the Insert Field dialog and then select either the Print Date or Print Date/Time options from the Field Name list box.

Note *ReportSmith automatically adds a page number field into every report.*

Inserting Summary Fields

In many applications, the ability to summarize data is crucial to satisfying end-users. It is not enough to just print reports. You have to be able to present information in a meaningful way to meet the demands of management, bookkeepers, accountants, and others. ReportSmith provides several ways in which you can crunch numbers in reports. The ability to group related information and summarize data are key strengths of ReportSmith.

Before trying to summarize a report, you may wish to select the Scale Page Width button from the toolbar to adjust the width of the report to the size of a printed page (see Figure 10.4). This will make it easier to view the report while you are working with it.

Once you have adjusted the report size, click anywhere on the EXCHANGE column to give the field focus. Afterwards, click on the Insert Header button to sort the EXCHANGE column in ascending order and to group the report by the EXCHANGE field. This will categorize the report by the EXCHANGE field (that is, all the records in the report will be grouped by the values in this field).

While creating groups is useful, the report will need some summary fields in order to fully crunch the information in the MASTER.DBF table. For example, you can use the Minimum or Maximum buttons to determine record highs and lows of the YRL_HIGH and YRL_LOW columns. Alternately, you could add a group total field or counter field to summarize other columns.

Before you can add a summary field into a group, you must insert a footer into each group section. Do this by opening the Insert menu and selecting the Header/Footer...

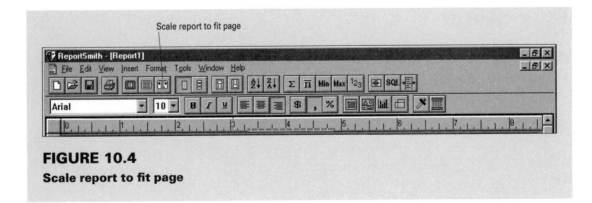

FIGURE 10.4
Scale report to fit page

command. Afterwards, from the Group Name list box, choose the EXCHANGE_Group. Then select the **Footer** check box. ReportSmith will respond by adding a footer section into each group section of the report.

Now that the report contains a footer to display summary information, try adding a summary field to compute the average of the CUR_PRICE column. Do this by clicking on the field (to give it focus) and then select the Average button from the toolbar (see Figure 10.5). ReportSmith will add the summary field to the report beneath the CUR_PRICE column in each group. Next to the summary field, a label that reads *Average of CUR_PRICE* is added to denote the summary field.

Adding a Drop Shadow Effect

As mentioned before, when you right-click on a report item, a pop-up menu appears that shows various formatting options available for the current report element. One very useful feature is the Border... option. This feature allows you to add single line, double line, and even drop shadows to areas of a report.

To add a drop shadow, click on the new summary field to give it focus. Then right-click on the same field to display the formatting options available for this field. Choose the Border... command and then in the dialog that appears, click on the Shadow option in the Border Type box. If you have a color printer, you may wish to also set the Border Color as well. Afterwards, click on OK to insert the drop shadow.

> **Note** *Before distributing a report that uses color, be sure to see how it looks on a black and white printer. Often what looks good in color may surprise you in gray-scale!*

Formatting Headings

ReportSmith makes it easy to format headings and other report items. Both the toolbar and the *ribbon* provide shortcuts to the options available in the Format menu (see Figure 10.6). For example, you can change the text style or point size of a selected font. Alternately, you can select many of the same options from the context menu that appears when you right-click on a report item.

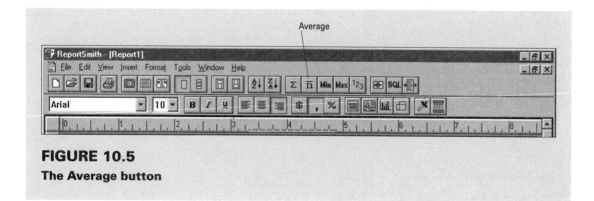

FIGURE 10.5
The Average button

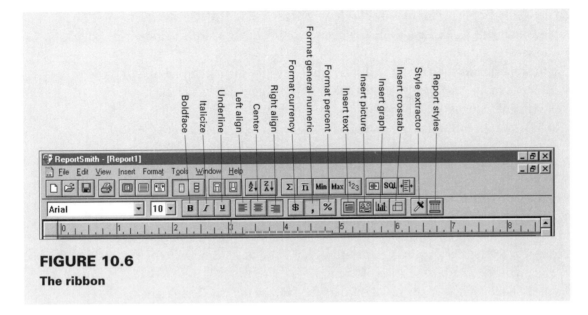

FIGURE 10.6
The ribbon

Setting Filters

Sometimes it becomes necessary to limit the scope of records that appear in a report. For example, you may wish to display only employees who live in New Jersey and who earn more than $30,000 a year. ReportSmith provides two ways in which you can set filters:

▶ Using the Field Selection Criteria dialog box

▶ Using the Selections dialog box

To set a filter using the Field Selection Criteria dialog, right-click on the report element you wish to filter and then choose Selection Criteria. If necessary, you can choose a different column to filter from the drop-down list that appears in the Field Selection

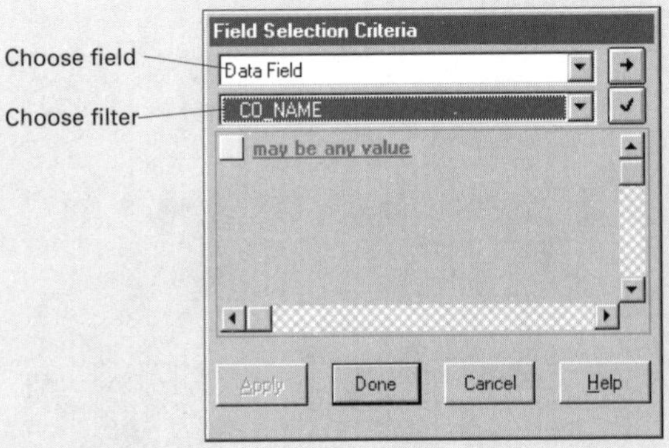

FIGURE 10.7
The Field Selection Criteria dialog box

Criteria dialog (see Figure 10.7). Afterwards, click on *may be any value* (the default filter) to display a list of other filters that can be applied. The following options are available:

may be any value	must be equal to
must be less than	must be less than or equal to
must be greater than	must be greater than or equal to
must be null	must be between
must be patterned like	must be in list
must not be equal to	must not be less than
must not be less than or equal to	must not be greater than
must not be greater than or equal to	must not be null
must not be between	must not be patterned like
must not be in list	

Alternately, you can set the same filter using the Tools | Field Selection Criteria... command. Regardless of how you set the filter, internally. ReportSmith handles the operation the same way—by building an SQL string. Although you can view this string using the Tools | SQL Text... command, you cannot modify the SQL string and preserve the report in its original state. In Delphi, however, you can use the TQuery component to create and edit reports using SQL.

Adding Derived Fields

A *derived field* is a field that is calculated from or based on other report fields. ReportSmith provides two ways to create derived fields. You can add a field derived from SQL or create a macro using ReportBasic, which is the language ReportSmith uses to build macros. For example, a derived field can be used to compute the total hours spent while consulting for different clients.

To define a derived field:

1 Open the Tools menu and choose the Derived Fields... command.

2 Enter a name for the new field in the Derived Field Name box.

3 Click on the Defined by SQL option.

Alternatively, you can:

1 Choose the Define by ReportBasic macro option to define a new macro.

2 Click on Add to define the macro or expression.

For most report needs, you do not need to know ReportBasic to define derived fields. You can compute the derived fields by choosing the Defined by SQL option and clicking on Add or Edit, where the Edit Derived Field dialog appears (see Figure 10.8). It is here that you enter the actual expression that will be used to compute the derived field. ReportSmith automatically displays a list of fields that are available in the report.

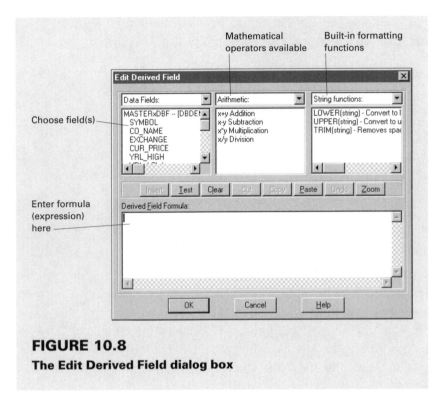

FIGURE 10.8
The Edit Derived Field dialog box

To use one of these in an expression, you merely have to drag the field from the list box into the Derived Field Formula box. Alternately, you can click on the field and choose the Insert button to add the field. To add a mathematical operator, either choose one from the above list of operators or simply type it. Then repeat this process for any other fields or operators in the report. For example:

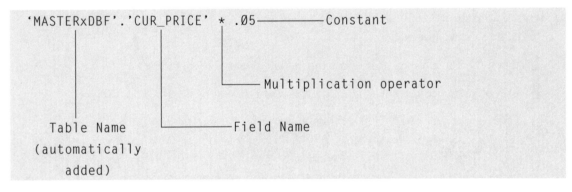

Note *ReportSmith automatically inserts the name of the table before each field in an expression.*

Once you have defined an expression, you can test it by choosing the Test button. If the expression evaluates OK, ReportSmith will inform you of this. Otherwise,

ReportSmith will report in a message box that an error occurred. Afterwards, you can click on OK and fix the error.

Once the formula is inserted into the report, it will appear in the first available column on the right. If the new column extends beyond the right margin, you can scroll over to it using the horizontal scroll bar. However, if the column is too far over to appear on a printed page, you will have to adjust the widths of the other columns to make room for the new field (using the Format | Column Width... command). If necessary, you can also reposition a column by dragging it to its new position.

Creating File Links

Many reports require that data be drawn from more than one table source. Unlike other report generators, ReportSmith makes it easy to create such links. To establish a relationship between files, the tables must be linked by a common field. ReportSmith allows you to establish *relations* among fields even if they have different names, provided that the fields are identical in structure.

To create a file link:

1 Choose File | New to create a link in a new report. Or, choose the Tools | Report Query... command to create a link in an already existing report.

2 Select the type of report you wish to create (Columnar, Crosstab, Form, or Label report).

3 Click on OK.

4 Choose the Add table... button to add the first table.

5 From the Files list box, choose a table (CLIENTS.DBF, for example).

6 Click on OK to add the table to the report and return to the Report Query— Tables dialog.

7 Optionally, select the Tables column... button to define the table columns that will appear in the report (default is all columns).

Repeat steps 4 through 7 to add the next table. You can use the HOLDING.DBF table to create a link with the CLIENTS.DBF table.

In the Report Query—Tables dialog, choose the Add new link... button. The Create New Table Link dialog will appear (see Figure 10.9). Note that ReportSmith automatically detects any common fields between the tables and highlights them.

To create a link, choose the field name that will be used to set the relation. Both the CLIENTS.DBF and HOLDINGS.DBF tables, for example, are linked by the ACCT_NBR field. Since ReportSmith has already detected the similarity in names, you only have to click on OK to confirm the link. By default, the report will contain only the records that are common between the two tables. If you wish to show records that do not match, click on **Include unmatched records** for each table you wish to include all the records from before clicking on OK. In the Report Query—Tables dialog, click on Done to build the multi-table report.

This will establish a *one-to-many* link between the tables—that is, for each record in the CLIENTS.DBF table, it will show any records that match in the HOLDING.DBF table. For example, it could link people listed alphabetically by common zip codes. You can also use this technique to print the phone number of each client from CLIENTS.DBF that has SHARES listed in the HOLDINGS.DBF table.

FIGURE 10.9
The Create New Table Link dialog box

Editing Links

After establishing a link, if you wish to edit or remove it, from the Report Query—Tables dialog click on the Edit link... or Remove link button. For example, instead of linking the tables by phone number or zip code, you can change this to area code or employee ID.

Saving Reports

Before printing the report, you should protect your work by saving it. To save a report, use the File | Save command (Shift+F12). Afterwards, you can print the report using the File Print command as a test before trying to link it into Delphi.

Printing Reports from Delphi

Once you have created a report, linking it to a program is a simple process. Before a report can be printed from a Delphi application, you must place a TReport component on the form (see Figure 10.10). Afterwards, add a button to the form and enter the following code into the Click event handler of the button. Then run the report and select the OK button. It's that simple!

```
{ Run a report using ReportSmith Runtime }


Report1.ReportName := 'C:\MYAPP\REPORTS\REP1.RPT';
Report1.Run;
```

Note *This example assumes that the report has been saved in the 'C:\MYAPP\REPORTS\REP1.RPT' path. You will most likely have to edit this path to make the example work in your program.*

Summary

In this chapter, you have learned how to create reports using the ReportSmith report generator. You have also learned how to:

▶ Create file links.

▶ Produce group totals.

▶ Set database filters.

▶ Format columns.

▶ Work with formulas.

▶ Display drop shadows.

▶ Print reports from Delphi programs.

FIGURE 10.10
The TReport Component

The MediaPlayer
Component

Graphics and
Multimedia

Distributing
Applications on
CD-ROMs

Exercise: Playing
a Video from
Delphi

Chapter 11

Developing Multimedia Applications

Delphi provides an abundance of tools that enable you to create multimedia applications. With these tools, you can display graphics on forms, play audio and video, access scanners and midi sequencers, and even produce CD-ROM applications. In this chapter, you will learn how to build powerful and robust programs in Delphi using its multimedia capabilities.

The MediaPlayer Component

The TMediaPlayer control provides an easy method of incorporating multimedia devices in programs. In the past, working with audio and video required special add-in tools or calls to DLLs. With the MediaPlayer component, playing a .WAV or .AVI file is as easy as specifying a device type, providing a file name and then opening the device. Best of all, the MediaPlayer component's device independent operation means that a single set of commands can control CD-ROM drives, VCRs, MIDI sequencers, sound cards, video drivers, and more. Figure 11.1 shows what the MediaPlayer control looks like.

The MediaPlayer component's buttons can be used to control various devices. The function of each is described below:

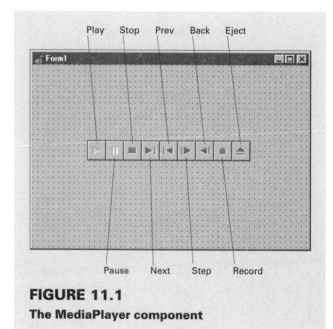

FIGURE 11.1
The MediaPlayer component

Button	Description
Play	Plays a Media Control Interface (MCI) device.
Pause	Pauses a device during a play or recording operation. This button works as a toggle—that is, clicking on Pause when the device is idle resumes normal playing or recording.
Stop	Ends device playing or recording.
Next	Skips a track or to the end of the medium if the device does not support tracks.
Prev	Skips to previous track or beginning of medium.

Step	Forwards device the specified number of frames.
Back	Rewinds a device.
Record	Begins a recording.
Eject	Ejects the current medium (if device supports operation).

Although it is great to have all this power at your fingertips, it is rare that an application supports all these devices. The VisibleButtons property of the MediaPlayer component controls the buttons that appear at run-time. The default value of this property is [btPlay, btPause, btStop, btNext, btPrev, btStep, btBack, btRecord, btEject].

The following example shows how to remove buttons from the control. When the form loads, only the Play, Pause, and Stop buttons appear:

```
procedure TForm1.FormCreate(Sender: TObject);


{ Show play, pause and stop buttons only }


begin
  MediaPlayer1.VisibleButtons := [btPlay, btPause, btStop];
end;
```

By default, the buttons on the MediaPlayer component appear in four colors. If you prefer black and white buttons instead, you can disable color in the control the following way:

```
MediaPlayer1.ColoredButtons := [];
```

Playing Audio

The following discussion assumes that your system is equipped with a sound card and that the appropriate drivers have already been installed. Playing audio with the MediaPlayer component requires no special coding or expertise. To play a wave file, only three steps are required: DeviceType, FileName, and AutoOpen. Here's an example:

```
DeviceType = dtAutoSelect
FileName = 'TEST.WAV'
AutoOpen = True
```

The dtAutoSelect constant sets the DeviceType property to auto detect. Although dtAutoSelect provides an easy way of specifying the device type, under certain circumstances it can cause conflict between devices. For this reason, it is better to specify the device yourself. The following device types are available: dtAutoSelect, dtAVIVideo, dtCDAudio, dtDAT, dtDigitalVideo, dtMMMovie, dtOther, dtOverlay, dtScanner, dtSequencer, dtVCR, dtVideodisc, or dtWaveAudio.

To play a wave file, for example, you set the DeviceType property to dtWaveAudio:

```
procedure TfrmMedia.btnAudioClick(Sender: TObject);

begin

{ Play .WAV file }

  MediaPlayer1.FileName := 'MY.WAV ';

  with MediaPlayer1 do
    if not AutoOpen then begin
      DeviceType := dtWaveAudio;
      Open;
      end;

end;
```

The **with** statement provides a shorthand way of accessing a component's properties and methods. In the preceding example, if AutoOpen is not set, the device is opened with the Open method. Although the device is ready to play the wave file, the control remains inactive until the user clicks on the Play button. If you prefer to automatically play the file upon initialization, modify the preceding code as follows:

```
{ Play .WAV file }

MediaPlayer1.FileName := 'MY.WAV';

with MediaPlayer1 do
    if not AutoOpen then begin
      DeviceType := dtWaveAudio;
      Open;
      Play;
    end;
```

The Play method informs the control to start playing the wave file. Note that if you execute the Play method this way, it is not necessary to show the Media Player control at run-time. Provided the proper initialization settings have been supplied, you can set the Visible property of the MediaPlayer component to **False** and still perform all the same operations using the Play, Pause, Step, Stop, StartRecording, and Eject methods of the control. For example:

```
procedure TForm1.FormCreate(Sender: TObject);

{ Hide Media Player component and play wave file }

begin

  with MediaPlayer1 do
    if not AutoOpen then begin
      DeviceType := dtWaveAudio;
      FileName := 'MY.WAV ';
      Visible := False;
      Open;
      Play;
      end;

end;

procedure TForm1.btnPauseClick(Sender: TObject);

{ Pause wave file }

begin
  MediaPlayer1.Pause;
end;

procedure TForm1.btnStopClick(Sender: TObject);

{ Stop wave file }

begin
  MediaPlayer1.Stop;
end;
```

Tip *Instead of using a button, place the code to stop the MediaPlayer control in the On Click event handler of the form or an image component.*

Playing Video

The procedure for playing a video is virtually identical to that of playing a wave file. For example, the following code demonstrates how to start playing an .AVI file from a procedure:

```
{ Play .AVI file }


MediaPlayer1.FileName := 'MY.AVI';


with MediaPlayer1 do
     if not AutoOpen then begin
        DeviceType := dtAVIVideo;
        Open;
        end;
```

To play the video automatically, modify the preceding example as follows:

```
{ Play .AVI file }


MediaPlayer1.FileName := 'MY.AVI';


with MediaPlayer1 do
    if not AutoOpen then begin
       DeviceType := dtAVIVideo;
       Open;
       Play;
       end;
```

Because your monitor can act as a display container, you do not have to purchase any special hardware to play .AVI files. However, if the video includes sound, you will not be able to hear the audio portion of the recording without a sound card. If your system does not have the appropriate software drivers to support playing .AVI files, you can use Microsoft Video for Windows for this purpose. These drivers are also provided with Windows 95 and multimedia utilities such as Adobe Premier, which allows you to create special effects in your videos.

While you do not need a special card to play .AVI files, you will need a video capture board or a program like Kai's Power Goo by MetaTools, Inc. to make your own videos. With Kai's Power Goo, you can generate "GOOVies" from personal photos and apply real-time distortion techniques using its built-in image-warping capabilities. The resultant demo can then be converted into an .AVI file and played from Delphi using the MediaPlayer component. The sample exercise later in this chapter will show you how to play a video created with Kai's Power Goo™. The source graphic used to produce this demo was created by PhotoSpin for MetaTools, Inc. For more information on Kai's Power Goo, see the GOO.TXT file included on the CD.

Graphics and Multimedia

Regardless of whether you decide to incorporate audio and video in your programs, one element that is almost always a part of multimedia applications is graphics. Delphi makes it easy to use graphics in projects. Table 11.1 shows a list of some common graphical components Delphi 3.0 provides.

The Image Control

One of the easiest ways to display graphics in Delphi is to use an image component. To show a graphic, you can set the Picture property of the control at design-time or perform the same operation using the **LoadFromFile** method. **LoadFromFile** takes one argument: the path of a bitmap, icon, or metafile. To generate the image, you can use a program like Microsoft Paint (included with Windows 95), the Delphi Image Editor, or any scanning utility that can save a graphic in .BMP (bitmap) format.

Once you have created the graphic, you use an image component to display the picture. To do this, draw an image component on the form, size it appropriately, and call **LoadFromFile** with the fully qualified path of the image. For example:

```
Image1.Picture.LoadFromFile(PathToApp + 'PICT1.BMP');
```

TABLE 11.1 COMMON GRAPHICAL COMPONENTS

Control	Description
Bevel	Displays a frame, panel or box over a form or image component.
BitBtn	Displays a picture on a push button.
CoolBar	Permits you to create a Delphi 3–style toolbar.
DBImage	Displays graphics stored in a database table.
Image	Displays a bitmap, icon, or metafile.
ImageList	Displays a group of graphic images.
PaintBox	Provides a rectangular area where graphics methods can be drawn.
ScrollBox	Provides a scrollable display container that can be used to house graphic and non-graphic components.
Shape	Displays one of six pre-defined shapes: rectangle, circle, ellipse, rounded rectangle, rounded square, or square
SpeedButton	A button-like component that can display a bitmap and is often used in combination with panels to produce toolbars.

Note *If you omit the path, Delphi will look for the graphic in the current directory.*

Sizing Graphics

A key issue of multimedia is how to display graphics without interfering with other components on a form. Sometimes it is not possible to determine the size of an image before it is displayed. Two special properties, AutoSize and Stretch, control the way that an image appears. By setting AutoSize to **True,** the picture will be resized automatically if the graphic is larger than the image control's boundaries. The Stretch property will also resize an image. If Stretch is set to **True,** the graphic will grow to the size of the image component if the control's boundaries are larger than the picture. Although you can use these properties to dynamically resize graphics, AutoResize will cause the image to overlap (or appear behind) other controls if you do not leave enough room on the form for its maximum display area. The effects of Stretch can be worse. A stretched image may appear distorted or out of proportion. Therefore, it is usually best to standardize the size of images displayed. For example, when scanning pictures, set the scan size of each graphic to a 4x4-inch area.

The one exception to this rule is with thumbnails. A *thumbnail* is a graphic that can be any size but is always displayed at the size of an icon. Thumbnails are often used to preview graphics (see Figure 11.2). Since they are small, a single display container can show many thumbnails (each being an image component with the Stretch property set to **True**). Although the effects of the Stretch property may not be desirable in all cases, Stretch is well suited for thumbnails. Rather than enlarging the bitmap, however, the graphic is proportionally reduced to the size of the image component. Without using Stretch, a large graphic would become truncated to the size of the image control.

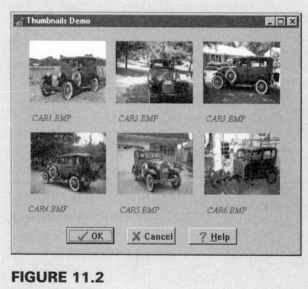

FIGURE 11.2
Thumbnails

Note *When you set the Picture property of an image component at design-time, the result will be a larger executable file. To avoid this problem, use the **LoadFromFile** method to dynamically incorporate the same graphics in your applications at run-time.*

Working with Color Palettes

When working with graphics, it is especially important to realize that the quality of graphics will vary dramatically depending on the installed video card. On one system, you may be able to display a high resolution scan at near photographic quality. The same graphic on another system with a low line video card or video driver set to display only 16 colors may be greatly obscured. Most video drivers (including the standard ones provided with Windows) handle color translation poorly. One solution to this problem is to use a third-party toolkit like ImageKnife by Olympus to scale 256 colors down to 16 colors or to scale a high density 32-bit graphic down to 256 colors. For example, the following code demonstrates how to reduce colors using the ImageKnife PicBuf component:

```
{ Reduce colors in PicBuf component down
  to 256 colors or 16 colors }

if radioReduce256.Checked then
    ikReduceColors(picbuf1.ctl, 256, False, True, False)
else if radioReduce16.Checked then
    ikReduceColors(picbuf1.ctl, 16, True, True, False)
else if radioNoReduction.Checked then
    { User has High Color or True Color video
      card - no color reduction required }
    .        .        .
```

Using this technique, you can ensure that regardless of what kind of video card the user has, the program will display the images so they will be optimized for the given hardware. By using a toolkit like ImageKnife, your programs will also be able to support other image formats such as .JPG, .TIF, .PCX, and more.

Avoiding Color Palette Conflicts

Due to limitations of the current VGA and Super VGA standard, most video cards are capable of displaying only 256 colors simultaneously on a screen. Although the video card may actually be capable of displaying many thousands of colors, only 256 colors can be selected at any given time. Thus, even if a picture contains an extremely wide spectrum of colors, the scan of the image will still be scaled down to 256 colors. This produces a reasonable simulation of the original graphic. Images saved this way are known as *palettized* images. Each color palette contains 256 colors.

With the advent of High Color (32,768 colors) and True Color (16.7 million colors) video cards, the need for palettized images is less of a problem today than in the past. However, non-palettized images require significantly more space to save. Furthermore, the large install base of lower line display cards mandates that developers familiarize themselves with different video card capabilities. Unfortunately, many programmers are not aware of how color palettes work and what they must do to ensure a reliable display of graphics on any video card.

When Windows encounters two or more images with different color palettes, it addresses the 256-color restriction by forcing background graphic components to use the same color palette as the image with focus. This can produce bizarre side effects. If the color palettes are different enough, only the image with focus will appear correctly. Although no tool has been developed yet to solve this problem, there are some things you can do. One solution is to invest in a commercial graphics utility like ImageKnife to scale the images down to 16 colors. Virtually all video cards today can reliably display 16 colors.

A better solution might be to display only one high resolution graphic at a time. This approach will work, provided the user's video driver is not set to display only 16 colors. If your application requires 256-color support, the best alternative may be to use the Edit | Bring to Front command in Delphi (or BringToFront method) to change the order in which graphic components are displayed. Although this approach is not infallible, you will at least be able to select the best color palette to use for all the graphics you wish to display.

For example, the following code loads three bitmaps from disk and then uses the BringToFront method to make the second bitmap that is loaded take precedence over the others by bringing it to the front of the *z-order*, or the order in which overlapping controls on a form are displayed:

```
Image1.Picture.LoadFromFile('PICTURE1.BMP');
Image2.Picture.LoadFromFile('PICTURE2.BMP');
Image3.Picture.LoadFromFile('PICTURE3.BMP');

{ Bring Image2 to front of z-order }

Image2.BringToFront;
```

Third-Party Voodoo Solutions

Some third-party component developers claim they can display multiple palettes on the screen without having to upgrade to a High Color or True Color video card. Using their proprietary components and color palette remapping functions, it is possible to remap the colors of a graphic displayed on the screen to another color palette (thus avoiding a color palette conflict).

By using the Delphi BringToFront and SetFocus methods, you can basically achieve similar results without having to invest in an expensive third-party toolkit. However, the same toolkits might be worth a consideration for their color reduction and multi-format image display capabilities.

Multimedia Routines of the Library

The developers' library included with this book provides an abundance of multimedia and related procedures that can be used to enhance the appearance and functionality of programs. These routines provide shorthand access to many common operations. Table 11.2 shows the multimedia and screen effect procedures and functions of the library.

In addition to multimedia and screen effects, the library provides several rich edit routines that allow you to display enhanced text in programs. These routines are designed to work with the RichEdit component. This control operates in two modes:

▶ *Read Only:* The RichEdit component acts as a non-editable display container that can show multiple fonts, colors, and other special formatting.

▶ *Editable:* This mode allows you to produce new documents with multiple text styles that can be saved or printed.

The sample program RTE.DPR is an enhanced memo editor written with the Rich Text Edit functions of the library. You can use this editor to create and display enhanced documents in Delphi or as a basis for developing your own custom editor. Table 11.3 summarizes the Rich Edit procedures and functions used to generate the sample editor. For more information on this example and how to use the Rich Edit control, see Chapter 16, "Rich Edit Routines."

Distributing Applications on CD-ROMs

With the ever-growing size of applications, many developers today feel it is necessary to distribute applications on CD-ROM. Because a single CD can easily hold over 600MB of data, CDs are often the only sensible way to distribute large applications.

TABLE 11.2   MULTIMEDIA AND SCREEN HANDLING ROUTINES OF THE LIBRARY

Routine	Description
BlockShadow	Displays a message with a block shadow effect.
ColorMessage	Shows a message with each letter in a different color.
CustomCursor	Displays a user-defined mouse cursor.
DelayMessage	Shows a message with a delay effect.
DisplayDirImages	Shows the next/previous graphic in a directory.
MessageBlink	Shows a message with three dots blinking after it.
PlayWaveFile	Plays a .WAV (wave audio) file.
PlayVideo	Plays an .AVI file.
ShowHotSpot	Defines a hotspot on a form or image control (automatically displays hand pointer when mouse cursor is over it).
ShowScrSaver	Displays a customizable screen saver.
SoundEnabled	Returns **True** if a sound card is installed.
Thumbnails	Loads a bitmap in an image component and proportionally reduces its size for viewing purposes.
TickerTape	Creates an animated scroll area for a message within a ticker tape.
TileBitmap	Tiles the screen with a user-defined graphic.
TransparentButton	Displays a transparent button over an image component or form.

To produce a CD, you need a CD-ROM archiver. The archiver typically comes with a separate hard drive you use as a working area while building the CD. You can treat the archiver's working drive just like any other disk. For example, the CD might contain an install program on the main root, some directories, and other files within those directories.

TABLE 11.3   RICH EDIT ROUTINES

Routine	Description
OpenRichEdit	Loads a RichEdit document from disk.
SetAlignment	Sets the paragraph alignment of a selected block.
SetBoldFace	Boldfaces a selected block.
SetBullet	Inserts or removes a bullet from a RichEdit document.
SetFontStyle	Sets the font style of a selected block.
SetUnderline	Underlines a selected block.
SaveRichEdit	Saves a RichEdit document to a file.
SetItalics	Italicizes a selected block.
UndoChange	Reverses the last edit operation in a RichEdit document.

Once you have copied all the necessary files to the archiver's hard drive, the next step is to test the install. Since CD-ROMs are read-only, any files your program uses that can be edited must be installed to the user's hard drive. Although not all CDs have to be installed, your users will appreciate at least having an icon in the program group to make accessing the program easier.

Note   *To install your programs, you can use InstallSHIELD Express, which comes with the Developer and Client Server editions of Delphi.*

Building the Pre-Master

After you are sure that the CD contains all the required files, you then build the pre-master. The archiver usually comes with some kind of utility that will automatically burn the CD for you. When burning the pre-master, the archiver software will usually prompt you for the CD volume name, the file type (DOS), the CD standard (such as ISO 9660), and the name of the data preparer (you). The ISO 9660 standard is usually adequate for producing CDs. The Hi-Sierra standard can also be specified. However, this setting is not recommended and is provided primarily for backward compatibility.

To create the CD, the archiver will first optimize the files on the working drive and then copy them to the CD-ROM disk. Once the files have been copied, the CD cannot be written to again. Therefore, you must be sure that all the required files are on the archiver's working drive before building the CD.

Note   *Some database engines like Access and Paradox provide file locking mechanisms which attempt to create locking files when you access tables. Since CD-ROMS are read-only, table locking must be disabled if you intend to access databases directly from a CD.*

Building the Glass Master

Once you have created the pre-master, the next step is to produce the *glass master*. You can burn the pre-master yourself, but the glass copy must be made in a dust-free environment. Therefore, this job is rarely done in-house. It is the glass master that is actually used to produce mass quantities of the CD. Since this requires a significant investment, you *must* be sure to test the pre-master on as many systems as possible before the duplicated copies are made.

Writing Code to Access CDs

Although CD-ROM production can be expensive, the good news is that as a developer, once you have overcome the technical concerns of physically producing a CD-ROM, you can write code to access the CD just as if it were a hard drive or floppy disk. For example, you can read a file by specifying the path where the file is located on the CD. The only difference is that you cannot write to the CD. Therefore, any files that can change must be installed to another drive.

Exercise: Playing a Video from Delphi

The following exercise demonstrates the basic code necessary to play an .AVI file from Delphi. For this lesson, you will run the CARTALK.AVI demo (included on the CD-ROM). After this exercise, you should be able to:

▶ Use the TOpenDialog component to select a video.

▶ Run an .AVI file using the TMediaPlayer component.

1 In a new project, add the following components to the form. Place each control as it appears in Figure 11.3.

Component	Page of Component Palette
MediaPlayer1	System
BitBtn1	Additional
BitBtn2	Additional

2 Set the Kind property of the first BitBtn component to OK.

3 Set the Kind property of the other BitBtn component to Close. Note that

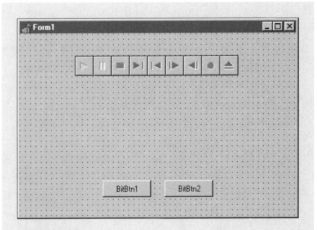

FIGURE 11.3

Positioning the components on the form

Delphi will automatically close the form when you click on this button at run-time.

4 From the Dialogs page of the Component Palette, choose the OpenDialog component.

5 Double click on the BitBtn1 control.

6 Add the following code to the Click event handler of the button:

```
if OpenDialog1.Execute then begin
   with MediaPlayer1 do begin
        FileName := OpenDialog1.FileName;
        if not AutoOpen then begin
           Open;
           Play;
           end;
   end;
end;
```

7 Run the project.

8 Click on the OK button. An Open dialog box will appear so you can choose a video to play.

9 Insert the CD that came with this book in your CD-ROM drive.

10 Use the Open dialog to find the CARTALK.AVI demo on the CD-ROM.

11 Click on the Open button now to run this video. The front of the car will morph into a face and then stick out its tongue and turn back into a car again.

Summary

In this chapter, you have learned how to build multimedia applications in Delphi. Specifically, you have learned how to:

▶ Play audio and video in Delphi.

▶ Work with graphic components.

▶ Display thumbnails.

▶ Avoid color palette conflicts.

▶ Produce CD-ROM applications.

▶ Incorporate third-party multimedia extensions in programs.

Why Create
Components?

Building
Components

Exercise: Creating
a Sample Component

Chapter 12
Building User-Defined Components

One of the great benefits of developing applications in Delphi is that you can create your own user-defined components. The Delphi Integrated Development Environment makes it easy to create and work with objects. Moreover, you can redefine property defaults and even add new properties, methods, and events to existing components. In this chapter, you will learn how to define, test, and install components in the Delphi IDE.

Why Create Components?

There are many reasons why you should write components. First, by building components, you avoid unnecessary repetition. For example, if you find yourself writing the same routines over and over for different projects, you will find that the use of a single component can save you from having to repeat code.

Another reason why you might want to create a component is to customize an already existing object. In most cases, Delphi's pre-defined controls will help you get the job done. However, if you find a particular component is not well-suited for your needs, you can define your own custom component to perform the same operation better.

Building Components

The Component Expert allows you to define new objects. It automatically generates the correct definitions you need to create and register classes in Delphi. After generating a new component, that component can be installed in the IDE and accessed from the Component Palette. Thus the controls you define become integrated parts of the Delphi environment and can be shared by any application.

To open the Component Expert:

1 Choose the File | New... command.

2 From the New Items dialog, click on Component.

3 Choose OK to create a new unit for the new type.

Defining a New Component

Figure 12.1 shows the Component Expert. To define a new component, the following items must be specified in the New Component dialog box:

▶ Ancestor type

▶ Class name

▶ Palette page

▶ Unit file name

▶ Search path

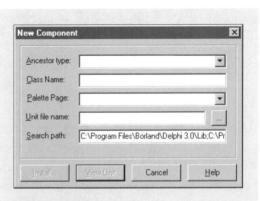

FIGURE 12.1
The Component Expert

Ancestor Type

The *ancestor type* is the class from which the component will be derived. A component can be derived from any class registered in Delphi. For instance, if you specify a TBevel component as the ancestor type, the new component will inherit all the properties, methods, and events of a TBevel control. If you do not know the ancestor type, you can choose it from the drop-down list (see Figure 12.2).

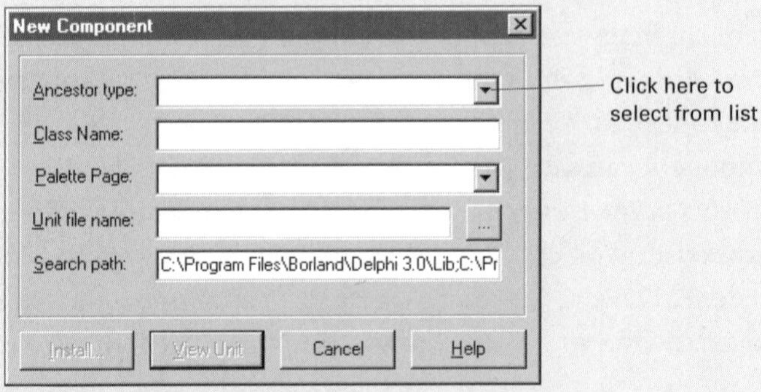

FIGURE 12.2
Choosing the ancestor type

Class Name

The *class name* you are defining. By convention, class names in Delphi begin with the letter "T". For example, TMyCompon is a valid class name. When you install the component, however, the object is referred to without the prefix, as in MyCompon1, MyCompon2, and so on.

The Palette Page

The *palette page* is the page on which the component will be installed. A drop-down combo box lists all the available pages for you to make this selection. Typically you would choose **Data Access** for new file-handling components, **Dialogs** for form-based components, the **System** page for environment objects, and so on.

> **Note** *Although Delphi permits you to add new components to its standard pages, to avoid confusion, you may wish to place all your user-defined components on the Samples page or create a new page specifically for these.*

Unit File Name

The *unit file name* provides the complete path and name of the file that will contain the definition for the new class. By default, Delphi will use the name of the component you specify as the ancestor type and add a .PAS file extension to the name. You can specify a different unit file name here as well.

Search Path

The search path is the path to search for the unit file. By default, Delphi will search the \DELPHI 3.0\LIB\ path first and then look in the \DELPHI 3.0\BIN\ subdirectory.

Generating the Unit

After specifying this information, when you click on View Unit, the Component Expert will automatically generate a new unit that contains the class definition. For example, if you defined a class called TMyCompon descended from TMemo, the new unit will look like this:

```
unit Memo1;


interface


uses
  Windows, Messages, SysUtils, Classes, Graphics, Controls, Forms,
  Dialogs, StdCtrls;


type
  TMyCompon = class(TMemo)
  private
    { Private declarations }
  protected
    { Protected declarations }
  public
    { Public declarations }
  published
    { Published declarations }
  end;


procedure Register;


implementation
```

```
procedure Register;
begin
  RegisterComponents('Samples', [TMyCompon]);
end;


end.
```

In this example, a new component called TMyCompon is defined as type TMemo. In addition to **private** and **public** definitions, the unit also contains two new sections, **protected** and **published**. You use *protected access* to hide implementation details from users. For example, if your component defines three variables, x, y, and z, you can use protected access to ensure that no user will inadvertently change any of their values. When you wish to make an object variable accessible to the user, you can define the variable in the **published** section of the unit. Any object reference defined for *published access* is made available to the user at design-time and at run-time.

Note that it is very important to understand the difference between a *component writer* and a *component user*. Up until now, the focus of this book has been primarily on how to use existing components. As a component writer, however, the user can be any party that makes use of your component(s), including yourself.

Like published object references, anything defined for public access becomes available to component users at run-time. Thus if you define a property for public access, your users will be able to set or inspect the property (depending on whether it is read-only or not) at run-time but not at design-time. This allows you to create a *run-time interface* for your component. If you wish to make the property available at both design-time and at run-time, define it in the **published** section instead. Only properties declared in this section will be available to users via the Object Inspector. Any such properties constitute the *design-time interface* of the object.

By declaring object variables for *private access,* the variables are hidden and inaccessible to end-users. Thus **private** definitions are useful for handling implementation details that you do not want your users to have access to.

Registering Components

In addition to adding a **protected** and a **published** section to the unit, the Component Expert also adds a new procedure header called Register to the **interface** section and procedure body in the **implementation** section. The Register procedure does exactly what you might expect: It registers a new component in the Delphi component library. The **implementation** section shows how the component is registered:

```
 .    .    .

 .    .    .

procedure Register;
```

```
implementation

procedure Register;
begin
  RegisterComponents('Samples', [TMyCompon]);
end;
```

RegisterComponents takes two arguments. The first argument defines the page on which the component will be installed. In the preceding example, the component will be added to the Samples page. The second argument indicates the component(s) to register. This parameter can be specified as a single argument or as a comma-separated list. In this case, TMyCompon is specified by including its name within the brackets. Since the Component Expert adds these references automatically, you do not have to do anything unless you edit the component's definition (or register more than one class in the unit).

The Visual Component Library

At the heart of Delphi's objects lies an invisible hierarchy of components. The Visual Component Library (VCL) establishes the relationship between classes. All components, for example, are descended from TComponent. Although you do not have to know all the ancestor types that can be specified in the Component Expert, it is important to understand that your custom component will inherit all the same properties, methods, and events of the ancestor type you provide. Although you can add new properties, methods, and so on, you cannot remove existing features from a component. Thus it is important to realize the capabilities of the ancestor type and to pick an ancestor that most closely resembles the component you wish to create.

Now that you are familiar with the basics, it is time to test your skills. For this exercise, you will use the Component Expert to generate a new class. Afterwards, you will define a new method and property that the component will utilize.

Exercise: Creating a Sample Component

1 To start the Component Expert, choose File | New. Afterwards, double click on Component. Then enter the following items:

```
Ancestor Type: TShape
Class Name: TBox
Palette Page: Samples
Unit File Name: C:\Program Files\Borland\Delphi 3.0\BIN\BoxObj.pas
```

Note *This assumes that you installed Delphi 3.0 in its default path. If this is not the case, be sure to specify the correct path here.*

2 When you are done, click on View Unit to generate the unit. Delphi will automatically produce the following code:

```
unit BoxObj;

interface

uses
  Windows, Messages, SysUtils, Classes, Graphics, Controls, Forms,
  Dialogs, ExtCtrls;

type
  TBox = class(TShape)
  private
    { Private declarations }
  protected
    { Protected declarations }
  public
    { Public declarations }
  published
    { Published declarations }
  end;

procedure Register;

implementation

procedure Register;
begin
  RegisterComponents('Samples', [TBox]);
end;

end.
```

Although TBox is a real type, it is essentially a clone of its ancestor type TShape. In order for it to be useful, the component must have at least one new feature. To see how easy it is to build upon an existing object, you are going to define a new method called Enlarge. The Enlarge method will increase the size of the enhanced shape control at run-time. Upon each call to Enlarge, the Height and Width of the object instance (occurrence) will be increased by the value stored in a new property called BoxInc.

The user-defined property BoxInc defines the number of pixels to increase the TBox component each time the Enlarge method is called. BoxInc will use a privately defined object variable called FBoxInc to store the value of the property. Enter the following definition in the **private** section of the unit to define this item:

```
private
  { Private declarations }
  FBoxInc: Integer;
```

To define the property and the method it acts upon, the following declarations must also be added:

```
    .     .      .
public
  { Public declarations }
  procedure Enlarge;

published
  { Published declarations }
  property BoxInc: Integer read FBoxInc write FBoxInc;
```

Note *Since the BoxInc property is defined for published access, the user will be able to change the property value at both design-time and at run-time.*

The read and write methods of a property declaration determine the variable used to access the property's value. Both the read and write methods use the FBoxInc object variable to set or get the value of the property. Internally, the Enlarge method and the BoxInc property are implemented the following way:

```
procedure TBox.Enlarge;

{ Define new method to enlarge box
  upon each method call }

begin

  { Assign default value to property
    used to control increment amount
    of user-defined method }
```

```
    if FBoxInc = 0 then
       FBoxInc := 10;

   Width := Width + FBoxInc;
   Height := Height + FBoxInc;

 end;
```

As with any Delphi unit, the procedure (or actually, method) must be coded in the **implementation** section of the unit. Notice that the Enlarge method is preceded by the name of the class TBox. The Object Pascal code that appears inside this block defines the operations that will be performed each time the method is called. By increasing the Height and Width properties (inherited from TShape), the component will be resized by the number of pixels specified by the FBoxInc object variable. The following listing shows how the completed unit should look:

```
unit BoxObj;

interface

uses
  Windows, Messages, SysUtils, Classes, Graphics, Controls, Forms,
  Dialogs, ExtCtrls;

type
  TBox = class(TShape)
  private
    { Private declarations }
    FBoxInc: Integer;
  protected
    { Protected declarations }
  public
    { Public declarations }
    procedure Enlarge;
  published
    { Published declarations }
    property BoxInc: Integer read FBoxInc write FBoxInc;
  end;

procedure Register;
```

```
implementation

procedure Register;
begin
  RegisterComponents('Samples', [TBox]);
end;

procedure TBox.Enlarge;

{ Define new method to enlarge box
  upon each method call }

begin

  { Assign default value to property
    used to control increment amount
    of user-defined method }

  if FBoxInc = 0 then
    FBoxInc := 10;

  Width := Width + FBoxInc;
  Height := Height + FBoxInc;

end;

end.
```

Testing Components without Installing

Although the process of creating components is fairly straightforward, Delphi permits
you to test new components without having to install them. To do this, save the unit
that contains the component definition. Then use the File | Close All command to close
the unit and anything else that may be loaded. Afterwards, create a new project and add
the BoxObj unit name to the **uses** clause of the form's unit:

```
uses
  Windows, Messages, SysUtils, Classes, Graphics, Controls, Forms,
  Dialogs, BoxObj;
```

Then in the **private** section of the unit, add the following definition:

```
Box1: TBox;
```

Afterwards, add this code to the OnCreate event handler of the form:

```
Box1 := TBox.Create(Self);
Box1.Parent:= Self;
Box1.Left := 50;
Box1.Top := 50;
Box1.Brush.Color := clBlue;
```

You are now ready to test the component. When you run the project, you should see a box appear on the form. If you receive an error at this point, first compare each line above and make sure you typed the code correctly. If you still receive errors even after checking the preceding listing, go back and check the code in the BOXOBJ.PAS unit and verify that each line matches the code presented in the "Creating a Sample Component" exercise.

To test a component without installing it, only three steps are required. First you add the component's unit to the **uses** clause of the form's unit. Then you declare an instance of that component in the program. Finally, you generate the actual instance of the component with the following two lines:

```
Box1 := TBox.Create(Self);
Box1.Parent:= Self;
```

The Create method will construct the new component instance and specify the object that houses the control. By passing Self here, the form will be assigned as the object that will destroy the component when it is no longer needed. Afterwards, you specify Self for the Parent of the control. If the component is not descended from TControl (that is, if it is not a control), you do not specify the Parent.

> **Caution** *Never set the form's Parent to Self as this may cause Windows to crash.*

Testing the Enlarge Method

Although the preceding code will work to test the component, it does not demonstrate the Enlarge method you defined. To see how this method works, in the **private** section of the unit add the missing definitions:

```
private
    { Private declarations }
    Box1, Box2: TBox;
    CountTimer: Integer;
```

Once you have done this, add a label control and a timer component to the form and change the code in the **implementation** section as follows:

```
procedure DrawBoxShadow (Box1, Box2: TBox; Label1: TLabel);

{ Frame box with shadow border }

begin
   Box2.Left := Box1.Left + 10;
   Box2.Top := Box1.Top + 10;
   Box1.BringToFront;
   Box1.Enlarge;
   Box2.Enlarge;
   Label1.Left := Box1.Left + (Box1.Width - Label1.Width) div 2;
   Label1.Top := Box1.Top + (Box1.Height - Label1.Height) div 2;
   Label1.BringToFront;
end;

procedure TForm1.FormCreate(Sender: TObject);

{ Declare two instances of box component }

begin
   Box1 := TBox.Create(Self);
   Box1.Parent:= Self;
   Box1.Left := 150;
   Box1.Top := 60;
   Box1.Brush.Color := clAqua;
   Box2 := TBox.Create(Self);
   Box2.Parent:= Self;
   Box2.Brush.Color := clBlack;
   Label1.Caption := 'Hello World';
   Label1.Transparent := True;
   DrawBoxShadow (Box1, Box2, Label1);
   Timer1.Interval := 200; { milliseconds }
   CountTimer := 0;
end;

procedure TForm1.Timer1Timer(Sender: TObject);
```

```
{ Enlarge shadow box until maximum size
  is reached }

begin

  CountTimer := CountTimer + 1;

  case CountTimer of
       1 : Label1.Font.Size := 10;
       2 : Label1.Font.Size := 12;
       3 : begin
             Label1.Font.Size := 14;
             Timer1.Enabled := False;
           end;
     end;

  Box1.Enlarge;
  DrawBoxShadow (Box1, Box2, Label1);
  Box2.Enlarge;

end;
```

This example declares two instances of the TBox component. The first is used to display a message. The other defines the shadow border that will appear around the first box. By positioning the second box at an offset from the first box and applying the BringToFront method, the illusion of a shadow box is created (see Figure 12.3). To make the example more interesting, upon each call to the DrawBoxShadow procedure, a call is also made to the Enlarge method which produces the effect of a growing shadow box on the form.

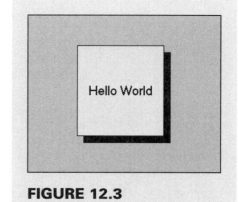

FIGURE 12.3
The shadow box

Installing Components

Once you have defined a class, you can install it in the Component Palette to see how it will work. To accomplish this, you must first create a package that will encompass the new component. Delphi 3.0 uses packages for all new components installed in the IDE. A *package* is a specially compiled dynamic link library (.DLL file) that permits you to access the properties, methods, and so on of a component.

In order to create a package, you must first make sure that DLLs can be viewed on your system. By default, Windows 95 hides .DLL files. To enable the display of DLLs, start the Windows 95 Explorer and use the Tools | Options... command to unhide these files. Afterwards, use the following steps to create the package:

1 Choose File | New.

2 Double click on Package.

3 In the New Package dialog box, enter the name you wish to save the package as in the File name box (for example, *PackTst*).

4 For the Description, type **My test component**.

5 Click on OK.

6 The Package Editor will now appear. Click on the Add button (see Figure 12.4).

7 In the Add dialog box, click on the three dots adjacent to the Unit file name prompt.

8 Afterwards, click on the name of the component's unit you wish to install and then choose the Open button.

9 Click on OK.

10 In Package Editor, choose the Build button.

11 Upon a successful compile, choose the Install button to install the new component/package in the Component Palette.

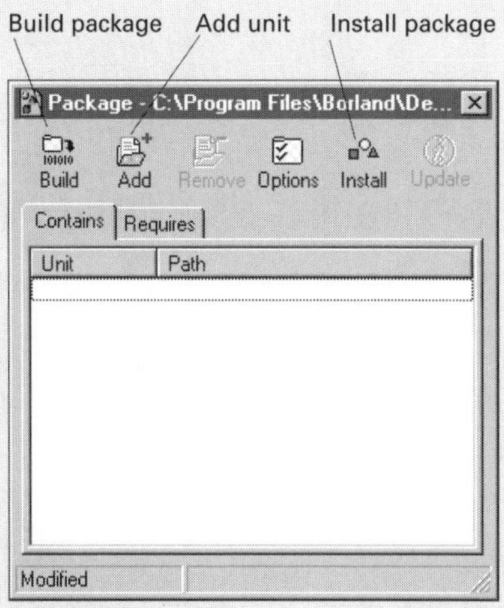

FIGURE 12.4
The Package Editor

Once installed, you can use your custom component the same way you use Delphi's components. For example, if the control has been installed on the Samples page of the Component Palette, then to add it to a form, you merely click on the tab labeled Samples and choose your custom component from the list. After adding the component to the form, the control can be tested by setting its properties, calling its methods and interpreting its events. In addition, any properties defined for published access will appear in the Object Inspector as well.

Summary

In this chapter, you have learned how to create custom components in Delphi. Specifically, you have learned how to:

▶ Create and register new components.

▶ Define properties and methods for components.

▶ Test components before they are installed.

▶ Compile and install packages in the Component Palette.

▶ Create shadow boxes.

A Brief History

Developing Internet Applications in Delphi

Sending E-Mail over the Internet

Making an FTP Connection

Other Internet-Related Issues

Exercise: Creating an E-Mail Application

Chapter 13

Delphi and the Internet

In the past, developing Internet applications was a time-consuming task limited to only a select group of professionals. With recent advancements in technologies, the learning curve for developing Internet-enabled software has been significantly reduced. Delphi provides state-of-the-art components to help you reach this end. This chapter provides an introduction to Delphi's Internet capabilities.

A Brief History

The concept of the Internet itself dates back to the '60s when it was originally conceived under the name ARPANET as a means for connecting four universities in the United States. The original idea came from Paul Baran of Rand Corporation who, at the height of the Cold War, proposed a communications network that U.S. authorities could use in the event of a nuclear attack. Unlike other communications networks of the time, Baran proposed a network that was not limited to the point-to-point connections of the day. Instead, his fishnet-like communications network could remain connected even if a major section had been destroyed. After a chain of events, the ARPANET eventually became known as the Internet and grew in popularity immensely throughout the '70s and '80s.

In 1989, the World Wide Web project was started by Tim Berners-Lee of the CERN high-energy physics laboratory. Designed to provide a way to permit researchers around the world to share information, the graphically oriented and hypertext-based system of the Web offered a more intuitive way of exchanging research and ideas. With the introduction of the Mosaic Web browser by the National Center for Supercomputing in November of 1992, the Web exploded in popularity and rapidly grew to immense proportions. Because the Web relies on the standard protocols of the Internet to exchange files and information, it is often used as a synonym for the Internet (though the Internet actually refers to the hardware links that connect the network).

Developing Internet Applications in Delphi

Enough history! You are probably wondering what Delphi can do for you. In the following sections, you will learn how to create a simple Web browser using the HTML component. Afterwards, you will learn how to send e-mail over the Internet from a Delphi program and how to develop an FTP client application.

The components discussed in this chapter are part of the Internet Solutions Pack (included with the Developer and the Client/Server Suite editions of Delphi). Table 13.1 shows some common terms key to understanding Delphi's relationship with the Internet.

TABLE 13.1   KEY INTERNET TERMS IN DELPHI

Term	Description
HTTP	The HyperText Transmission Protocol is the language that Web servers and clients use to communicate with each other and provides the ability to exchange multimedia files such as graphics, sound, video, and more.
TCP/IP	Acronym for Transmission Control Protocol and Internet Protocol. TCP/IP is a set of rules and commands that permits different types of computers to communicate over the Internet.
URL	Uniform Resource Locator, a network address.
WinSock	A standard for implementing TCP/IP network protocols in Windows.

Creating Web Viewers

With the HTML ActiveX component, you can create a simple Web browser to view Web pages in minutes. Figure 13.1 shows how this control appears in the Component Palette. HTML or *HyperText Markup Language* is a standard for developing Web pages. The following example demonstrates how to create a simple Web viewer. The OnClick event of the btnOK button shows the basic code needed to retrieve an HTML document:

```
procedure TForm1.btnOKClick(Sender: TObject);

{ Start Web Browser if not already running and
  go to page indicated by ComboBox1.Text }

begin
  Screen.Cursor := crHourGlass;
  Timer1.Enabled := True;
  BrowseWebPage (HTML1, ComboBox1);
end;
```

Note *To test the Internet features discussed in this chapter using Delphi 3.0, your Internet service provider must support a 32-bit WinSock. CompuServe 3x, for example, uses a 32-bit WinSock connection.*

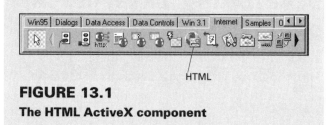

FIGURE 13.1
The HTML ActiveX component

The BrowseWebPage procedure, defined in the LMWebBrw unit, retrieves the document indicated by the Text property of ComboBox1. Upon each call to BrowseWebPage, the library routine adds the URL to the list (thereby permitting you to quickly return to any page visited during a session). For example, if you type www.borland.com, the program will load Borland's home page when you click on OK. After visiting another Web site, you can easily return back to www.borland.com by selecting the URL from the list (see Figure 13.2).

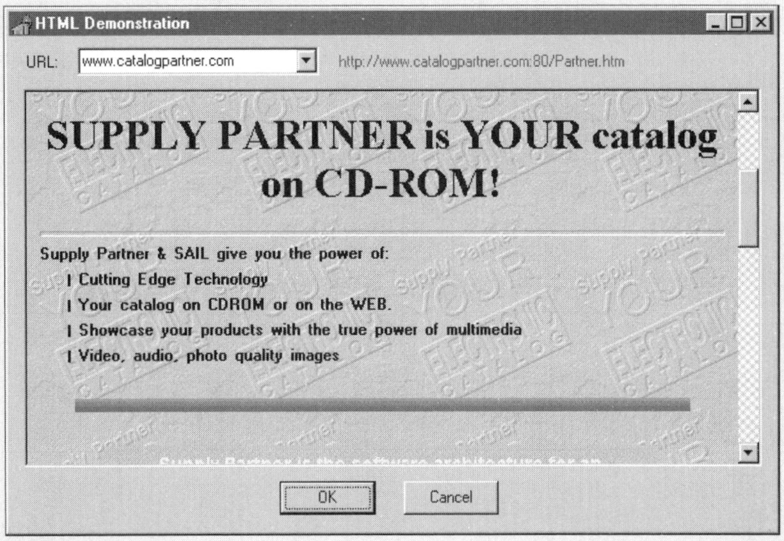

FIGURE 13.2
A sample Web browser

Retrieving an HTML Document

While waiting for a page to load, you can monitor the status of the current HTML operation. Since most of this work is handled automatically, you need only include a few lines of code to add the professional touch to your custom Web browser. Before calling BrowseWebPage, the OnClick event of the btnOK button changes the cursor shape to an hourglass. Afterwards, the timer (previously disabled at design-time) is enabled:

```
Screen.Cursor := crHourGlass;
Timer1.Enabled := True;
```

Inside the OnTimer event handler, a call is made to the MessageBlink library procedure (defined in the LMScreen unit). MessageBlink shows a *Loading page* status message in the lblStatus label component with three dots blinking after it while the document is being retrieved:

```
procedure TForm1.Timer1Timer(Sender: TObject);
begin
  MessageBlink ('Loading page', lblStatus);
end;
```

Note *Before calling BrowseWebPage, you must start your Internet dialer service.*

To determine when to stop showing the *Loading page* message, the program uses the OnEndRetrieval event handler of the HTML component to disable the timer and to display the name of the requested URL. Afterwards, the mouse cursor is reset back to its default shape:

```
procedure TForm1.HTML1EndRetrieval(Sender: TObject);

{ Show requested URL after document retrieval
  and disable timer }

begin
  Timer1.Enabled := False;
  lblStatus.Caption := HTML1.RequestURL;
  Screen.Cursor := crDefault;
end;
```

Canceling an HTML Operation

Any time you want to stop loading an HTML document, use the Cancel method to terminate the operation. An optional message can also be provided that will be appended to the partially loaded page. For example:

```
procedure TForm1.btnCancelClick(Sender: TObject);

{ Cancel HTML operation }

begin
  HTML1.Cancel('Operation canceled by user.');
  Close;
end;
```

Below is the complete source listing for the sample Web browser project. The boldfaced lines indicate the significant lines of code for the project (though only the call to BrowseWebPage is required). If you wish to recreate this example, you will need to add two modules to the project (LMWEBBRW.PAS and LMSCREEN.PAS) which are part of the developers' library included with this book.

> **Note** *When recreating the example, be sure to add the library modules to the project before entering this code. Otherwise, Delphi will rebuild the unit and remove the references to the LMWebbrw and LMScreen modules when the project is compiled the first time.*

```
unit uWebBrow;

interface

uses
  Windows, Messages, SysUtils, Classes, Graphics, Controls, Forms,
  Dialogs, StdCtrls, OleCtrls, ISP3, Buttons, ExtCtrls;

type
  TForm1 = class(TForm)
    HTML1: THTML;
    ComboBox1: TComboBox;
    Label1: TLabel;
    btnOK: TButton;
    btnCancel: TButton;
    lblStatus: TLabel;
    Timer1: TTimer;
    procedure FormCreate(Sender: TObject);
    procedure btnOKClick(Sender: TObject);
    procedure btnCancelClick(Sender: TObject);
    procedure HTML1EndRetrieval(Sender: TObject);
    procedure Timer1Timer(Sender: TObject);
  private
    { Private declarations }
  public
    { Public declarations }
  end;

var
  Form1: TForm1;

implementation

Uses
  LMWebBrw, LMScreen;

{$R *.DFM}
```

```
procedure TForm1.FormCreate(Sender: TObject);

begin

  { Fill combo box with test URL's }

  ComboBox1.Items.Add ('www.borland.com');
  ComboBox1.Items.Add ('www.shareware.com');
  ComboBox1.Text := 'www.borland.com';

end;

procedure TForm1.btnOKClick(Sender: TObject);

{ Start Web Browser if not already running and
  go to page indicated by ComboBox1.Text }

begin
  Screen.Cursor := crHourGlass;
  Timer1.Enabled := True;
  BrowseWebPage (HTML1, ComboBox1);
end;

procedure TForm1.btnCancelClick(Sender: TObject);

{ Cancel HTML operation }

begin
  HTML1.Cancel('Operation canceled by user.');
  Close;
end;

procedure TForm1.HTML1EndRetrieval(Sender: TObject);

{ Show requested URL after document retrieval and
  disable timer }

begin
```

```
    Timer1.Enabled := False;
    lblStatus.Caption := HTML1.RequestURL;
    Screen.Cursor := crDefault;
end;


procedure TForm1.Timer1Timer(Sender: TObject);
begin
    MessageBlink ('Loading page', lblStatus);
end;


end.
```

Sending E-Mail over the Internet

With the SMTP Client ActiveX Control, electronic mail can be sent over the Internet using the *Simple Mail Transfer Protocol*. The component is easy to use as well as fast and reliable. Figure 13.3 shows how the SMTP Client Control appears in the Component Palette.

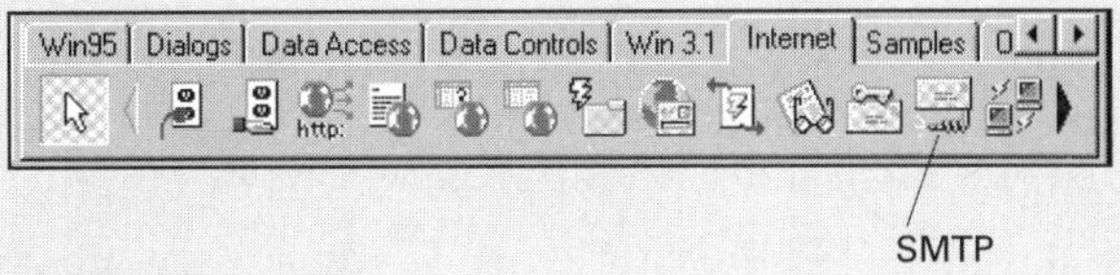

FIGURE 13.3
The SMTP Client component

The following example demonstrates how to send e-mail over the Internet (see Figure 13.4). To make a connection to an SMTP server, the following code is used:

```
procedure TForm1.btnConnectClick(Sender: TObject);

{ Make connection to SMTP server }

begin

    Screen.Cursor := crHourGlass;

    if SMTP1.State = prcConnected then
        SMTP1.Quit
    else
        if SMTP1.State = prcDisconnected then begin
            SMTP1.RemoteHost := editServName.Text;
            SMTP1.Connect(GetNoParam, GetNoParam);
```

```
        Application.ProcessMessages;
        Screen.Cursor := crDefault;
        btnSend.Enabled := True;
      end;

  end;
```

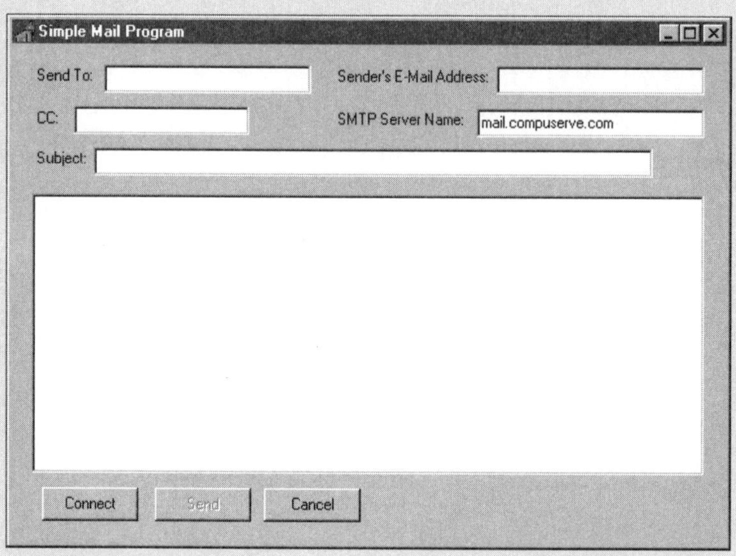

The State property determines the status of the component. The OnClick event handler of the Connect button either establishes or terminates a connection. If a connection has already been made, the Quit method is applied to disconnect from the server. Otherwise, the RemoteHost property specifies the SMTP server to connect to. The default value for this property is *mail*. If this is not applicable to your server, you will need to provide the correct SMTP server name before a connection can be made. For CompuServe, you would specify this parameter as *mail.compuserve.com*. If you do not

FIGURE 13.4
A sample mail project

know the name of your SMTP server, your Internet service provider should be able to supply you with this information.

After indicating the server name, the Connect method establishes the actual connection. Connect accepts two optional parameters: RemoteHost and RemotePort. If a value for either of these two parameters is supplied, that value will take precedence over the RemoteHost or RemotePort properties. Since these properties are optional, the connection is made by calling the GetNoParam function (defined in the LMMail unit) to provide default variant values as placeholder arguments.

Once a connection is established, the code inside the Send button performs the actual transmission:

```
procedure TForm1.btnSendClick(Sender: TObject);

begin
```

```
{ Make sure user is connected }

if not (SMTP1.State = prcConnected) then begin
   MessageDlg('Not connected to SMTP server', mtError, [mbOK], 0);
   exit;
   end;


while SMTP1.Busy do
     Application.ProcessMessages;


{ Send the message }


SendEMailMsg (SMTP1, editSendTo, editFrom, editRedirectTo,
            editSubject, Memo1);


end;
```

The State property of the SMTP component determines the status of the component. If State is not equal to prcConnected, an error message is displayed and control exits from the event handler:

```
{ Make sure user is connected }

if not (SMTP1.State = prcConnected) then begin
   MessageDlg('Not connected to SMTP server', mtError, [mbOK], 0);
   exit;
   end;
```

To ensure that all pending events have been processed, the following code is applied to delay the sending of the message until the component is ready:

```
while SMTP1.Busy do
     Application.ProcessMessages;
```

Otherwise all systems are go and the program calls the SendEMailMsg library routine defined in the LMMail unit to transmit the message:

```
{ Send the message }


SendEMailMsg (SMTP1, editSendTo, editFrom, editRedirectTo,
            editSubject, Memo1);
```

SendEMailMsg accepts the following arguments:

▶ ctrlSMTP: Name of TSMTP component that specifies the connection parameters

▶ editFrom: Edit control which holds the e-mail address of the message composer

▶ editCC: Edit control providing an optional e-mail address for redirecting mail

▶ editSubject: Edit control indicating the title (a description of the message)

▶ ctrlMemo: Name of TMemo component containing memo to send

SendEMailMsg handles the details of the operation automatically. Upon a successful transmission, the library procedure will display a modal dialog box and inform you that the message has been sent.

Making an FTP Connection

In addition to sending e-mail and creating Web browsers, the components provided in the Internet Solutions Pack allow you to establish connections to FTP servers. FTP, or the *File Transfer Protocol*, represents the older and more traditional way of connecting to the Internet. Although this protocol has been around for quite a while, it is still relevant and is widely used in many applications.

The FTP Client ActiveX Control provides an interface between a local machine and a remote machine. At run-time, the component is invisible on a form (see Figure 13.5). To build an FTP client, you do not have to be an expert at WinSock. By setting properties and calling the methods of the component, you can easily establish an FTP connection with minimal coding effort. For example:

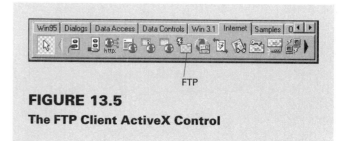

FIGURE 13.5
The FTP Client ActiveX Control

```
procedure TForm1.btnConnectClick(Sender: Tobject);
begin
  with FTP1 do begin
      RemoteHost := 'ftp.borland.com';
      RemotePort := 21;
      Connect(RemoteHost, RemotePort);
      end;
end;


procedure TForm1.FTP1ProtocolStateChanged(Sender: TObject;
        ProtocolState: Smallint);
```

```
begin

  case ProtocolState of

    { Indicate user id and password }

    ftpAuthentication: FTP1.Authenticate('anonymous', 'emailaddr');

    { Invoke list method to get current directory info. }

    ftpTransaction: FTP1.List('/');

    end;

end;

procedure TForm1.FTP1StateChanged(Sender: TObject; State: Smallint);

{ Get status of control and display in label }

begin
  case FTP1.State of
      prcConnecting   : Label1.Caption := 'Connecting to server...';
      prcResolvingHost: Label1.Caption := 'Resolving host...';
      prcHostResolved : Label1.Caption := 'Host resolved';
      prcConnected    : Label1.Caption := 'Connected to server';
      prcDisconnecting: Label1.Caption := 'Disconnecting...';
      prcDisconnected : Label1.Caption := 'Disconnected';
  end;

  { Use delay to see message }

  Sleep (1000);
  Application.ProcessMessages;

end;
```

This example connects to Borland's FTP server. By convention, the File Transfer Protocol uses port number 21 to make a connection. Thus by setting RemoteHost to "ftp.borland.com" and RemotePort to 21, a connection is made by invoking the Connect method.

Notice the use of the Sleep function. Sleep accepts one parameter—the number of milliseconds to wait. By pausing 1,000 milliseconds, each status message in the OnStateChanged event handler will be displayed for one second. Also notice the use of the ProcessMessages method of the Application object (included by default in every Delphi application). Since the Sleep function does not automatically process pending events, you must call ProcessMessages to ensure the user will see all the status messages.

Getting Directory Information from an FTP Server

Once you have established a connection, you can get directory information from an FTP server by invoking the List or NameList methods. For example:

```
procedure TForm1.FTP1ProtocolStateChanged(Sender: TObject;
          ProtocolState: Smallint);

begin

  case ProtocolState of

    { Indicate user id and password }

    ftpAuthentication: FTP1.Authenticate('anonymous', 'emailaddr');

    { Invoke list method to get current directory info. }

    ftpTransaction: FTP1.List('/');

    end;

end;
```

Many FTP servers (including Borland's, fortunately) support an *anonymous* login. If the server you are trying to access does not support this, you will have to contact the party in question for a valid ID before you can log in. For the password, you would normally provide your e-mail address or home page URL. Since Borland's server does not require a real password, a fake address is used here, although virtually any string will work with the exception of a blank string, which will cause the server to hang.

Afterwards, a detailed listing of the current directory will be returned from the server. If the ListItemNotify property of the FTP Client ActiveX Control is set to **True** (default), the OnListItem event handler will be invoked:

```
procedure TForm1.FTP1ListItem(Sender: TObject; const Item: Variant);

{ Get file and directory information from FTP server }
var
   NL:String;


begin

  NL := Chr(10) + Chr(13);

  { Get file information and convert to a string }

  Label1.Caption := Label1.Caption + VarToStr (Item.Filename) +
      ', ' +
      VarToStr (Item.Size) + ', ' +
      VarToStr (Item.Date) + ', ' +
      VarToStr (Item.Attributes) + ', ' +
      VarToStr (Item.Detail) + NL;

end;
```

NL is declared as Chr(13) plus Chr(10). This code will generate a new line character that will be used to format the output on multiple lines. Before this, a constant called Item is passed to the event handler as an argument. Item is actually an object itself that can be queried to determine the attributes of a file. For instance:

Item.Filename	Returns name of file
Item.Size	Returns the byte size of the file
Item.Date	Returns the file creation date
Item.Attributes	Returns the file attributes

Although it is not required, the OnBusy event handler of the FTP Client ActiveX Control can also be applied to determine when an operation is being performed and to provide the user with visual feedback on the status of a transaction. For instance, the following code will change the shape of the mouse cursor to an hourglass while the component is busy and restore it back to its default pointer shape when the action is completed:

```
procedure TForm1.FTP1Busy(Sender: TObject; isBusy: WordBool);

{ Change mouse cursor shape to hourglass while busy }

begin
  if isBusy then
    Screen.Cursor := crHourGlass
  else
    Screen.Cursor := crDefault;
end;
```

Adding Directory Items to a Tree

The preceding technique for getting directory information from a server and displaying it in a label will work for a basic test. However, for "real" Internet programming, you will most likely have to do more to provide your users with an easier way of viewing directory information on the server. Typically, you would add the directory/file information to a TTreeView component and create a list of *nodes* that represent the directory structure. Although this may sound complicated, Delphi provides an easy way of accomplishing this with just a few adjustments to the preceding source code.

To create a tree to view a directory structure, place a TTreeView component on the form (see Figure 13.6). Afterwards, add the following declarations to the **private** section of the unit:

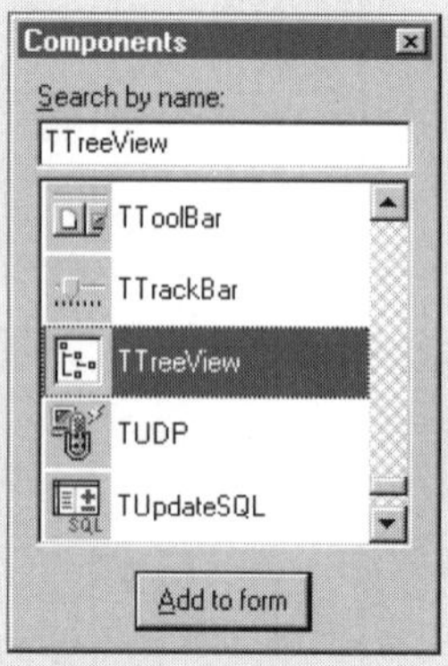

FIGURE 13.6
The TTreeView component

```
private
    { Private declarations }
    DriveRoot: TTreeNode;
    PathItem: TTreeNode;
```

Once you have done this, replace the code in the OnClick event handler of the btnConnect button and the OnListItem event handler of the FTP component with the highlighted lines below:

```
procedure TForm1.btnConnectClick(Sender: TObject);

{ Connect to FTP server and add name of host to root of
  TreeView component }

begin
```

Making an FTP Connection

```
  with FTP1 do begin
      RemoteHost := 'ftp.borland.com';
      RemotePort := 21;
      Connect(RemoteHost, RemotePort);
      DriveRoot := TreeView1.Items.AddChild(nil, RemoteHost);
      DriveRoot.ImageIndex := 0;
      DriveRoot.SelectedIndex := 0;
      TreeView1.Selected := DriveRoot;
      end;
end;


procedure TForm1.FTP1ListItem(Sender: TObject; const Item: Variant);

{ Get file and directory information from FTP server and add to tree }

begin
  PathItem := TreeView1.Items.AddChild(DriveRoot, Item.Filename);
end;
```

Figure 13.7 shows how the directory listing will appear after connecting to the
server. If you want to take this one step further, you can call the GetFTPDir library procedure to get a listing of files in the current directory. For example, the following code
will display all the files in the *pub* directory on the server:

```
  .    .    .
private
    { Private declarations }
    DriveRoot: TTreeNode;
    PathItem: TTreeNode;
    CurrentNode: String;
    RefreshStatus: Boolean;
public
    { Public declarations }
  end;

var
  Form1: TForm1;
  CurrentFile: Integer;
  .    .    .
```

```
procedure TForm1.Button1Click(Sender: TObject);

{ Switch to directory specified by List method }

begin
  Screen.Cursor := crHourGlass;
  RefreshStatus := True;
  FTP1.List('./pub/');
  Screen.Cursor := crDefault;
end;


procedure TForm1.FTP1ListItem(Sender: TObject; const Item: Variant);

begin
  GetFTPDir (ListView1, Item.FileName, Item.Size, RefreshStatus);
  RefreshStatus := False;
end;
```

This code will display a list of files in a ListView component (see Figure 13.8). Before calling GetFTPDir, you must add a TListView component to the form (Figure 13.9) and call SetListViewHeadings to initialize the ListView component. Here's an example:

```
procedure TForm1.FormCreate(Sender: TObject);
begin
  CurrentFile := 0;
```

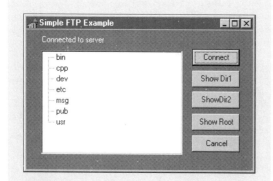

FIGURE 13.7

Displaying directories on the server

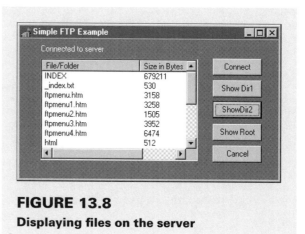

FIGURE 13.8

Displaying files on the server

```
    SetListViewHeadings (ListView1);
end;
```

FIGURE 13.9
The TListView component

Both GetFTPDir and SetListViewHeadings are defined in the LMFTP unit included with this book. By adding this unit to your project, you can easily retrieve directory information from the server.

Accessing UNIX Hosts

Since many FTP servers are written on UNIX hosts, it is helpful to know something about how UNIX directories are laid out. While you don't have to be an expert at UNIX, it is important at least to know that a "." (a period) means the current directory. The preceding example demonstrated how to retrieve file information from a server by passing a directory specification like this:

```
FTP1.List('./pub/');
```

After viewing a directory, to switch back to the root of the server, you would type:

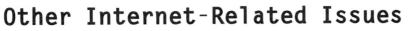

```
procedure TForm1.Button1Click(Sender: TObject);

{ Return back to root }

begin
  Screen.Cursor := crHourGlass;
  RefreshStatus := True;
  FTP1.List('/');
  Screen.Cursor := crDefault;
end;
```

Other Internet-Related Issues

Delphi also provides support for other protocols for establishing connections to the Internet. The following section provides a brief overview of some of Delphi's other Internet capabilities.

Using TCP/IP

The WinSock TCP ActiveX Control provides support for the *WinSock Transmission Control Protocol* (TCP), which can be used to generate chat and simple Web server applications. At run-time, the WinSock TCP ActiveX Control is invisible on a form. Like the FTP Client ActiveX Control, you do not need to be an expert at WinSock to use this component. By setting properties and invoking the methods of the component, transmissions can be established between the client and server.

Making a TCP Connection

The WinSock TCP ActiveX Control can be used to establish connections from a client to a server and to exchange data in both directions. The client initiates the connection to the remote server by calling the Connect method. Upon a successful connection, a Connect event will occur. If the host rejects the connection, the OnError event handler will be called instead. To determine what type of error has occurred, use the MessageDlg function to show the value of the Description parameter passed to this handler. For example:

```
procedure TChatForm.TCP1Error(Sender: TObject; Number: Smallint;
  var Description: string; Scode: Integer; const Source, HelpFile:
  string; HelpContext: Integer; var CancelDisplay: Wordbool);
begin
  MessageDlg(Description, mtWarning, [mbOk], 0);
end;
```

Once you have established a connection, the SendData method will transmit data to the remote machine. Upon arrival, the DataArrival event handler will execute in the server. By setting the WinSock TCP ActiveX Control to listen in on port 80 (the standard Web socket port) with another instance (occurrence) of the component, you can then display incoming data as it arrives:

```
procedure TChatForm.TCP1DataArrival(Sender: TObject; bytesTotal:
          Integer);

var
  DataRead: Variant;

begin

  { Get and display incoming data }

  TCP2.GetData(DataRead, VT_BSTR, bytesTotal);
  lblIncoming.Caption := lblIncoming.Caption + VarToStr (DataRead);
end;
```

Getting Network News

Delphi also provides support for retrieving news events from a news server. In order to retrieve news, you must specify the news server your Internet service provider uses. For example, in CompuServe 3x you would specify this as *news.spry.com*. The NNTP Client ActiveX Control provides support for getting news using the Networking News Transfer Protocol.

The Borland example application, NNTPDEMO.DPR, demonstrates how to use this component. To try this example, start your Internet service dialer and execute the NNTPDEMO.DPR application. Then choose the File | News command and enter the name of your news server. The program will respond by showing a *connecting...* message and then a *resolving host...* message. Afterwards, you will receive another message stating that the program is *retrieving news groups...* and at the bottom of the screen (in the status bar), you should see the total number of bytes downloaded. Once the messages have been sent, the application will build a listing of news events (see Figure 13.10). By clicking on one of the nodes that represents a news item, the current news event will be expanded to provide you with additional information on that topic.

Packages and the Internet

In Delphi 3.0, packages have been added to facilitate the distribution of applications. By compiling your programs into packages (the default compiler option), you can easily upload just the part (or parts) of your program that have changed after a software revision. Thus by using packages, uploads will be quicker and the resulting executable size of your applications will also be smaller and easier to distribute.

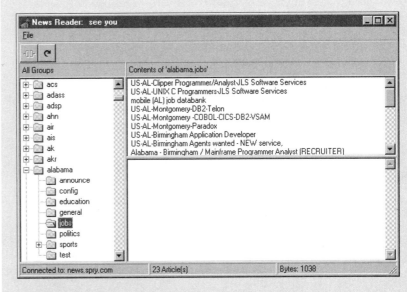

FIGURE 13.10
The Borland NNTPDEMO.DPR project

Exercise: Creating an E-Mail Application

In the following exercise, you will build a project to send e-mail over the Internet using the SendEMailMsg library procedure and the SMTP component. After this lesson, you should be able to:

▶ Connect to an SMTP server.

▶ Use the ProcessMessages method to process pending events.

▶ Send e-mail from a Delphi application.

1 Create a new project by choosing File | New Application.

2 Using the Object Inspector, set the properties of the form as indicated below:

Caption	Simple Mail Program
Height	400
Width	562
Position	poScreenCenter

3 From the Standard page of the Component Palette, add the following controls to the form. Place each component as it appears in Figure 13.11.

Label1	Edit1	Memo1
Label2	Edit2	Button1
Label3	Edit3	Button2
Label4	Edit4	Button3
Label5	Edit5	
Label6		

4 From the Internet page of the Component Palette, add an SMTP component to the form. If you do not remember what this component looks like, use the help hints to find it in the Component Palette or use the View | Component List command to find it.

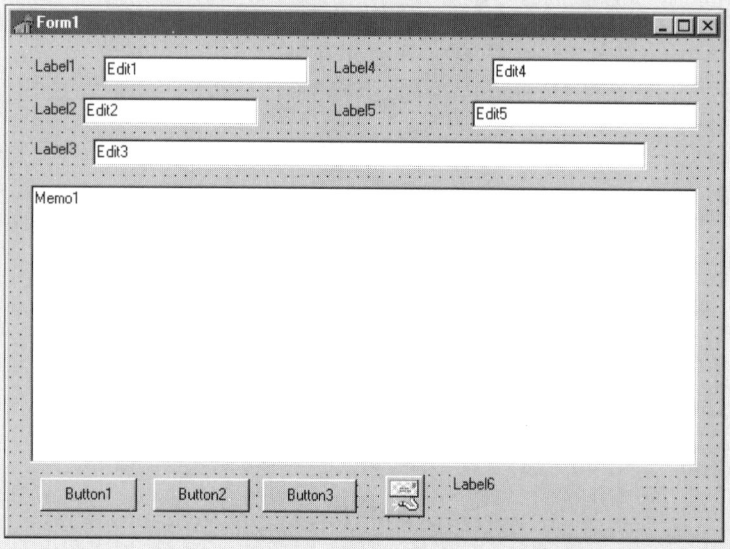

FIGURE 13.11
Positioning the components on the form

5 Set the properties of each component as follows:

Component	Property	Value
Edit1	Name	editSendTo
	Text	null string
Edit2	Name	editRedirectTo
	Text	null string
Edit3	Name	editSubject
	Text	null string
Edit4	Name	editFrom
	Text	null string
Edit5	Name	editServName
	Text	null string
Button1	Name	btnConnect
	Caption	Connect
Button2	Name	btnSend
	Caption	Send
	Enabled	False
Button3	Name	btnCancel
	Caption	Cancel
Label1	Caption	Send To:
Label2	Caption	CC:
Label3	Caption	Subject:
Label4	Caption	Sender's EMail Address
Label5	Caption	SMTP Server Name:
lblStatus	AutoSize	False
	Caption	null string

6 In the event handler of the Connect button, add the following code:

```
Screen.Cursor := crHourGlass;

if SMTP1.State = prcConnected then
    SMTP1.Quit
else
    if SMTP1.State = prcDisconnected then begin
        SMTP1.RemoteHost := editServName.Text;
        SMTP1.Connect(GetNoParam, GetNoParam);
```

```
      Application.ProcessMessages;
      Screen.Cursor := crDefault;
      btnSend.Enabled := True;
      end;
```

7 In the OnClick event handler of the btnSend button, type:

```
{ Make sure user is connected }

if not (SMTP1.State = prcConnected) then begin
   MessageDlg('Not connected to SMTP server', mtError, [mbOK], 0);
   exit;
   end;


while SMTP1.Busy do
      Application.ProcessMessages;


{ Send the message }


SendEMailMsg (SMTP1, editSendTo, editFrom, editRedirectTo,
              editSubject, Memo1);
```

8 Add the following code to the OnClick event handler of the Cancel button:

```
SMTP1.Quit;
while SMTP1.Busy do begin
      Application.ProcessMessages;
      Label1.Caption := 'Terminating session...';
      end;
Close;
```

9 In the OnCreate event handler of the *form*, add the following code:

```
Memo1.Lines.Clear;
```

10 From the File menu, choose the Add to Project... command.

11 In the File name box, type **C:\DLIB\LMMAIL.PAS** and then click on the Open button.

12 Switch back to the Unit1 unit by clicking on the Unit1 tab in the Code editor window.

13 Add the following lines directly below the **implementation** reserved word:

```
Uses
   LMMail;
```

To test the program, first start your Internet dialer service. Then run the program. Afterwards, type the send-to address, optional CC, the subject (or title) of the message, your e-mail address, and the name of your SMTP server. For example:

Send To: someone@aol.com
CC: 123456.7890@compuserve.com
Subject: E-Mail Test
Sender's E-Mail Address: 555555.5555@compuserve.com
SMTP Server Name: mail.compuserve.com

When you are done, type the message in the memo component and click on the Connect button. After a successful connection has been made, the Send button will be enabled. Click on Send to begin the transmission. Upon a successful upload, you should receive the following message:

```
Message has been sent!
```

If you experience problems trying to connect, make sure you have a 32-bit WinSock connection and that you have correctly configured and specified the name of your SMTP server. If you do not know this information, check with your Internet service provider.

Summary

In this chapter, you have learned how to establish WinSock connections using the components provided in the Internet Solutions Pack. Specifically, you have learned how to:

▶ Create a custom Web browser to load, view, and scroll HTML documents.

▶ Create a program for sending e-mail over the Internet.

▶ Connect to FTP servers and display listings of files.

▶ Work with other protocols for the transmission of data.

▶ Use packages to simplify the distribution of applications.

Over the entran...
temple a...
was a famous in...

Part 2
The Library

Chapter 14: Database Routines

Chapter 15: Multimedia Routines

Chapter 16: Rich Edit Routines

Chapter 17: Spreadsheet Routines

Chapter 18: String Routines

Chapter 19: String Grid Routines

Chapter 20: System Routines

Chapter 21: Utility and Web Connectivity
Routines

The ancient
Greeks believed
that they could
consult the
famous oracle
at D

AddField

DisplayQueryRecs

IsEmpty

LoadQuery

SortTable

Chapter 14
Database Routines

The developers' library included with this book includes five special routines for maintaining databases. These routines let you:

▶ Display the results of queries on grids.

▶ Dynamically modify table structures.

▶ Quickly sort records in tables.

▶ Load and execute saved queries.

▶ Determine whether a table is empty.

The database routines of the library are contained in the LMDB unit. Before a routine from the library can be used in a program, you must add the name of the unit that contains the procedure or function to your **uses** clause. You can then call any routine in that unit provided that the unit (LMDB.DCU) resides in the same DOS directory. Optionally, you may wish to include the source code for the unit in your project (using the File | Add to Project... command in Delphi). By doing this, you will be able to modify the code and include units from other directories.

You can use the library routines for your own custom needs and even modify the source code, provided that you agree to the terms in the licensing agreement and that you also agree not to use the code to market a competing developers' library or other reusable code system.

AddField

AddField inserts a new field into a database table. The function provides an easy way of modifying table structures at run-time. Use it to perform software updates on your customers' machines.

Syntax
```
function AddField (qryCtrl: TQuery; tblName: String; FieldName,
FieldType, FieldSize, FieldDec: String): Integer;
```

Parameters: qryCtrl: Name of TQuery component
tblName: Table to which field is added
FieldName: Field to insert
FieldType: Data type of field that is added
FieldSize: Size of field
FieldDec: Optional decimal places

Uses: LMDB

Returns: 1 if successful, 0 if not

Example

The DBADDFLD.DPR project demonstrates how to incorporate the AddField library routine in an application. When the user clicks on the Add Field button, the program prompts the user for the name of the field to add. Afterwards, a message dialog reports the status of the operation.

```
procedure TForm1.btnAddFieldClick(Sender: TObject);

var
  tblName, FieldName, FieldType, FieldSize, FieldDec: string;
  RetVal: integer;

begin

  { Define new field in BioLife table }

  Query1.DatabaseName := 'DBDEMOS';
  tblName := 'BioLife';
  FieldName := InputBox('Field Name', 'Field name to add:', '');
  FieldType := 'Character';
  FieldSize := '20';
  FieldDec := '0';

  if FieldName = '' then
    exit;

  RetVal := AddField (Query1, tblName, FieldName, FieldType, FieldSize,
                      FieldDec);

  if RetVal <> 1 then
    MessageDlg('Field already defined in table.',
    mtWarning, [mbOk], 0)
  else
    MessageDlg('Field has been added.',
    mtInformation, [mbOk], 0);

end;
```

DisplayQueryRecs

DisplayQueryRecs displays the results of a query on a grid. The SQLStr parameter lets you specify the conditions in which data will be drawn from the table. For example, to display all the records from the BioLife table where the Category field begins with the letter *S*, you could pass a string like this:

```
SQLStr := 'SELECT * FROM BioLife WHERE Category LIKE "S%"';
```

Of course, if you wish to display all the records in the table, you can omit the **WHERE** clause:

```
'SELECT * FROM BioLife';
```

For more information on SQL and how to create selection criteria, see Chapter 9.

Syntax:
```
procedure DisplayQueryRecs (qryCtrl: TQuery; DataSource: TDataSource;
                            DBGrid: TDBGrid; DBName, SQLStr: String);
```

Parameters: qryCtrl: Name of TQuery component to use
DataSource: Name of TDataSource component to use
DBGrid: Name of TDBGrid component to use
DBName: Database alias
SQLStr: SQL string to display

Uses: LMDB

Returns: Nothing

Example

The following example, taken from the DBPROJ.DPR sample project, shows how to use the library routine. When the project loads, the FormCreate procedure calls DisplayQueryRecs to read the records onto the grid. Figure 14.1 shows how the output appears.

```
procedure TForm1.FormCreate(Sender: TObject);

var
  DBName, SQLStr: string;

begin

  { Bind data components together and display
    results of query on grid }

  DBName := 'DBDEMOS';
  SQLStr := 'SELECT * FROM BioLife';
```

```
DisplayQueryRecs (Query1, DataSource1, DBGrid1, DBName, SQLStr);

btnSorted.Enabled := True;
DBImage1.DataField := 'Graphic';

end;
```

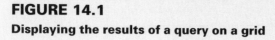

FIGURE 14.1
Displaying the results of a query on a grid

IsEmpty

IsEmpty provides a quick and easy way of determining whether a table is empty by re-turning **True** if a table is empty. It performs the same basic task as checking to see whether a table is both **BOF** and **EOF**. Although simple, the function demonstrates how you can create simple handlers for common tasks and also how a function can be used to improve the readability of code.

Syntax:	`function IsEmpty (tbl_Object: TTable);`
Parameters:	tbl_Object: Name of table component
Uses:	LMDB
Returns:	**True** if table is empty, **False** if not

Example

DBPROJ.DPR shows how to apply the library routine. When the user clicks on the CheckEmpty button, a modal dialog appears showing the status of the table (see Figure 14.2).

```
procedure TForm1.btnEmptyClick(Sender: TObject);


begin

  { Check if table is empty }

  if IsEmpty (Table1) then
     MessageDlg('Table contains no records.', mtInformation, [mbOk], 0)
  else
     MessageDlg('Table is not empty.', mtInformation, [mbOk], 0);

end;
```

FIGURE 14.2
The modal dialog box

LoadQuery

LoadQuery loads and executes a saved query. The query can be any valid SQL string but must be saved in a plain ASCII file—that is, one that contains no special formatting or codes. You can use Notepad or the MSDOS editor for this purpose.

Syntax: `procedure LoadQuery (FileToLoad: String; qryCtrl: TQuery);`

Parameters: FileToLoad: Text file containing query specification
              qryCtrl: Name of query component

Uses: LMDB

Returns: Nothing

Example

The DBPROJ.DPR project demonstrates how to use the library routine. When the user clicks on the Load Query button, the MYQUERY.TXT query is read from disk and executed. MYQUERY.TXT contains the following SELECT statement:

```
SELECT * FROM Customer WHERE Company LIKE "Ma%"
```

Since the query is contained in a text file, the SELECT statement can be modified without having to recompile the program. This system is useful for providing an open architecture to high-end users who need to be able to define their own queries. Note that if a user makes a mistake in the query specification, LoadQuery will trap the error, report the message "Cannot perform query," and recover from the error.

```
procedure TForm1.btnLoadClick(Sender: TObject);

{ Load and execute saved query  }

var
  FileToLoad: string;

begin
  FileToLoad := 'MyQuery.Txt';
  LoadQuery (FileToLoad, Query1);
end;
```

SortTable

SortTable provides a quick and convenient way of ordering records in a table. The *optSort* parameter determines whether the records are arranged in ascending order (ASC) or descending order (DESC). If *optSort* contains an empty string, ascending order is assumed.

Syntax:
```
procedure SortTable (qryCtrl: TQuery; FieldScope, tblName,
                     SortField, optSort: String);
```

Parameters: qryCtrl: Name of query component
FieldScope: Comma-separated field list of fields to return after sort, or use the * wildcard to include all fields
tblName: Name of table to sort
SortField: Name of field to sort by
optSort:
  ASC = Sort records in ascending order
  DESC = Sort records in descending order

Defaults: Sorts by ascending order if optSort is an empty string

Uses: LMDB

Returns: Nothing

Example

The DBPROJ.DPR project demonstrates how to use the library routine. When the user clicks on the Sort Table button, the BioLife table is sorted in ascending order by the Category field:

```
procedure TForm1.btnSortedClick(Sender: TObject);

var
  FieldScope, tblName, SortField, optSort: string;

begin

  { include all fields in sort }

  FieldScope := '*';
  tblName := 'BioLife';
  SortField := 'Category';
  optSort := '';

  { Organize records by category and length }

  SortTable (Query1, FieldScope, tblName, SortField, optSort);

end;
```

BlockShadow

ColorMsg

CustomCursor

DisplayDirImages

MessageBlink

PlayVideoFile

PlayWaveFile

ShowHotSpot

ShowScrSaver

ShowTNail

SlowPrint

SoundEnabled

TickerTape

TileBitmap

TransparentButton

Chapter 15
Multimedia Routines

With thousands of multimedia titles on the market today, developers need a way to stand out among the competition. The library provides several routines that allow you to enhance the appearance and functionality of programs. These routines let you play wave files and videos, display transparent buttons over bitmaps, simulate ticker tape machines, cycle through graphics in a directory, define hotspots on forms, and more. In addition, the library provides several reusable screen handling procedures. These library resources provide extra support for creating unique effects in programs, such as displaying messages with shadow effects, defining your own custom mouse cursors, creating screen savers, tiling bitmaps, and more. Table 15.1 lists the multimedia and screen handling procedures and functions of the library.

TABLE 15.1   MULTIMEDIA PROCEDURES OF THE LIBRARY

Routine	Description
BlockShadow	Displays a message with a block shadow effect.
ColorMsg	Shows a message with each letter in a different color.
CustomCursor	Displays a user-defined mouse cursor.
DisplayDirImages	Shows the next/previous graphic in a directory.
MessageBlink	Displays a message with three dots blinking after it.
PlayVideoFile	Plays an .AVI file.
PlayWaveFile	Plays a wave audio file.
ShowHotSpot	Defines a hotspot on a form or image control (automatically displays hand pointer when mouse cursor is over it).
ShowScrSaver	Displays a customizable screen saver.
ShowTNail	Displays a bitmap the size of an icon.
SlowPrint	Displays a message with a delay effect.
SoundEnabled	Returns **True** if a sound card is installed.
TickerTape	Creates an animated scroll area for a message within a ticker tape.
TileBitmap	Displays a user-defined graphic on a form with a tiling effect.
TransparentButton	Displays a transparent button over a user-defined graphic.

BlockShadow

BlockShadow displays a message with a block shadow effect on a form's canvas (see Figure 15.1). Use it to add visual appeal to any program.

Syntax:
```
procedure BlockShadow (Canvas: TCanvas; StrMsg: String; X, Y: Integer;
          FColor, BColor, CColor: TColor);
```

Parameters: Canvas: Name of canvas on which to display message
StrMsg: Message to show
X: Relative horizontal coordinate (in pixels) from left edge of form to display message
Y: Relative vertical coordinate (in pixels) from top of form to display message
FColor = Foreground color of message
BColor = Background color of message
CColor = Canvas color

Uses: LMScreen

Returns: Nothing

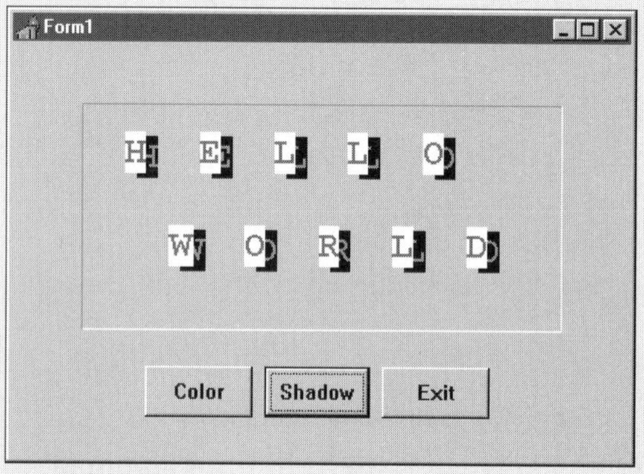

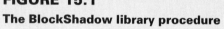

FIGURE 15.1
The BlockShadow library procedure

Example

The STRCOLR.DPR project shows how to use the library procedure. When the user clicks on the Shadow button, a message appears with each character over a shadow block.

```
procedure TForm1.btnShadowMsgClick(Sender: TObject);


var
  X, Y: Integer;
```

```
      FColor, BColor, CColor: TColor;

begin

   X := 80; Y := 60;
   Canvas.Font.Size := 18;
   Form1.Refresh;

   FColor := clBlack;
   BColor := clWhite;
   CColor := clSilver;

   { Display message with block shadow effect }

   BlockShadow (Canvas, 'HELLO', X, Y, FColor, BColor, CColor);

   X := 110; Y := 120;

   BlockShadow (Canvas, 'WORLD', X, Y, FColor, BColor, CColor);

end;
```

ColorMsg

ColorMsg provides a unique and interesting way of displaying messages to users—it shows a message with each letter in a different color. Use it to add a professional touch to any application.

Syntax:
```
procedure ColorMsg (Canvas: TCanvas; MsgToPrint: String; X, Y: Integer;
                    BColor, CColor: TColor);
```

Parameters:
Canvas = Canvas on which to display message
MsgToPrint = String to display
X = Relative horizontal coordinate (in pixels) from left edge of form to display message
Y = Relative vertical coordinate (in pixels) from top of form to display message
BColor = Background color
CColor = Canvas color

Uses: LMScreen

Returns: Nothing

Example

The sample project STRCOLR.DPR demonstrates how to use the library routine. When the btnColorClick button is selected, a message appears on the canvas in several contrasting colors (see Figure 15.2).

```
procedure TForm1.btnColorClick(Sender: TObject);

var
  BkColor, BlankSpaceColor: TColor;
  xCoord, yCoord : integer;
  MsgToPrint: string;

begin

  { Display color message on form's canvas }

  xCoord := 100; yCoord := 70;
  BkColor := clSilver;
  BlankSpaceColor := clSilver;
  MsgToPrint := 'Sample color';

  Canvas.Font.Size := 18;

  Form1.Refresh;
```

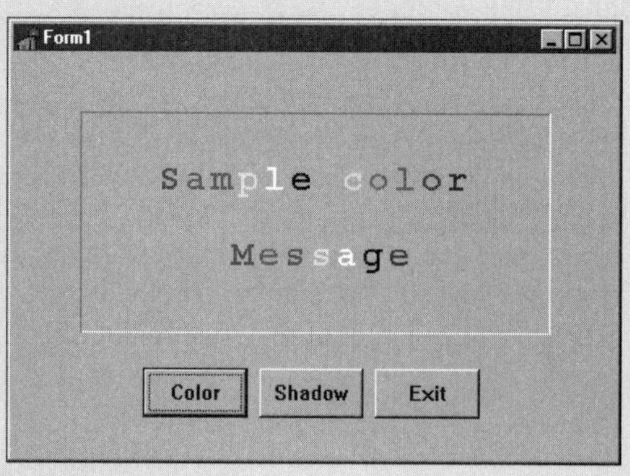

FIGURE 15.2
The ColorMsg library procedure

```
    ColorMsg (Canvas, MsgToPrint, xCoord, yCoord, BkColor,
              BlankSpaceColor);


    xCoord := 150; yCoord := 120;
    MsgToPrint := 'Message';


    ColorMsg (Canvas, MsgToPrint, xCoord, yCoord, BkColor,
              BlankSpaceColor);


  end;
```

CustomCursor

CustomCursor displays a user-defined mouse cursor on a form. The library provides three custom mouse cursors you can use (GUNSCOPE, CHECKMARK, and DRAG-FOLDER). You can also specify a custom cursor of your own. To create a mouse pointer, use the Delphi Image Editor to add a new cursor to the CUR32.RES resource file (the LMScr32.PAS unit automatically links this resource file to your project when you create an application that uses CustomCursor). Each cursor must be saved under a unique name. If you do not assign a name to a cursor, Delphi will automatically name it as CURSOR_1, CURSOR_2, CURSOR_3, and so on. To display the cursor in a program, you associate the cursor image in the resource file with a numeric constant you define. Since the standard cursors in Delphi are all associated with negative numbers, any positive integer can be used.

Syntax:
```
procedure CustomCursor (crCustom: Integer; CursorName: PChar; frmCtrl:
                        TForm);
```

Parameters: crCustom: Number to assign to cursor
CursorName: GUNSCOPE, CHECKMARK, DRAGFOLDER, or user-defined cursor name
frmCtrl: Form to associate with cursor

Uses: LMScr32

Returns: Nothing

Example

CUSTCUR.DPR demonstrates how to apply the library routine. When the form loads, the standard cursor is replaced with a gun scope.

```
procedure TForm1.FormCreate(Sender: TObject);


{ Set mouse cursor shape to gunscope }
```

```
const
  crGScope = 1;
var
  X, Y: integer;

begin
  CustomCursor (crGScope, 'GUNSCOPE', Form1);
  X := 320; Y := 230;
  SetMouse (X, Y);
end;
```

```
procedure TForm1.BitBtn1Click(Sender: TObject);

{ Reset default mouse cursor shape }

begin
  CustomCursor (crDefault, 'crDefault', Form1);
end;
```

Note *When you distribute programs that use the CustomCursor library procedure, you must also include the CUR32.RES resource file with your application.*

DisplayDirImages

DisplayDirImage shows the next or previous bitmap in a directory. Use it to quickly preview graphics or in programs that require the sequential display of file images. For example, you can use DisplayDirImage for a custom screen saver that loads bitmaps from disk.

Syntax:
```
function DisplayDirImage (GraphicsPath: TString: imgCtrl: Timage:
            fileCtrl: TFileListBox: DisplayOption: Integer);
```

Parameters: GraphicsPath: Path to bitmap images
imgCtrl: Image component to display pictures on
fileCtrl: File list box
DisplayOption: 1 = Show next graphic in directory; 2 = Show previous graphic in directory

Uses: LMScreen

Returns: Name of current bitmap

Example

PICVIEW.DPR shows how to use the DisplayDirImage function. The arrow buttons (implemented as two image components) determine which bitmap to show (see Figure 15.3). When the user clicks on the left arrow button, the previous bitmap in the directory is shown. When the user clicks on the right arrow button, the next bitmap in the directory is shown.

```
procedure TForm1.FormCreate(Sender: TObject);

var
  optWin: integer;

begin

  { Set default path }

  optWin := 0;
  FileListBox1.Directory := WinDir (optWin);
  edit1.Text := WinDir (optWin);

  { Show first bitmap when form loads }

  FileListBox1.Mask := '*.bmp';
  FileListBox1.ItemIndex := FileListBox1.ItemIndex + 1;
  Image1.Picture.LoadFromFile (FileListBox1.FileName);

  { Display bitmap name }

  Label1.Caption := FileListBox1.FileName;
  FileListBox1.Visible := False;

  chkProportional.Checked := True;

end;

procedure TForm1.imgNextClick(Sender: TObject);

{ Show next graphic in directory }
```

```
var
  GraphicsPath: string;
  optDisplay: integer;

begin

  GraphicsPath := Edit1.Text;
  optDisplay := 1;

  Label1.Caption := DisplayDirImage (GraphicsPath, Image1,
                  FileListBox1, optDisplay);

end;

procedure TForm1.imgPrevClick(Sender: TObject);

{ Show previous graphic in directory }

var
  GraphicsPath: string;
  optDisplay: integer;
```

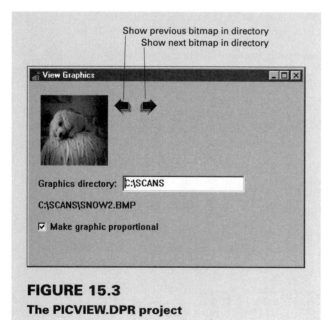

FIGURE 15.3
The PICVIEW.DPR project

```
begin

  GraphicsPath := Edit1.Text;
  optDisplay := 2;

  Label1.Caption := DisplayDirImage (GraphicsPath, Image1,
                FileListBox1, optDisplay);

end;
```

Note *The WinDir function is defined in the LMString unit.*

MessageBlink

MessageBlink displays a message with three dots blinking after it. To show the dots blinking, the call to MessageBlink must be placed in the OnTimer event handler. The library routine provides an elegant way of showing status messages to users. Use it during lengthy operations to give users extra information while routine processing is being performed.

Syntax:	`procedure MessageBlink (Msg: String; ctrlLabel: TLabel);`
Parameters:	Msg = Message to show ctrlLabel = Label component on which to display message
Uses:	LMString
Returns:	Nothing

Example

The following example shows how MessageBlink can be applied. When the DBPROJ.DPR sample application loads, the message "Initializing tables..." appears while the program is starting.

```
procedure TForm1.Timer1Timer(Sender: TObject);

const
  MAX_SECONDS = 7;

var
  MsgToShow: String;

begin
```

```
{ Display message with 3 dots blinking
  after it }

MsgToShow := ' Initializing tables';
MessageBlink (MsgToShow, Label1);
TimerCount := TimerCount + 1;

if TimerCount >= MAX_SECONDS then
  begin
    Label1.Visible := False;
    Timer1.Enabled := False;
    Screen.Cursor := crDefault;
  end;

end;
```

PlayVideoFile

Although PlayVideoFile uses the TMediaPlayer component to play videos, the control does not actually have to be visible on a form to play an .AVI file. Therefore, if you wish to hide the component (by setting its Visible property to **False**), you can use PlayVideoFile to launch the video from another handler.

Syntax: `procedure PlayVideoFile (ctrlMedia: TMediaPlayer: PathName: String);`

Parameters: ctrlMedia: Name of Media Player component
                 PathName: Path to .AVI file

Uses: LMMedia

Returns: Nothing

Example

The following example shows how to apply the library procedure. When the user clicks on the OK button of the PLAYVIDEO.DRP project, the program shows a video of a puzzle assembling in the air. The puzzle then morphs into a CD and flies through the air and lands in a disk drive[1]. In order to play videos on a PC, you must have the proper video drivers installed. You can use Microsoft Video for Windows for this purpose.

---

[1] The SAIL.AVI, which features a music sound track by Mike Donnelly, was provided courtesy of Software Assistance International, LTD.

These drivers are also included in Windows 95. For more information about how to play and create .AVI files, see Chapter 11, "Developing Multimedia Applications."

```
procedure TForm1.btnPlayMediaClick(Sender: TObject);

begin

  { Play audio or video }

  if radioVideo.Checked then
     PlayVideoFile (MediaPlayer1, 'SAIL.AVI')
  else
     PlayWaveFile (MediaPlayer1,  'thatsa.wav');

end;

procedure TForm1.MediaPlayer1Exit(Sender: TObject);

{ Close device after playing }

begin
  MediaPlayer1.Stop;
  MediaPlayer1.Close;
end;
```

PlayWaveFile

PlayWaveFile provides an easy and convenient way of incorporating sound in applications. In order to play a wave (.WAV) file, your system must be equipped with a sound card.

> **Note** *To determine whether a sound card is present, use the SoundEnabled library procedure.*

Syntax:	`procedure PlayWaveFile (ctrlMedia: TMediaPlayer: PathName: String);`
Parameters:	ctrlMedia: Name of Media Player component
	PathName: Path to wave file
Uses:	LMMedia
Returns:	Nothing

Example

PLAYVIDEO.DRP demonstrates how to incorporate audio in applications. The program provides two ways to play wave files. When the chkVisible check box is selected, clicking on the Play button of the Media Player component plays the wave file. When the chkVisible check box is not selected, clicking on the OK button plays the same wave file without showing the Media Player component. After playing the wave file, the MediaPlayer1Exit procedure of the Media Player component closes the device so the next audio or video recording can be played. The following example shows the basic code needed to play a wave file:

```
procedure TForm1.btnPlayMediaClick(Sender: TObject);

begin

  { Play audio or video }

  if radioVideo.Checked then
    PlayVideoFile (MediaPlayer1, 'SAIL.AVI')
  else
    PlayWaveFile (MediaPlayer1, 'thatsa.wav');

end;

procedure TForm1.MediaPlayer1Exit(Sender: TObject);

{ Close device after playing }

begin
  MediaPlayer1.Stop;
  MediaPlayer1.Close;
end;
```

ShowHotSpot

ShowHotSpot allows you to define your own custom hotspots on a form or image component. At run-time, the mouse cursor shape changes to a hand pointer while positioned over the hotspots. The library procedure takes as an argument a label component. To determine whether the hotspot has been selected, place the code to interpret this event in the OnClick event handler of the label.

Syntax:	`procedure ShowHotSpot (lblCtrl: TLabel);`
Parameters:	lblCtrl: Name of label component to use as hotspot
Uses:	LMScr32
Returns:	Nothing

Example

The following example demonstrates how to apply the ShowHotSpot routine in a program. CUR32PRJ.DPR uses the library procedure to display three hotspots over a bitmap. When the program runs, the ShowHint method of the Application object (defined in the Forms unit) is applied to display a help hint next to each hotspot. When one of the labels that defines a hotspot is selected, the MessageDlg procedure displays a message to the user indicating which hotspot was selected.

```
  .    .    .
implementation

uses
  LMScr32;

{$R *.DFM}

procedure TForm1.FormCreate(Sender: TObject);

begin

  { Define 3 hotspots implemented as labels }

  ShowHotSpot (Label1);
  ShowHotSpot (Label2);
  ShowHotSpot (Label3);

  { Bring hotspots (labels) to front of z-order
    to ensure hotspots can be selected }

  Label1.BringToFront;
  Label2.BringToFront;
  Label3.BringToFront;

  { Make hotspots transparent }
```

```
   Label1.Transparent := True;
   Label2.Transparent := True;
   Label3.Transparent := True;

   { Define help hints }

   Application.ShowHint := True;
   Application.HintColor := clAqua;
   Application.HintPause := 200;

   Label1.ShowHint := True; Label2.ShowHint := True;
   Label3.ShowHint := True;

   Label1.Hint := 'Delphi Way RAD!';
   Label2.Hint := 'Hotspots are easy to develop with the library!';
   Label3.Hint := 'Can you take a hint?';

end;

procedure TForm1.Label1Click(Sender: TObject);

{ Show message to indicate which hotspot
  was selected }

begin
  MessageDlg('Hotspot #1 selected', mtInformation, [mbOk], 0);
end;

procedure TForm1.Label2Click(Sender: TObject);

{ Show message to indicate which hotspot
  was selected }

begin
  MessageDlg('Hotspot #2 selected', mtInformation, [mbOk], 0);
end;
```

```
procedure TForm1.Label3Click(Sender: TObject);

{ Show message to indicate which hotspot
  was selected }

begin
  MessageDlg('Hotspot #3 selected', mtInformation, [mbOk], 0);
end;


end.
```

Note *When you distribute programs that use the ShowHotSpot library procedure, you must also include the CUR32.RES resource file with your application.*

ShowScrSaver

ShowScrSaver displays a customizable screen saver on a form. By varying the LineWidth and LineStyle parameters, the screen saver can be customized in several different ways. In Windows 95, the screen saver can be installed by renaming the .EXE file as a .SCR file and copying it to the Windows\System directory. Once this is done, the screen saver will appear in the list of screen savers available in the Control Panel.

Syntax: `procedure ShowScrSaver (LineWidth, LineStyle: Integer; ctrlForm: Form);`

Parameters: LineWidth: Pixel width of lines drawn by screen saver
              LineStyle: 0 = Solid lines; 1 = Mixed colored lines with dotted pattern
              ctrlForm = Form to display screen saver on

Uses: LMScreen

Returns: Nothing

Example

The sample project SBLANKER.DPR demonstrates how to write a screen saver application. When the blanker starts, the code in the OnCreate event handler of the form initializes the program by recording the initial coordinates of the mouse cursor when the project loads and by setting the mouse cursor style to crNone. Afterwards, the code in the OnTimer event handler is where the actual call for the ShowScrSaver procedure is placed:

```
procedure TForm1.Timer1Timer(Sender: TObject);

var
```

```
  LineWidth, LineStyle: Integer;

{ Show custom screen saver }

begin
  LineWidth := 2;
  LineStyle := 1;
  ShowScrSaver (LineWidth, LineStyle, Form1);
end;
```

The following code shows how to end the screen blanker run when a key is pressed. Notice that you *must* reset the mouse pointer shape. This is extremely important or else you will not be able to use your mouse!

```
procedure TForm1.FormKeyPress(Sender: TObject; var Key: Char);
begin
  Screen.Cursor := crDefault;
  Close;
end;
```

The screen blanker also stops running if the user moves the mouse. To determine whether the mouse has been moved, the Abs function is applied in the form's OnMouseMove event handler to calculate the relative number of pixels the mouse cursor position has shifted since the screen saver was started:

```
procedure TForm1.FormMouseMove(Sender: TObject; Shift: TShiftState; X,
                               Y: Integer);

begin

  { Terminate screen saver if mouse has moved
    since screen saver kicked in }

  if Abs (X) - Abs (StartPos_X) > 5 then begin
    close;
  end;

  if Abs (Y) - Abs (StartPos_Y) > 5 then begin
    close;
  end;

end;
```

Initially, if you recall, the position of the mouse cursor was recorded in two private variables (StartPos_X and StartPos_Y). If the mouse has moved more than five pixels either vertically or horizontally since the program started, the Close method is applied to end the run. Below is the complete source listing of the SBLANKER.DPR project:

```
private
  StartPos_X, StartPos_Y: Integer;
public
  { Public declarations }
end;

var
  Form1: TForm1;

implementation

uses
  LMScreen;

{$R *.DFM}

implementation

uses
  LMScreen;

{$R *.DFM}

procedure TForm1.FormCreate(Sender: TObject);
begin
  Screen.Cursor := crNone;
  StartPos_X := 100;
  StartPos_Y := 100;
  SetMouse (StartPos_X , StartPos_Y);
end;

procedure TForm1.Timer1Timer(Sender: TObject);

var
```

```
  LineWidth, LineStyle: integer;

{ Show custom screen saver }

begin
  LineWidth := 2;
  LineStyle := 1;
  ShowScrSaver (LineWidth, LineStyle, Form1);
end;


procedure TForm1.FormKeyPress(Sender: TObject; var Key: Char);
begin
  Screen.Cursor := crDefault;
  Close;
end;


procedure TForm1.FormMouseMove(Sender: TObject; Shift: TShiftState; X,
  Y: Integer);

begin

  { Terminate screen saver if mouse has moved
    since screen saver kicked in }

  if Abs (X) - Abs (StartPos_X) > 5 then begin
    close;
  end;

  if Abs (Y) - Abs (StartPos_Y) > 5 then begin
    close;
  end;

end;
```

ShowTNail

ShowTNail displays a bitmap on a form and proportionally reduces its size for viewing purposes. By displaying the image at the size of an icon, multiple bitmaps can be previewed on a form simultaneously.

Syntax: `function ShowTNail (GraphicsPath: String; imgCtrl: TImage) : String;`

Parameters: GraphicsPath: Path to bitmap
imgCtrl: Image component to display bitmap

Uses: LMScreen

Returns: Name of bitmap

Example

The following code demonstrates how to incorporate the library procedure in an application. When the project runs, the first six bitmaps in the \Windows directory are shown as thumbnails (see Figure 15.4).

```
implementation

uses
  LMScreen, LMSys;

{$R *.DFM}

procedure TForm1.FormCreate(Sender: TObject);

var
  GraphicsPath: String;
  I, LastElem: Integer;

begin

  { Display first 6 bitmaps in directory as thumbnails }

  GraphicsPath := WinDir(0) + FileListBox1.FileName;
  FileListBox1.Directory := GraphicsPath;
  LastElem := FileListBox1.Items.Count;

  if LastElem > 6 then
    LastElem := 6;
```

FIGURE 15.4
The ShowTNail library procedure

```
for I := 1 to LastElem do begin
    FileListBox1.ItemIndex := FileListBox1.ItemIndex + 1;
    case I of
        1 : Label1.Caption := ShowTNail (FileListBox1.FileName,
            Image1);
        2 : Label2.Caption := ShowTNail (FileListBox1.FileName,
            Image2);
        3 : Label3.Caption := ShowTNail (FileListBox1.FileName,
            Image3);
        4 : Label4.Caption := ShowTNail (FileListBox1.FileName,
            Image4);
        5 : Label5.Caption := ShowTNail (FileListBox1.FileName,
            Image5);
        6 : Label6.Caption := ShowTNail (FileListBox1.FileName,
            Image6);
    end;
  end;

end;
```

SlowPrint

SlowPrint displays a delayed message on a form. Use it to draw attention to your programs and to emphasize important messages. SlowPrint accepts as an argument the name of a timer control contained on the form. To show the message, the call to SlowPrint must be placed in the Timer1Timer procedure.

Syntax:
```
procedure SlowPrint (Canvas: TCanvas; Msg: String; X, Y: Integer;
                     ctrlTimer: TTimer; FColor, BColor, CColor:
                     TColor);
```

Parameters: Canvas: Canvas on which to display message
Msg: Message to show
X: Relative horizontal coordinate (in pixels) from left edge of form to display message
Y: Relative vertical coordinate (in pixels) from top of form to display message
ctrlTimer: Name of timer component
FColor: Foreground color of message
BColor: Background color of message
CColor: Canvas color

Uses: LMScreen

Returns: Nothing

Example

STRPROC.DPR demonstrates how to use the library routine. When the user clicks on the Slow Print button, a delayed message appears.

```
var
  Form1: TForm1;
  Str2: String;
  xCoord, yCoord, CountIndex : Integer;
  MsgToPrint: String;
  TextColor, BkColor, BlankSpaceColor: TColor;


implementation


{$R *.DFM}


uses
  LMScreen, LMString;


procedure TForm1.btnStrScrollClick(Sender: TObject);
```

```
{ Initialize program for displaying a message
  with a delay effect }

begin

    xCoord := 50;
    yCoord := 100;
    MsgToPrint := 'Hello World!';
    TextColor := clWhite;
    BkColor := clBlue;
    BlankSpaceColor := clAqua;
    timer1.enabled := True;
    btnStrScroll.Enabled := False;

end;

procedure TForm1.Timer1Timer(Sender: TObject);

{ Call library to display message with a delay effect }

begin

  SlowPrint (Canvas, MsgToPrint, xCoord, yCoord, Timer1, TextColor,
            BkColor, BlankSpaceColor);
end;
```

SoundEnabled

SoundEnabled checks whether a sound card is present and capable of playing on a given system. Use it to determine whether the Play button for sound routines in an application should be enabled or visible. SoundEnabled works by testing the capabilities of a machine. To do this, a test wave file must be passed as a parameter to SoundEnabled. This file, however, is only necessary for the test and is not actually played by the library routine.

Syntax:
```
function SoundEnabled (PathName: String; MediaPlayer: TMediaPlayer):
                        Boolean;
```

Parameters: PathName: Path to a test wave file
ctrlMedia: Name of Media Player component

Uses: LMMedia

Returns: **True** if a sound card is present, **False** if not

Example

PLAYVIDEO.DRP shows how to use SoundEnabled. When the program starts, the library function checks for the existence of a sound card. If no sound card is present, a message is shown to report this and the radioAudio radio button is disabled.

```
implementation

uses
  LMMedia;

{$R *.DFM}

procedure TForm1.FormCreate(Sender: TObject);

begin

  { Check whether sound card is present }

  if not (SoundEnabled ('thatsa.wav', MediaPlayer1)) then
        begin
            radioAudio.Enabled := False;
            MessageDlg('No sound card detected.', mtInformation,
                    mbOk], 0);
        end;

end;
```

TickerTape

TickerTape shows an animated message within a ticker tape. Specifically, the message scrolls from the right edge of the ticker tape to the left edge until it disappears. The message then slowly reappears at the right side of the ticker tape and scrolls leftward again.

Syntax: `procedure TickerTape (ScrollMsg: String: imgCtrl: TImage: timerCtrl:`
                                `TTimer);`

Parameters: ScrollMsg: Message to show in ticker tape
                imgCtrl: Image component to use for ticker tape
                timerCtrl: Timer control to time ticker tape

Uses:	LMScreen
Returns:	Nothing

Example

TTICKET.DPR shows how to apply the library procedure. When the program runs, a call to TickerTape is called from the OnTimer event handler. Whenever the timer executes, the TickerTape procedure is called again, creating the illusion of an animated message scrolling within a ticker tape machine (see Figure 15.5).

```
procedure TForm1.Timer1Timer(Sender: TObject);

{ Show animated message scrolling within a
  ticker tape }

var
  ScrollMsg: String;
begin
  ScrollMsg := 'Sample ticker tape message.';
  TickerTape (ScrollMsg, Image1, Timer1);
end;
```

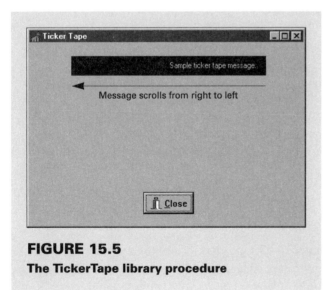

FIGURE 15.5
The TickerTape library procedure

TileBitmap

TileBitmap displays a user-defined graphic on a form with a tiling effect. Use it to create more interesting wallpapers and to give your programs a unique look and feel.

Syntax: `procedure TileBitmap (TileImage: TGraphic; frmCtrl: TForm);`

Parameters: TileImage: Bitmap to display
frmCtrl: Form on which to show tiles

Uses: LMScreen

Returns: Nothing

Example

TILES.DPR shows how to incorporate the library routine in a project. Upon loading, the program generates a new bitmap object and initializes it with a graphic loaded from disk (SEAWEED.BMP). The TileImage object is then passed to the TileBitmap procedure in the FormPaint event handler to create the tiling effect. (When a project runs, Delphi automatically executes the code in the On Paint event handler after the OnCreate, OnShow, and OnActivate events occur.) Figure 15.6 shows how the output appears.

```
var
  Form1: TForm1;
  TileImage: TBitmap;

implementation

uses
  LMScreen;

{$R *.DFM}

procedure TForm1.FormCreate(Sender: TObject);

begin

  { Generate a new bitmap object }

  TileImage := TBitmap.Create;

  Form1.Color := clBlack;

  { Load bitmap from disk }
```

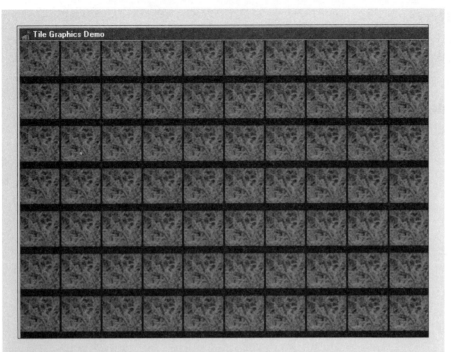

FIGURE 15.6
The TileBitmap library procedure

```
   TileImage.LoadFromFile('seaweed.bmp');

end;

procedure TForm1.FormPaint(Sender: TObject);

{ Show tile effect on form }

begin
   TileBitmap (TileImage, Form1);
end;
```

TransparentButton

The TransparentButton procedure allows you to display clear buttons over a user-defined bitmap. Use this procedure to add elegance to any application. TransparentButton accepts as an argument a label and a bevel component. When placing label controls over image components, often it becomes necessary to use the Edit | Bring to Front command (or BringToFront method) in Delphi so that the labels do not appear behind the image components. This will also ensure that the buttons can be selected at run-time.

Syntax:	`procedure TransparentButton (bevelCtrl: TBevel: lblCtrl: Tlabel:` `btnCaption: String btnColor: TColor);`
Parameters:	bevelCtrl: Bevel component lblCtrl: Label component btnCaption: Caption to appear on button btnColor: Button caption color
Uses:	LMMedia
Returns:	Nothing

Example

BTNCLR.DPR demonstrates how to include the library procedure in an application. The project contains a single form. An image component stretches the inner boundaries of the form and is used to display a background graphic. When the project runs, two transparent buttons appear over the bitmap (see Figure 15.7). These buttons are actually bevel components that use labels to display the button captions. Since a bevel component does not have an OnClick event, the code to determine whether a button is selected is placed instead in the OnClick event handler of the labels.

```
  .    .    .
  .    .    .
implementation

Uses
  LMMedia;

{$R *.DFM}

procedure TForm1.FormCreate(Sender: TObject);

begin

  { Display two transparent buttons over a bitmap }

  TransparentButton(bevel1, label1, 'OK', clYellow);
  TransparentButton(bevel2, label2, 'Exit', clYellow);

end;
```

FIGURE 15.7
The TransparentButton library procedure

```
procedure TForm1.Label1Click(Sender: TObject);
begin
  MessageDlg('OK button selected', mtInformation, [mbOk], 0);
end;


procedure TForm1.label2Click(Sender: TObject);
begin
  MessageDlg('Exit button selected', mtInformation, [mbOk], 0);
  close;
end;
```

OpenRichEdit

SaveRichEdit

SetAlignment

SetBoldFace

SetBullet

SetBlockStyle

SetItalics

SetUnderline

UndoChange

Chapter 16
Rich Edit Routines

The developers' library included with this book incorporates several reusable procedures and functions to make working with memos easier. These routines let you open and save documents, apply text formatting, insert bullets in memos, add boldfacing and underlining, change paragraph alignments, and more. To use these routines, you must add the LMREdit unit to your project. Table 16.1 lists the Rich Edit memo handling routines of the library.

OpenRichEdit

OpenRichEdit loads a Rich Text Format memo from disk. The function uses the Open common dialog to display a list of file choices to the user (see Figure 16.1). The Open dialog lets you retrieve both Rich Text Format documents and plain ASCII files. By default, only files that have an .RTF file extension are displayed. To see a list of text files available, click on the Files of type drop-down list and select the Text Files (.txt) filter.

Syntax: `function OpenRichEdit (rEditCtrl: TRichEdit; OpenDialog: TOpenDialog): String;`

Parameters: rEditCtrl: Name of Rich Edit component that will display the document
                  OpenDialog: Name of TOpenDialog component to use to open document

Uses: LMREdit

Returns: Name of document opened

TABLE 16.1   RICH EDIT MEMO HANDLING ROUTINES OF THE LIBRARY

Library Routine	Description
OpenRichEdit	Loads a RichEdit document from disk.
SaveRichEdit	Saves a RichEdit document to a file.
SetAlignment	Sets the paragraph alignment of a selected block.
SetBoldFace	Boldfaces a selected block.
SetBullet	Inserts or removes a bullet from a RichEdit document.
SetBlockStyle	Sets the font style of a selected block.
SetItalics	Italicizes a selected block.
SetUnderline	Underlines a selected block.
UndoChange	Reverses the last edit operation in a RichEdit document.

Example

The sample Rich Text Editor program (RTE.DPR) demonstrates how to retrieve a document. When the user selects the File | Open... command, the Open dialog appears with a list of file choices. Choosing a file subsequently from the list and clicking on the Open button then causes the document to be loaded into the RichEdit control.

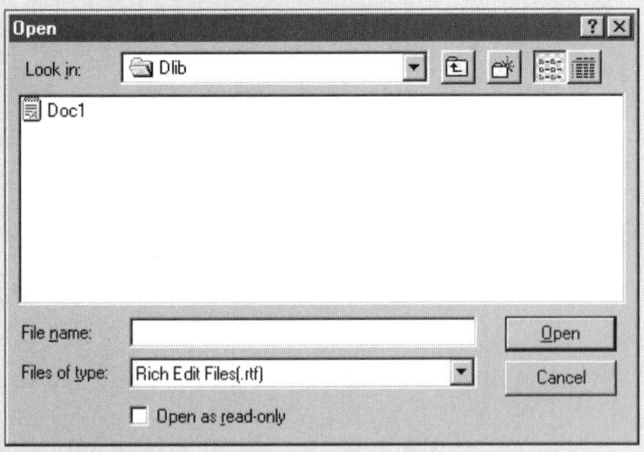

Once a document has been loaded, the name of the file is displayed in the title bar of the active window to remind the user which document is open. The Modified property of the RichEdit component is then set to **False**. This property is useful for keeping track of the file's status. If RichEdit1.Modified = **True**, it means the file has been changed and needs to be updated.

FIGURE 16.1
The Open common dialog

```
procedure TForm1.mnuOpenFileClick(Sender: TObject);

var
  DocFileName: String;

begin

  { Open a Rich Text document }

  DocFileName := OpenRichEdit (RichEdit1, OpenDialog1);

  if DocFileName <> '' then
    begin
      Form1.Caption := DocFileName;
      RichEdit1.Modified := False;
    end;

end;
```

SaveRichEdit

SaveRichEdit saves a Rich Text Format memo to a file. When the *SaveOption* parameter is set to 1 (assist mode), the function displays the Save common dialog. When the *SaveOption* parameter is set to 2 (auto save), the memo is saved without using the Save common dialog. Use this option to update memos that have previously been saved.

Syntax:
```
function SaveRichEdit (rEditCtrl: TRichEdit; SaveDialog: TSaveDialog;
            SaveOption: Integer; FileToSave: String): String;
```

Parameters: rEditCtrl: Name of Rich Edit component containing text to save
SaveDialog: Name of TSaveDialog component to use to display when saving file
SaveOption: 1 = Save document without showing the Save dialog;
    2 = Show Save common dialog
FileToSave: Name of file to create or update

Uses: LMREdit

Returns: Name of file saved

Example

The sample editor (RTE.DPR) demonstrates how to use the SaveRichEdit library routine. When the user selects the File | Save command, the program first checks to see if the document has been saved. As you may recall, when a file is opened, the title bar of the edit window is set to the name of the document retrieved. Ergo, the following code can be used to retrieve this name:

```
{ Get caption on title bar to determine the current
  document's name }

FileToSave := Form1.Caption;
```

The Pos function is then used to determine whether *FileToSave* contains the substring "Untitled". If so, it means the document has not been named and the Save common dialog is displayed to get the name of the file. If *FileToSave* is set to any other value, it means the document has been named and the SaveRichEdit function is called to update the file without showing the Save common dialog.

```
if Pos ('Untitled', FileToSave) = 0 then begin

    { File has NOT been named, so invoke Save As routine }

    SaveOption := 2;

    SaveAs (RichEdit1, SaveDialog1, SaveOption, '');

    end
```

Below is the complete source listing for the save routine:

```
procedure SaveAs (rEdit: TRichEdit; SaveDialog1: TSaveDialog;
         SaveOption: Integer; FileToSave: String);

{ Display Save As dialog so document can either be
  named the first time or renamed }

var
  RetVal: String;

begin

  RetVal := SaveRichEdit (rEdit, SaveDialog1, SaveOption, '');

  If RetVal <> '' then
    Form1.Caption := RetVal;

end;

procedure TForm1.mnuSaveFileClick(Sender: TObject);

{ Save RichEdit document - automatically invoke Save As
  routine if file has not been named }

var
  RetVal, FileToSave: String;
  SaveOption: Integer;

begin

  { Get caption on title bar to determine the current
    document's name }

  FileToSave := Form1.Caption;

  if Pos ('Untitled', FileToSave) = 0 then begin
```

```
            { File has NOT been named, so invoke Save As routine }

            SaveOption := 2;

            SaveAs (RichEdit1, SaveDialog1, SaveOption, '');

            end

        else begin

            { File already has a name, so just save it }

            SaveOption := 1;

            RetVal := SaveRichEdit (RichEdit1, SaveDialog1,
                        SaveOption, FileToSave);

            If RetVal <> '' then
                Form1.Caption := RetVal

        end;

    end;
```

SetAlignment

SetAlignment aligns selected text in a Rich Edit memo. To select the range, you must hold the left mouse button down while dragging the mouse over the range. Alternately, you can select a range by holding the Shift key down and then pressing the left, right, up or down arrow keys.

Syntax: `procedure SetAlignment (rEditCtrl: TRichEdit; AlignOption: Integer);`

Parameters: rEditCtrl: Name of Rich Edit component that contains selected text to align
            AlignOption: 0 = Left justify; 1 = Right justify; 2 = Center

Uses: LMREdit

Returns: Nothing

Example

RTE.DPR demonstrates how to use the library procedure. At run-time, when the user selects a range and clicks on the Left Justify, Right Justify, or Center command, the selected area is reformatted with that alignment (see Figure 16.2).

```
procedure TForm1.mnuLeftJustifyClick(Sender: TObject);

{ Left justify the selected text block }

begin
  SetAlignment (RichEdit1, 0);
end;


procedure TForm1.mnuRightJustifyClick(Sender: TObject);

{ Right justify the selected text block }

begin
  SetAlignment (RichEdit1, 1);
end;


procedure TForm1.mnuCenterClick(Sender: TObject);
```

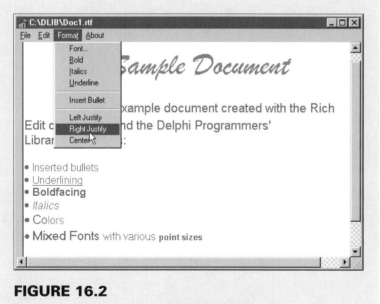

FIGURE 16.2
The Format menu of the RTE.DPR project

```
{ Center the selected text block }


begin
  SetAlignment (RichEdit1, 2);
end;
```

SetBoldFace

SetBoldFace provides an easy way of adding boldfacing to a memo. To apply boldfacing to a range, you must first select the area you wish to format. SetBoldFace works as a toggle—that is, when you call the procedure the first time, the text you select is bold-faced. Afterwards, calling the library procedure again removes the boldfacing.

Syntax: `procedure SetBoldFace (rEditCtrl: TRichEdit);`

Parameters: rEditCtrl: Name of Rich Edit component that contains text to boldface

Uses: LMREdit

Returns: Nothing

Example

The following example, taken from the RTE.DPR project, shows how to use the SetBoldFace procedure. When the user selects a text block and chooses the Format | Bold command, the block is formatted for boldfacing.

```
procedure TForm1.mnuBoldClick(Sender: TObject);


{ Boldface current block }


begin
  SetBoldface (RichEdit1);
end;
```

SetBullet

The SetBullet procedure inserts a bullet into a Rich Edit memo. Like SetBoldFace, the SetBullet procedure works as a toggle permitting you to add/remove bullets with the same handler.

Syntax: `procedure SetBullet (rEditCtrl: TRichEdit);`

Parameters: rEditCtrl: Name of Rich Edit component to insert bullet into

Uses: LMREdit

Returns: Nothing

Example

The following example, taken from RTE.DPR, shows how to incorporate the library routine in an application. When the user selects a range and chooses the Format | Insert Bullet command, a bullet is inserted into the memo. Figure 16.3 shows how the memo appears.

```
procedure TForm1.mnuInsertBullet1Click(Sender: TObject);

{ Insert bullet in RichEdit document }

begin
  SetBullet (RichEdit1);
end;
```

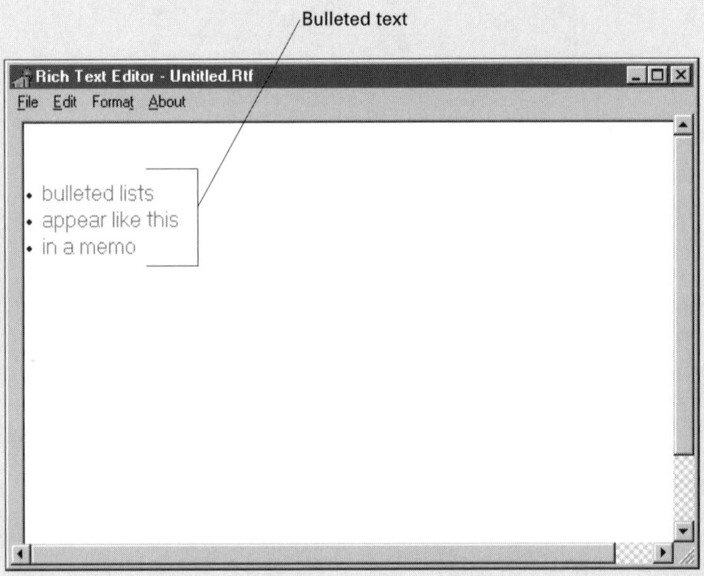

FIGURE 16.3
Inserting bullets into a Rich Edit memo

SetBlockStyle

SetBlockStyle lets you set the style of selected text in a Rich Edit memo. The library procedure accepts as an argument the name of a TFontDialog component. SetBlockStyle uses the component to display the Font common dialog. In addition to the font name and point size, you can set the color of text by clicking on the Color drop-down list (see Figure 16.4).

Syntax:
```
procedure SetBlockStyle (rEditCtrl: TRichEdit; ctrlFontDialog:
                TFontDialog);
```

Parameters: rEditCtrl: Name of Rich Edit component containing memo to format
ctrlFontDialog: Name of TFontDialog on the form

Uses: LMREdit

Returns: Nothing

Example

RTE.DPR shows how to incorporate SetBlockStyle in an application. When the user selects a block and chooses the Format | Font... option, the Font common dialog appears to make a style selection.

```
procedure TForm1.mnuFontClick(Sender: TObject);


{ Set current font, color and point size }


begin
  SetBlockStyle (RichEdit1, FontDialog1);
end;
```

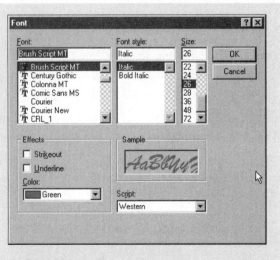

FIGURE 16.4
The Font common dialog

SetItalics

SetItalics provides an easy and convenient way of adding fancy formatting to a memo. To italicize a block, you must first select the text you wish to format. SetItalics works like a toggle switch—that is, when you call the routine the first time, the tagged block will be formatted to appear in an italics style. Upon a subsequent call to the library routine, the italics style will be removed.

Syntax: `procedure SetItalics (rEditCtrl: TRichEdit);`

Parameters: rEditCtrl: Name of Rich Edit component containing block to italicize

Uses: LMREdit

Returns: Nothing

Example

This next example taken from RTE.DPR shows how to add italics style formatting to a memo using the library. When the user selects a block and chooses the Format | Italics command, the block is reformatted in the new style.

```
procedure TForm1.mnuItalicsClick(Sender: TObject);


{ Italicize the currently selected block }


begin
  SetItalics (RichEdit1);
end;
```

SetUnderline

SetUnderline provides an easy way of adding underlining to a memo. To underline text, you must first select the area you wish to format. SetUnderline works like a toggle switch—that is, when you call the procedure the first time, the text you select is underlined. Afterwards, calling the library procedure again removes the underlining.

Syntax: `procedure SetUnderline (rEditCtrl: TRichEdit);`

Parameters: rEditCtrl: Name of Rich Edit component to add underlining to

Uses: LMREdit

Returns: Nothing

Example

The following example, taken from the RTE.DPR project, shows how to use the SetUnderline procedure. When the user selects a text block and chooses the Format | Underline command, the block is formatted with the new style.

```
procedure TForm1.Underline1Click(Sender: TObject);


{ Underline current block }


begin
  SetUnderline (RichEdit1);
end;
```

UndoChange

UndoChange restores a Rich Edit memo back to its previous state after a change has been made by reversing the last editing operation. Specifically, it restores previous formatting, deleted text, line spacing, styles, colors, and more. Use it in all your memo handlers to add an elegant touch to your programs.

Syntax: `procedure UndoChange (rEditCtrl: TRichEdit);`

Parameters: rEditCtrl: Name of Rich Edit component containing memo

Uses: LMREdit

Returns: Nothing

Example

This next example taken from RTE.DPR demonstrates how to use the library routine. After accidentally deleting a line, the user can choose the Edit | Undo command to reverse the operation.

```
procedure TForm1.mnuUndoClick(Sender: TObject);


{ Undo last edit operation }


begin
  UndoChange (RichEdit1);
end;
```

CreateChart

DrawObject

FormatWorksheet

PrintWorksheet

Chapter 17
Spreadsheet Routines

The Developer and Client-Server editions of Delphi include a special ActiveX control called the Formula One component. With Formula One, you can develop your own custom spreadsheet programs. This remarkable custom control provides powerful calculating, formatting, and graphing capabilities. In addition, the Formula One control can both read and write Excel 5.0 spreadsheets.

The developers' library included with this book provides shorthand access to many common spreadsheet operations. Table 17.1 summarizes the spreadsheet procedures discussed in this chapter. In addition to these library routines, Appendix B provides a more detailed look at the component. For more information on how to use the Formula One custom control, see Appendix B.

CreateChart

CreateChart provides an easy way of adding charts to worksheets. Use it to quickly graph data and to add a professional touch to your custom spreadsheet programs. To create a chart, you must first type the values you wish to graph in a worksheet. Afterwards, you indicate the range of data to be included in the graph by selecting the range with a mouse. Once this is done, call the CreateChart procedure to generate the new chart object.

Syntax: `procedure CreateChart (FormulaCtrl: TF1Book);`

Parameters: FormulaCtrl: Name of Formula One component on which to show graph

Uses: LMWSheet

Returns: Nothing

TABLE 17.1   SPREADSHEET ROUTINES OF THE LIBRARY

Procedure	Description
CreateChart	Generates a new chart.
DrawObject	Draws a line, rectangle, circle or arc.
FormatWorksheet	Formats a cell range in a Formula One worksheet.
PrintWorksheet	Prints a Formula One worksheet.

Before the chart is actually created, the Chart Wizard will appear with a list of graph types for you to select from (see Figure 17.1). Clicking on the 3D radio button will display a list of additional 3D chart types. Afterwards, choose Finish to insert the new chart object into the worksheet. The graph will appear minimized until you size it.

To resize the graph:

1 Click on the chart to give it focus.

2 Use the mouse to resize the chart by dragging its size handles.

Example

The following example shows how to apply the library procedure. When the user selects a data range in the worksheet and clicks on the Create Chart button, the Chart Wizard appears with a list of available graph options. Afterwards, by choosing a graph style, the new graph is inserted into the worksheet (see Figure 17.2).

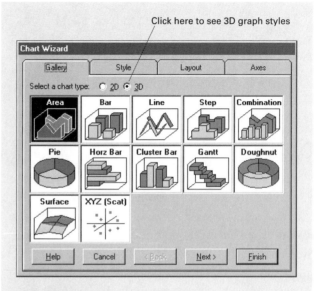

FIGURE 17.1
The Chart Wizard

```
procedure TForm1.btnChartClick(Sender: TObject);


{ Create a new chart object }
```

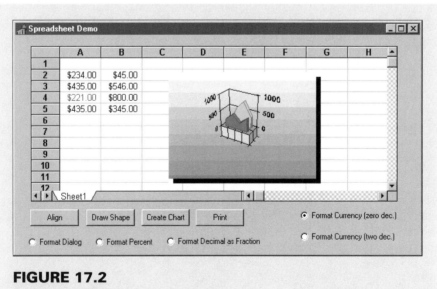

FIGURE 17.2
A sample graph

```
begin
  CreateChart (F1Book1);
end;
```

DrawObject

DrawObject dynamically creates a graphical object from a selected spreadsheet area. Use it to dress up worksheets and to emphasize important data (see Figure 17.3). The wsObjectType parameter determines the type of object that is drawn. Specifically, the procedure permits you to create the following objects: line, rectangle, oval, or arc.

Syntax: `procedure DrawObject (FormulaCtrl: TF1Book; wsObjectType: Integer);`

Parameters: FormulaCtrl: Name of Formula One component
wsObjectType: 1 = Draw line; 2 = Draw rectangle; 3 = Draw oval; 4 = Draw arc

Uses: LMWSheet

Returns: Nothing

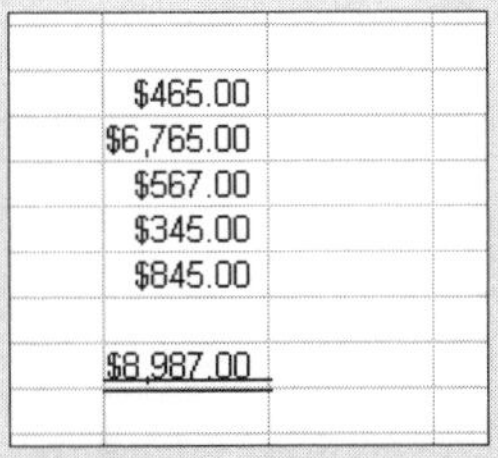

FIGURE 17.3
Sample output for the DrawObject library routine

Example

This next example shows how to insert an object into a worksheet. When the user highlights a cell range, a circle is drawn around the specified area.

```
procedure TForm1.btmCloseClick(Sender: TObject);

{ Draw circle from selected range }

const wsCIRCLE = 3;
```

```
begin
  DrawObject (F1Book1, wsCIRCLE);
end;
```

FormatWorksheet

FormatWorksheet provides a central way of formatting spreadsheet data. Use it to dress up a worksheet before printing. When the FormatOption parameter is set to 4, the Format dialog appears. You can use the Format dialog to change font styles and point sizes and even to add color to worksheets (see Figure 17.4).

Syntax: `procedure FormatWorksheet (FormulaCtrl: TF1Book; FormatOption: Integer);`

Parameters: FormulaCtrl: Name of Formula One component

FormatOption: 0 = Format cells for currency (no decimal places); 1 = Format cells for currency (two decimal places); 2 = Format decimals to appear as fractions; 3 = Format cell range as percent; 4 = Display Format dialog

Uses: LMWSheet

Returns: Nothing

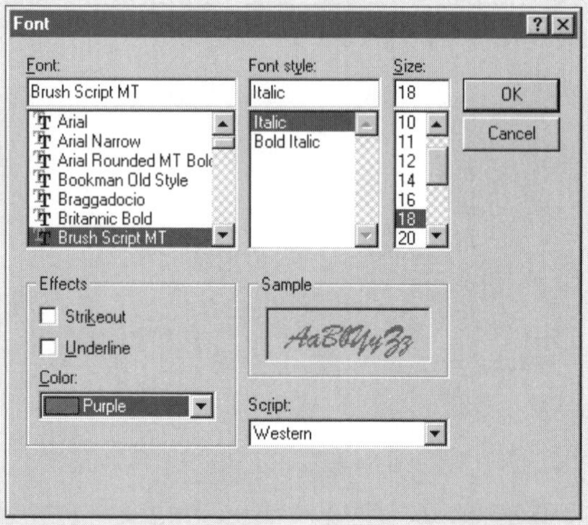

FIGURE 17.4
The Format dialog

Example 1

The following example demonstrates how to incorporate the library procedure in a program. When the user selects a data range and clicks on the Format Currency (two decimal places) radio button, the values in the cells appear formatted as currency with two decimal places.

```
procedure TForm1.RadiobtnFormatCurZer2Click(Sender: TObject);


{ Format spreadsheet range for currency two
  decimal places }


const
  FORMAT_DEC2 = 1;


begin
  FormatWorksheet (F1Book1, FORMAT_DEC2);
end;
```

Example 2

This next example shows how easy it is to expand upon the previous code and achieve other formatting options. Figure 17.5 shows a formatted worksheet created with the library routine.

```
procedure TForm1.RadiobtnFormatCurZer0Click(Sender: TObject);


{ Format spreadsheet range for currency zero
```

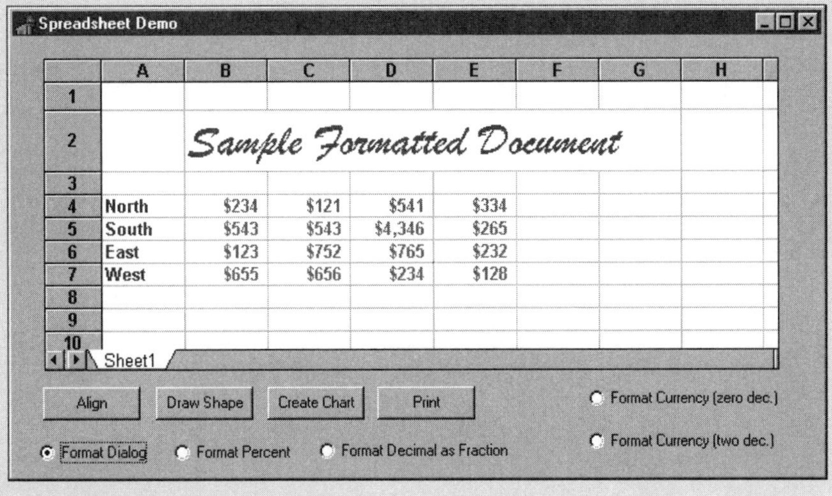

FIGURE 17.5

A formatted worksheet

```
    decimal places }

const
  FORMATZERO = 0;

begin
  FormatWorksheet (F1Book1, FORMATZERO);
end;

procedure TForm1.RadiobtnFormatTextClick(Sender: TObject);

{ Use format dialog to format range }

const
  FORMAT_DIALOG = 4;

begin
  FormatWorksheet (F1Book1, FORMAT_DIALOG);
end;

procedure TForm1.RadiobtnFormatPercentClick(Sender: TObject);

{ Format spreadsheet range for percent }

const
  FORMAT_PERCENT = 3;

begin
  FormatWorksheet (F1Book1, FORMAT_PERCENT);
end;

procedure TForm1.RadiobtnFormatDectoFracClick(Sender: TObject);

{ Format decimals to appear as fractions }

const
  FORMAT_FRAC = 2;
```

```
begin
  FormatWorksheet (F1Book1, FORMAT_FRAC);
end;
```

PrintWorksheet

PrintWorksheet prints a Formula One worksheet with the print options you provide. For draft printing, you may prefer to set the prtBorders and prtGridLines options to **False**. This will cause the worksheets to print faster. The prtColor option can also be disabled to make color formatting appear clearer on a non-color printer.

Syntax:
```
procedure PrintWorksheet (FormulaCtrl: TF1Book; prtBorders,
                          prtGridLines, prtColor: Boolean);
```

Parameters: FormulaCtrl: Name of Formula One component
prtBorders: **True** = Print borders; **False** = Do not print borders
prtGridLines: **True** = Print grid lines; **False** = Do not print grid lines
prtColor: **True** = Print color; **False** = Do not print color

Uses: LMWSheet

Returns: Nothing

Example

This next example shows how to use the PrintWorksheet library procedure. When the user clicks on Print, the Print dialog appears (see Figure 17.6). Afterwards, clicking on OK sends the output to the printer device.

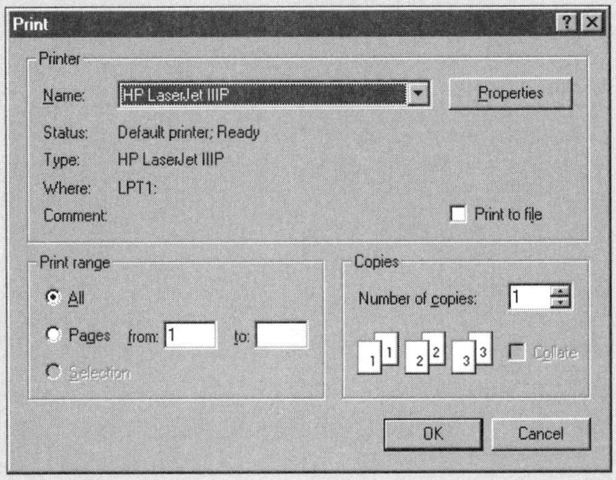

FIGURE 17.6
The Print dialog

```
procedure TForm1.btnPrintClick(Sender: TObject);

{ Print worksheet quickly with borders, grid lines
  and color printing disabled }

var
  prtColor, prtBorders, prtGridLines: Boolean;

begin
  prtBorders := False;
  prtGridLines := False;
  prtColor := False;

  PrintWorksheet (F1Book1, prtBorders, prtGridLines,
                  prtColor);
end;
```

IsNumVal

StrCenter

StrDeleteAll

StrExtractCmd

StrFormatUpper

StrReplaceAll

StrReverse

StrRightChar

StrStripSpaces

Chapter 18
String Routines

The ability to manipulate strings is a key skill among programmers. Often, for example, you may find it is necessary to parse (that is, break down) a string and analyze its different parts. A typical example would be the need to extract a particular item such as a code, drive letter, or search item in a memo. In some cases, you may have to rebuild the string entirely. For instance, some UNIX serial communication programs require you to remove tildes (~) from strings. Delphi provides the low-level tools you need to gain access to the "raw bytes" of a string. The library provides even more functions to help you manipulate strings. Table 18.1 describes the string-handling routines of the library.

IsNumVal

IsNumVal checks a string and returns **True** if the value it holds does not consist of any non-numeric characters. Specifically, for a value to be considered numeric, it must consist only of numbers and an optional decimal point. If more than one decimal point is contained in the string, IsNumVal returns **False**.

Syntax: `IsNumVal (StrVal: String);`

Parameters: StrVal: String to check

Uses: LMString

Returns: **True** if string contains an implicit numeric value, **False** if not

---

TABLE 18.1   STRING MANIPULATION ROUTINES OF THE LIBRARY

Routine	Description
IsNumVal	Returns **True** if a string contains only numeric characters.
StrCenter	Correctly centers a variable length string on a form at run-time.
StrDeleteAll	Deletes all occurrences of a character from a string.
StrExtractCmd	Extracts and returns an argument from a command string.
StrFormatUpper	Capitalizes the first letter of each word in a string.
StrReplaceAll	Replaces all occurrences of a character in a string with another character.
StrReverse	Reverses a string.
StrRightChar	Returns the rightmost character from a string.
StrStripSpaces	Removes blank spaces from a string.

Example

VNUMCHK.DPR shows how to use IsNumVal. When the user enters a value in the edit box, the program tests the value and reports whether the underlying value contained in the string is numeric.

```
procedure TForm1.BitBtn1Click(Sender: TObject);

var
  StrVal: String;

begin

  { Read value from edit component and
    check if it is numeric }

  StrVal := Edit1.Text;

  if IsNumVal (StrVal) then
    MessageDlg('Value is numeric.', mtInformation, [mbOk], 0)
  else
    MessageDlg('Value is not numeric.', mtWarning,
    [mbOk], 0);

end;
```

StrCenter

StrCenter correctly displays a message centered on a form. Although Delphi provides a way of centering objects on a form using the Alignment dialog, Delphi's method fails to recalculate the correct centering after the width of the control has changed at run-time. To avoid this problem, use StrCenter to dynamically center labels after setting the Caption property.

Syntax:	`procedure StrCenter (frmCtrl: TForm; lblCtrl: TLabel);`
Parameters:	frmCtrl: Form to show message
	lblCtrl: Label to use to show message
Uses:	LMMedia
Returns:	Nothing

Example

The following code uses StrCenter to center a message at run-time. When the user clicks on the chkVisible check box, a message is displayed on the form centered within the window (see Figure 18.1).

```
procedure TForm1.chkVisibleClick(Sender: TObject);

{ Play audio/video without displaying
  media player component }

begin

  MediaPlayer1.Visible := not MediaPlayer1.Visible;
  Label1.Caption := 'Click OK to play audio/video  ';

  if not (MediaPlayer1.Visible) then begin
     StrCenter (Form1, Label1);
     Label1.Visible := True;
     end
  else
     Label1.Visible := False;

end;
```

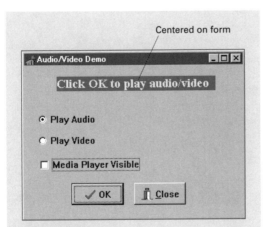

FIGURE 18.1

Centering a string at run-time using the library

StrDeleteAll

StrDeleteAll removes all occurrences of a specified character from a string. Use it in general utility procedures that require the manipulation of strings.

Syntax: `function StrDeleteAll (S: String; DelChar: Char): String;`

Parameters: S: String to purge characters from
DelChar: Character to remove from string

Uses: LMString

Returns: String with all occurrences of *DelChar* removed

Example

STRPROC.DPR demonstrates how to use the library routine. When the user clicks on the Del. Char. button, a message containing the purge character is displayed in a modal dialog box (see Figure 18.2). After calling the library function, the same message is displayed again, this time without the invalid character.

```
procedure TForm1.btnDelCharClick(Sender: TObject);


var
  S: String;
  DelChar: Char;


begin

  { Delete all occurrences of the specified
    character from string }
```

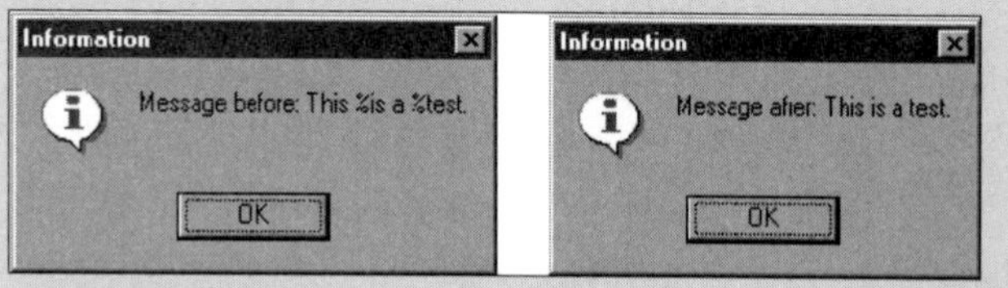

FIGURE 18.2
The message after calling StrDeleteAll

```
   S := 'This %is a %test.';
   DelChar := '%';

   MessageDlg('Message before: ' + S, mtInformation, [mbOk], 0);

   S := StrDeleteAll (S, DelChar);

   MessageDlg('Message after: ' + S, mtInformation, [mbOk], 0);

end;
```

StrExtractCmd

StrExtractCmd provides a quick and simple way of retrieving command parameters
from a string. Use it to read .INI file options and to parse strings. For example, if the
.INI file contains the following command:

```
GraphicsPath=C:\ProgImg
```

setting the optParam option to 1 will return the substring "GraphicsPath". Likewise,
setting the optParam option to 2 returns the substring "C:\ProgImg".

Syntax: `function StrExtractCmd (CommandStr: String; optParam: Integer): String;`

Parameters: CommandStr: Command string to check
optParam: 1 = Extract command name from string; 2 = Extract command value
from string

Uses: LMString

Returns: Extracted command or its associated value

Example

The following example demonstrates how to use the StrExtractCmd library routine.
When the user clicks on the Get Cmd button in STRPROC.DPR, the program reads the
command from an edit component and returns the command portion of the string
(see Figure 18.3). Afterwards, a subsequent call to the StrExtractCmd function retrieves
the command argument.

```
procedure TForm1.btnGetCmdClick(Sender: TObject);
```

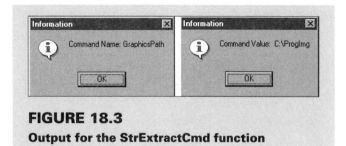

FIGURE 18.3
Output for the StrExtractCmd function

```
var
    CommandStr, CommandName, CommandValue, Msg1, Msg2: String;

begin

    CommandStr := Edit2.Text;

    CommandName := StrExtractCmd (CommandStr, 1);
    CommandValue := StrExtractCmd (CommandStr, 2);

    MessageDlg('Command Name: ' + CommandName,
            mtInformation, [mbOk], 0);

    MessageDlg('Command Value: '+ CommandValue,
            mtInformation, [mbOk], 0);
    .     .     .
```

StrFormatUpper

FormatUpper formats a string by capitalizing the first letter of each word in the string. Use it to format names and messages. For example, if the string is "john smith", FormatUpper will reformat this as "John Smith".

Syntax: `function FormatUpper (Str1: String): String;`

Parameters: Str1: String to format

Uses: LMString

Returns: Formatted string

Example

STRPROC.DPR demonstrates how to use the library routine. When the user clicks on the Format button, the string in the Edit1 edit component is read and formatted (see Figure 18.4).

```
procedure TForm1.btnFormatStrClick(Sender: TObject);

var
  Str1: String;

begin

  { Capitalize first letter of each word in message }

  Str1 := Edit1.Text;
  Edit1.Text := FormatUpper (Str1);
  btnFormatStr.Enabled := False;
```

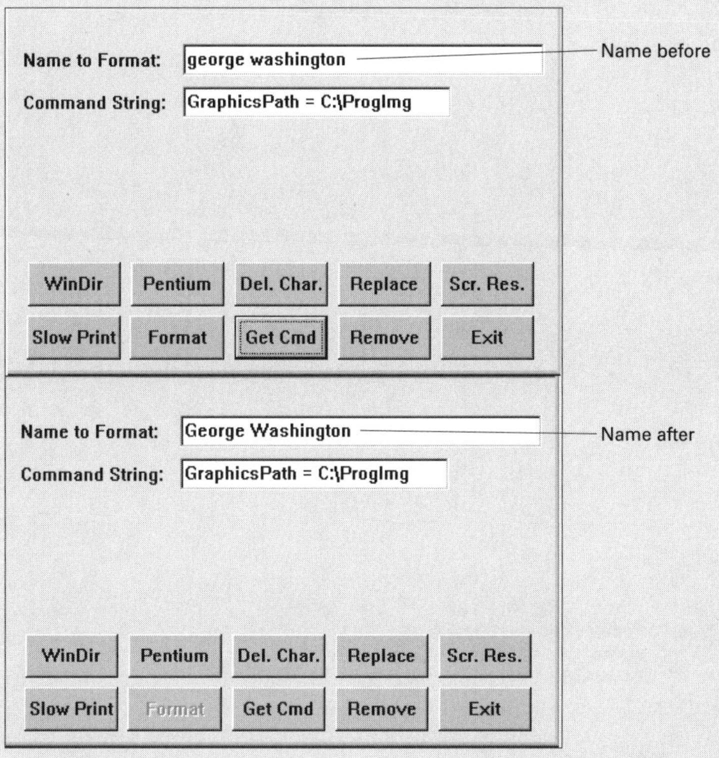

FIGURE 18.4
Output for the FormatUpper library routine

```
end;
```

StrReplaceAll

StrReplaceAll replaces all occurrences of a character in a string with another character.
Use it in general utility procedures that require the manipulation of strings.

Syntax: `function StrReplaceAll (S: String; OldChar, NewChar: Char): String;`

Parameters: S: String to search
OldChar: Character to replace
NewChar: Character to replace OldChar

Uses: LMString

Returns: String with replaced characters

Example

STRPROC.DPR demonstrates how to use the library routine. When the user clicks on
the Replace button, a message containing the character to replace is displayed in a
modal dialog box (see Figure 18.5). After calling the library function, the same message
is displayed again with the replaced character.

```
procedure TForm1.btnReplaceClick(Sender: TObject);

var
  S: String;
  OldChar, NewChar: Char;

begin

  { Replace all occurrences of the specified
```

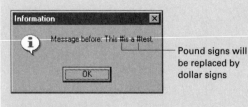

FIGURE 18.5
The message before calling
StrReplaceAll

```
      character with new character }

  S := 'This #is a #test.';
  OldChar := '#';
  NewChar := '$';

  MessageDlg('Message before: ' + S, mtInformation, [mbOk], 0);

  S := StrReplaceAll (S, OldChar, NewChar);

  MessageDlg('Message after: ' + S, mtInformation, [mbOk], 0);

end;
```

StrReverse

StrReverse returns a string with its characters in reverse order. Use it in your security and in your general handlers that require the manipulation of strings.

Syntax: `function StrReverse (S: String): String;`

Parameters: S: String to reverse

Uses: LMString

Returns: Reversed string

Example

STRPRJ.DPR shows how to incorporate StrReverse in a program. When the user clicks on the Encrypt button, a test message is read from an edit component and reversed. Afterwards, the EncryptMsg library function is called to encode the string for security purposes. Figure 18.6 shows how the output appears.

```
procedure TForm1.btnEncryptClick(Sender: TObject);

var
  Msg1, EncodedStr, Temp: String;
  EncryptNo: Integer;

begin

  Msg1 := Edit1.Text;
```

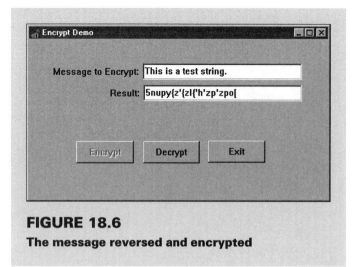

FIGURE 18.6
The message reversed and encrypted

```
    EncryptNo := 7;


    { Encrypt message using the library }


    Msg1 := StrReverse (Msg1);


    EncodedStr := EncryptMsg (Msg1, EncryptNo);
    Edit2.Text := EncodedStr;
    btnDecrypt.Enabled := True;
    btnEncrypt.Enabled := False;


end;
```

StrRightChar

StrRightChar returns the rightmost character in a string. Use it to check paths in your general string handlers.

Syntax: function StrRightChar (S: String): String;

Parameters: S: String to search

Uses: LMSys

Returns: Right character in a string

Example

This next example shows how to use the StrRightChar function. The FileCopyList procedure of the LMSys unit uses StrRightChar to check whether the path the user supplies contains a backslash. If not, the FileCopyList procedure automatically adds a backslash to the path.

```
procedure FileCopyList (ctrlList: TFileListBox; tPath: string);

{ Copy list of files to target path }

var
  SourceFile, TargetPath: String;
  I: Integer;

begin

  Screen.Cursor := crHourGlass;

  if StrRightChar (tPath) <> '\' then
    tPath := tPath + '\';

  for I := 0 to ctrlList.Items.Count - 1 do begin
    SourceFile := ExtractFileName (ctrlList.Items[I]);
    TargetPath := tPath + SourceFile;
    libFileCopy (SourceFile, TargetPath);
    end;

  Screen.Cursor := crDefault;

end;
```

StrStripSpaces

StrStripSpaces purges blank spaces from strings. It is useful for validating purchase order numbers and codes where blank spaces in strings cannot be processed by programs.

Syntax: `function StrStripSpaces (StrMsg: String): String;`

Parameters: StrMsg: String to delete blank spaces from

Uses: LMString

Returns: String with blank spaces removed

Example

This next example shows how to apply StrStripSpaces in an application. When the user clicks on the Remove button in STRPROC.DPR, a string is read in from an edit component and passed to the library to purge the blank spaces. Afterwards, the same string is displayed again in the edit control without the spaces.

```
procedure TForm1.btnStripClick(Sender: TObject);

{ Remove blank spaces from string }

var
  Msg1: String;

begin

  Msg1 := Edit2.Text;
  Edit2.Text := StrStripSpaces (Msg1);
  btnStrip.Enabled := False;

end;
```

ClrStrGrid

InitStringGrid

OpenStringGrid

SaveStringGrid

WeeklySchedule

Chapter 19

String Grid Routines

This chapter focuses on the string grid manipulation routines of the library. With these routines, you will be able to save the contents of a string grid to a file, restore a string grid from a file, quickly clear the cells of a string grid, display weekly date headings at the top of a string grid, and even show a 24-hour time schedule on a grid. Table 19.1 summarizes the string grid handling procedures of the library and explains what each routine does.

ClrStrGrid

ClrStrGrid clears the cell contents of a string grid. Use it whenever you need to change the information you wish to display on a grid.

Syntax:	`procedure ClrStrGrid (strGrid: TStringGrid; optClear: Integer);`
Parameters:	strGrid: Name of StringGrid to clear
	optClear: 0 = Clears only non-fixed rows and columns; 1 = Clears all cells
Uses:	LMGrid
Returns:	Nothing

Example

The GRIDPRJ.DPR project demonstrates how to use the ClrStrGrid procedure. When the user clicks on the Clear Grid button, the contents of the grid are erased so that new appointments can be displayed.

```
procedure TForm1.btnClearGridClick(Sender: TObject);
```

TABLE 19.1 STRING GRID ROUTINES

Routine	Description
ClrStrGrid	Clears a string grid.
InitStringGrid	Initializes a string grid.
OpenStringGrid	Restores a string grid saved with SaveStringGrid.
SaveStringGrid	Saves a string grid to a file.
WeeklySchedule	Displays a weekly time schedule on a string grid.

```
{ Clear the grid }

var
  optclear: Integer;

begin
  optClear := 0;
  ClrStrGrid (StringGrid1, optClear);
  btnRead.Enabled := True;
end;
```

InitStringGrid

InitStringGrid quickly initializes a string grid. Specifically, it sets the number of rows and columns in the grid and also the width for each column.

Syntax:
```
procedure InitStringGrid (strGrid: TStringGrid; TotalCols,
            TotalRows, ColPixels: Integer);
```

Parameters: strGrid: Name of string grid to initialize

TotalCols: Total columns to show

TotalRows: Total rows to show

ColPixels: Number of pixels per column

Uses: LMGrid

Returns: Nothing

Example

This example, taken from the sample application GRIDPRJ.DPR demonstrates how to apply the library routine. When the program loads, the OnCreate event handler calls InitStringGrid to set the grid size to 8 columns, 25 rows, and 90 pixels per column.

```
procedure TForm1.FormCreate(Sender: TObject);

{ Initialize string grid }

var
  TotalCols, TotalRows, ColPixels: Integer;

begin
```

```
  TotalCols := 8;
  TotalRows := 25;
  ColPixels := 90;


  InitStringGrid (StringGrid1, TotalCols, TotalRows, ColPixels);


  Form1.Caption := GetDay + ' ' + DateToStr (Date);


end;
```

Note *The GetDay library routine is included in the LMUtil unit.*

OpenStringGrid

OpenStringGrid restores the contents of a grid previously saved with SaveStringGrid.
Use it to quickly restore information saved to a file.

Syntax: `procedure OpenStringGrid (strGrid: TStringGrid; FileToOpen: String);`

Parameters: strGrid: Name of string grid to restore
              FileToOpen: Name of file to load

Uses: LMGrid

Returns: Nothing

Example

GRIDPRJ.DPR shows how to use the OpenStringGrid procedure. At run-time when
the user clicks on the Read button, the grid is restored from a text file.

```
procedure TForm1.btnReadClick(Sender: TObject);


{ Restore string grid from a file }


begin
  OpenStringGrid (StringGrid1, 'StrGrid.Txt');
end;
```

SaveStringGrid

SaveStringGrid saves the contents of a grid to a text file. By recording the relative row and column numbers of the cells with their associated string values, the file can later be read back using OpenStringGrid.

Syntax: `procedure SaveStringGrid (strGrid: TStringGrid; FileToSave: String);`

Parameters: strGrid: Name of string grid to save
FileToOpen: Name of file to save output to

Uses: LMGrid

Returns: Nothing

Example

The sample appointment scheduling application (GRIDPRJ.DPR), demonstrates how to use the SaveStringGrid library routine. When the user clicks on a cell at run-time, the program automatically schedules a test appointment and displays it on the grid. Afterwards, by choosing the Save command, the weekly appointments are then written to an output file.

```
procedure TForm1.StringGrid1MouseDown(Sender: Tobject; Button:
        TMouseButton; Shift: TShiftState; X, Y: Integer);

{ Create and display test appointment on grid }

var
  ColPos, RowPos: Longint;
  S: String;
begin
  AppointNo := AppointNo + 1;
  S := IntToStr(AppointNo);
  StringGrid1.MouseToCell(X, Y, ColPos, RowPos);
  StringGrid1.Cells[ColPos, RowPos] := 'Appointment' + S;
end;

procedure TForm1.btnSaveClick(Sender: TObject);

{ Save string grid to a file }

begin
  SaveStringGrid (StringGrid1, 'StrGrid.Txt');
  btnClearGrid.Enabled := True;
end;
```

WeeklySchedule

WeeklySchedule displays a weekly time schedule on a string grid. Specifically, it shows an hourly time schedule and the days/dates of the week in the fixed rows and columns of the grid (see Figure 19.1).

Syntax: `procedure WeeklySchedule (strGrid: TStringGrid);`

Parameters: strGrid: Name of StringGrid to show schedule

Uses: LMGrid

Returns: Nothing

Example

GRIDPRJ.DPR uses WeeklySchedule to display the date and time headings for an appointment scheduling application. At run-time, when the user clicks on the Schedule button, the schedule for the current week is displayed.

```
procedure TForm1.btnSchedClick(Sender: TObject);


{ Display weekly schedule }


begin
  WeeklySchedule (StringGrid1);
  btnSave.Enabled := True;
  MessageDlg('Click on a cell to schedule an appointment',
             mtInformation, [mbOk], 0);
end;
```

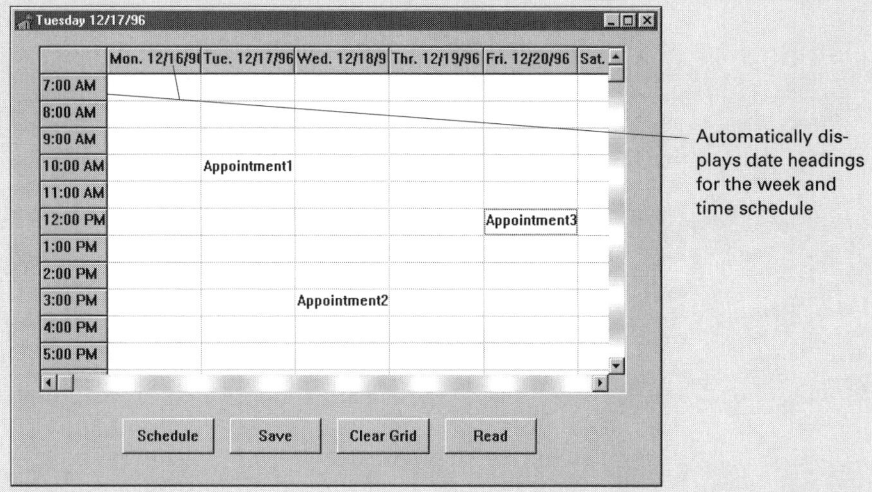

FIGURE 19.1

Output for the WeeklySchedule library routine

ChangeSearchPath

CheckPentium

FileCopyList

WinDir

Chapter 20

System Routines

This chapter introduces the library routines that return information about the hardware, operating environment, and other system parameters. With these routines, you will be able to copy file lists, quickly change search paths, determine the path where Windows is installed, and more. Table 20.1 summarizes the System procedures and functions of the library.

ChangeSearchPath

ChangeSearchPath switches a search path from one drive to another. This routine was written to provide a quick way of substituting the path where a program will look for files that may not be present on a given drive. For example, if you have a program that makes extensive use of graphics, videos, wave files, and so on, some end-users may prefer accessing these files from a CD-ROM. Other users may decide to install the full program for the faster file access speed. With ChangeSearchPath, you can do both. If the files are not found on the CD-ROM, the program can then check an alternate path for the existence of the required (or optional) files.

Syntax: `function ChangeSearchPath (SPath: String): String;`

Parameters: SPath: Search path to change

Uses: LMSys

Returns: New search path

TABLE 20.1   SYSTEM ROUTINES OF THE LIBRARY

Routine	Description
ChangeSearchPath	Changes the drive letter of a search path from a CD-ROM path to the equivalent path on a local hard drive.
CheckPentium	Reports whether a Pentium processor is faulty.
FileCopyList	Copies a list of files in a directory to an alternate drive.
WinDir	Returns the Windows or Windows\System directory.

Example

The following example demonstrates how to use ChangeSearchPath. When the user clicks on the Help button, the application first looks for the help file on the network. If the file is not found, the program will search for the same file on the local hard drive.

```
procedure TForm1.btnShowHelpClick(Sender: TObject);

Var
  SPath: String;

begin

  SPath := 'V:\MYPATH\';

  { Change search path if file not found
    on network drive }

  if not (FileExists (SPath + 'APP.HLP')) then
    SPath := ChangeSearchPath (SPath);

  ShowMessage (SPath);

end;
```

CheckPentium

CheckPentium reports whether a Pentium processor contains a floating-point math error. Some people get nervous at the thought of anything being wrong with their systems. However, if you do discover that your system has this problem, relax! Unless you do a great deal of floating-point arithmetic, chances are you would never even know you had the problem.

Syntax: `function CheckPentium: Integer;`

Parameters: None

Uses: LMString

Returns: 0 if faulty, 1 if not

Example

The following handler demonstrates how to test whether a system has a floating-point math error. At run-time, by clicking on the Pentium button, the program will report the microprocessor status.

```
procedure TForm1.btnPentiumCheckClick(Sender: TObject);

begin

  { Check Pentium processor for floating-point
    arithmetic error}

  if CheckPentium = 0 then
    MessageDlg('uhOwe!', mtWarning, [mbOk], 0)
  else
    MessageDlg('Relax, your system is fine!', mtInformation,
               [mbOk], 0);

end;
```

FileCopyList

The FileCopyList library routine provides a quick and easy way of backing up files in a directory. The procedure accepts as a parameter the name of a file list box that holds the list of files to be copied. The Mask property of the file list box determines which files will be included in the copy. By default, all files listed in the directory specified by the *tPath* parameter will be copied. To limit the scope of files copied, you can specify your own mask. For example, to backup all files ending with a .DAT file extension, you could supply a mask like this *.DAT.

Syntax: `procedure FileCopyList (ctrlList: TFileListBox; tPath: String);`

Parameters: ctrlList: File list box containing list of files to copy
                           tPath: Path indicating where to copy files from

Uses: LMSys

Returns: Nothing

Example

SYS1.DPR shows how to back up the library modules to a floppy. At design-time, the Mask property of FileListBox1 is set to LM*.PAS. When the user clicks on the Backup command, the program asks whether the disk drive is ready for the copy. Upon confirmation, all files in the current directory that begin with the letters *LM* (that is, Library Modules) and end with a .PAS file extension are copied to the floppy drive (see Figure 20.1).

```
procedure TForm1.btnBackupClick(Sender: TObject);

{ Backup list of files in directory matching
  file mask }

Var
  TargetPath: String;

begin

  if MessageDlg('Is disk drive ready?', mtInformation,
     [mbYes, mbNo], 0) = mrYes then begin
     TargetPath := 'A:\';
     FileCopyList (FileListBox1, TargetPath);
     end;

end;
```

Tip *By setting the Visible property of the TFileListBox control to **False**, you can copy files without displaying them to the user.*

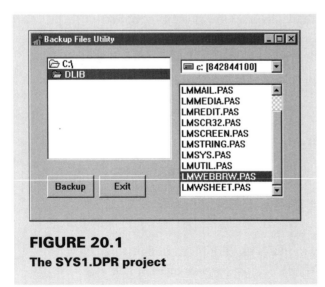

FIGURE 20.1
The SYS1.DPR project

WinDir

WinDir returns the path where Windows is installed on a system. The function is easy to use and provides an alternative to the awkward Windows API function GetWindowsDirectory.

Syntax: `function WinDir (optWin: Integer ): String;`

Parameters: optWin: 0 = Return \Windows path; 1 = Return \Windows\System path

Uses: LMString

Returns: Path where Windows is installed

Example

STRPROC.DPR shows how to incorporate the library routine in an application. When the user clicks on the WinDir button, the program reports the path where Windows is installed in a modal dialog box.

```
procedure TForm1.btnGetWinClick(Sender: TObject);

{ Get Windows path }

begin
  MessageDlg(WinDir(0), mtInformation, [mbOk], 0);
end;
```

BrowseWebPage

ComparePaths

ConvertFraction

DecryptMsg

EncryptMsg

GetDay

GetFTPDir

NextControl

SearchListItem

SendEMailMsg

ShowHelpTopic

Chapter 21

Utility and Web Connectivity Routines

This chapter discusses the various ad hoc procedures and functions of the library. Although discussed last, the routines presented here are by no means the least significant. In this chapter, you will learn how to create custom Web browsers, send e-mail over the Internet, connect to FTP servers, create context-sensitive Help for applications, create high-level security handlers, and more. Table 21.1 discusses the library routines discussed in this chapter.

BrowseWebPage

With the BrowseWebPage library procedure, you can create your own custom Web browser in less than five minutes! The one-line procedure call makes the library routine easy to use and virtually effortless to implement.

Syntax:
```
procedure BrowseWebPage (ctrlHTML: THTML; ctrlComboBox:
            TComboBox);
```

Parameters: ctrlHTML: HTML component to use for connection
ctrlComboBox: Combo box to hold list of URLs visited during session

Uses: LMWebBrw

Returns: Nothing

TABLE 21.1   UTILITY AND WEB CONNECTIVITY ROUTINES OF THE LIBRARY

Subroutine	Description
BrowseWebPage	Loads and displays an HTML document.
ComparePaths	Compares two directories and creates a list of files that are not common between paths.
ConvertFraction	Converts a decimal to a fraction.
DecryptMsg	Decrypts a string encrypted with EncryptMsg.
EncryptMsg	Encrypts a message for security purposes.
GetDay	Returns the current day of the week.
GetFTPDir	Returns directory information from an FTP server.
NextControl	Enables tabbing with the Enter key.
SearchListItem	Searches a list box and returns the closest match to keys typed in an edit component.
SendEMailMsg	Sends e-mail over the Internet.
ShowHelpTopic	Displays context-sensitive Help for an application.

Example

The following code fragment shows how to create a simple Web browser (see Figure 21.1). The btnOK event handler shows the basic code needed to activate the browser and load a Web page.

```
procedure TForm1.btnOKClick(Sender: TObject);

{ Start Web Browser if not already running and
  go to page indicated by ComboBox1.Text }

begin
  Screen.Cursor := crHourGlass;
  Timer1.Enabled := True;
  BrowseWebPage (HTML1, ComboBox1);
end;
```

The complete source listing for this project is discussed in Chapter 13, "Delphi and the Internet." To perform a simple test, however, only the call to BrowseWebPage is needed:

```
BrowseWebPage (HTML1, ComboBox1);
```

BrowseWebPage uses the THTML component to load HTML pages. By passing a combo box on the form that contains the name of a URL, BrowseWebPage will load the

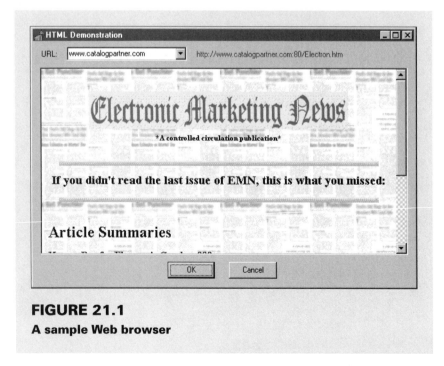

FIGURE 21.1

A sample Web browser

page associated with the URL. For example, if the Text property of ComboBox1 is set to www.borland.com, the program will load Borland's home page.

> **Note** *Before running this example, you must start your Internet dialer service.*

ComparePaths

ComparePaths compares two paths and creates a list of files not common between them. This procedure can be useful when trying to determine the difference between versions of a program or in daily backups.

Syntax: `procedure ComparePaths (ctrlFileList: TFileListBox; ctrlListBox:`
                                `TListBox; ComparePath: String);`

Parameters: ctrlFileList: File list box containing files to compare against
                ctrlListBox: List box to show output
                ComparePath: Path to comparison directory

Uses: LMSys

Returns: Nothing

Example

COMPARE.DPR uses the library routine to display a list of files not common between paths. When the Compare button is selected by the user, the program displays a list of files in the current directory that are not present in the other directory.

```
procedure TForm1.btnCompareClick(Sender: TObject);

{ Compare files in directories and return list
  of files not common between paths }

var
  ComparePath: String;

begin
  ComparePath := Edit1.Text;
  ComparePaths (FileListBox1, ListBox1, ComparePath);
end;
```

ConvertFraction

ConvertFraction returns the closest fraction to a floating-point expression. For example, if the number is 23.5, then ConvertFraction returns 1/2. To display the whole part of the number with the answer, use the Trunc function.

Syntax:	`function ConvertFraction (N: Extended): String;`
Parameters:	N: Number to format
Uses:	LMUtil
Returns:	The decimal part of a number formatted as a fraction

Example

The following event handler demonstrates how to incorporate the library routine in an application. When the btnConvert button is selected, the program reads a number from an edit control. Afterwards, the value is converted to a string with the decimal part of the answer appearing as a fraction. Figure 21.2 shows how the output appears.

```
procedure TForm1.btnConvertClick(Sender: TObject);


{ Get real-type number and format the decimal
  part of the value as a fraction }


var
  N: Extended;
  S: String;
  WholeNum: Integer;
begin
  N := StrToFloat(Edit1.Text);
  S := ConvertFraction (N);
  WholeNum := Trunc (N);
```

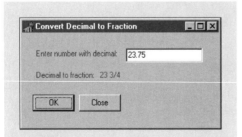

FIGURE 21.2

Output for the ConvertFraction function

```
    lblAnswer.Caption := IntToStr (WholeNum) + ' ' + S;
end;
```

DecryptMsg

DecryptMsg decrypts a string encrypted with the library function EncryptMsg. To successfully decrypt a message, the same value used to encrypt the message must be applied. For example, if the message was originally encrypted by seven characters, you must also decrypt it by the same number of characters.

> **Caution** *Never experiment using EncryptMsg or DecryptMsg without backing up your files.*

Syntax: `function DecryptMsg (Msg1: String; DecryptNo: Integer): String;`

Parameters: Msg1: String to decrypt

Uses: LMString

Returns: String decrypted

Example

The STRPRJ.DPR project shows how to decrypt a string encrypted with EncryptMsg. When the Decrypt button is selected, the program reads the string to decrypt from an edit control. For security purposes, the string has been reversed, using the StrReverse function. Therefore, before decrypting the string, a call is made to StrReverse again. Afterwards, the string is decrypted and displayed back to the user.

```
procedure TForm1.btnDecryptClick(Sender: TObject);

var
  Msg1, DecodedStr: String;
  DecryptNo: Integer;

begin

  Msg1 := Edit2.Text;
  DecryptNo := 7;

  { Decrypt message using the library }

  Msg1 := StrReverse (Msg1);
```

```
    DecodedStr := DecryptMsg (Msg1, DecryptNo);
    Edit2.Text := DecodedStr;


    btnEncrypt.Enabled := True;
    btnDecrypt.Enabled := False;


end;
```

EncryptMsg

EncryptMsg encrypts a message for security purposes. The value of the *EncryptNo* parameter indicates how much each character in the string should be encrpyted by. To maximize your security, you can make use of other library functions as well, such as StrReverse, FormatUpper, StrReplaceAll, and so on. For example, after encrypting the message, you can reverse the string with StrReverse, then reformat it with StrFormatUpper, and encrypt the string again with a different encryption amount. By combining library routines this way, you can devise your own unique security system. Since encrypting a string once is not enough to guarantee an airtight security system, for high-level security, you will probably want to do more.

Keep in mind, however, that anything you encrypt and encode you must also be able to decrypt and decode. Therefore, it is important that you *always* keep a backup of any important data files, programs, and so on and *never* experiment on important files until you are sure that you know what you are doing and have thoroughly tested your security system.

> **Tip** *Use the Library function GetDay (discussed below) and the FileCopyList procedure to back up files to a different path each day of the week. For example, on Monday copy files to the \BACKUP\MONDAY directory, on Tuesday copy files to the \BACKUP\TUESDAY directory, and so on. By placing the executable program in your Windows Startup group, the program will automatically back up files whenever you load Windows.*

Syntax:	`function EncryptMsg (Msg1: String; EncryptNo: Integer): String;`
Parameters:	Msg1: String to encrypt
	EncryptNo: Value used to encrpyt string
Uses:	LMString
Returns:	Encrypted string

Example

The following code, taken from the STRPRJ.DPR project, demonstrates how to encrypt a message. At run-time, when the btnEncrypt button is selected, a test string is reversed and encrpyted. Figure 21.3 shows how the output appears.

```
procedure TForm1.btnEncryptClick(Sender: TObject);

var
  Msg1, EncodedStr: String;
  EncryptNo: Integer;

begin

  Msg1 := Edit1.Text;

  EncryptNo := 7;

  { Encrypt message using the library }

  Msg1 := StrReverse (Msg1);

  EncodedStr := EncryptMsg (Msg1, EncryptNo);
  Edit2.Text := EncodedStr;
  btnDecrypt.Enabled := True;
  btnEncrypt.Enabled := False;

end;
```

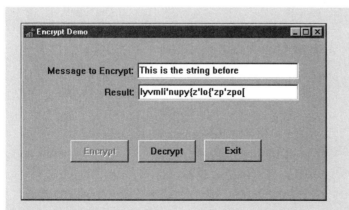

FIGURE 21.3

A message encrypted with the EncryptMsg function

GetDay

GetDay provides an easy way of determining the current day of the week. Use it in any application that displays date headings or maintains a log of weekly events.

Syntax: `function GetDay: String;`

Parameters: None

Uses: LMUtil

Returns: Current day of week

Example

GRIDPRJ.DPR uses GetDay to display the current day of the week in the title bar of a form. Figure 21.4 shows how the output appears.

```
procedure TForm1.FormCreate(Sender: TObject);


{ Initialize string grid }


var
  TotalCols, TotalRows, ColPixels: Integer;


begin

  TotalCols := 8;
```

FIGURE 21.4
Output for the GetDay function

```
    TotalRows := 25;
    ColPixels := 90;

    InitStringGrid (StringGrid1, TotalCols, TotalRows,
                  ColPixels);

    Form1.Caption := GetDay + ' ' + DateToStr (date);

end;
```

GetFTPDir

GetFTPDir displays a list of file information on an FTP server. The library routine is easy to use and provides quick access to directory structures residing on a remote host.

Syntax:
```
procedure GetFTPDir (ctrlListView: TListView; File_Name: Variant; File_Size:
                    Variant; RefreshStatus: Boolean);
```

Parameters: ctrlListView: Name of TListView component to show directory information

File_Name: Variant that indicates name of current file (use the OnListItem event of the FTP Client ActiveX Control to get this value)

File_Size: Variant that indicates size of current file (use the OnListItem event of the FTP Client ActiveX Control to get this value)

RefreshStatus: **True** = Clear list before showing current file; **False** = Append file to active directory listing

Uses: LMFTP

Returns: Nothing

Example

The following example demonstrates how to retrieve directory information from a server using the File Transfer Protocol and the library. Below is the basic code used to get the directory/file listings. For more information on FTP, see Chapter 13, "Delphi and the Internet."

```
  .         .          .
private
   { Private declarations }
   RefreshStatus: Boolean;
public
   { Public declarations }
```

```
end;

var
  Form1: TForm1;

implementation

Uses
  LMFTP;

{$R *.DFM}

procedure TForm1.btnConnectClick(Sender: TObject);

{ Connect to FTP server }

begin

  with FTP1 do begin
      RemoteHost := 'ftp.borland.com';
      RemotePort := 21;
      Connect(RemoteHost, RemotePort);
      end;

end;

procedure TForm1.FTP1ListItem(Sender: TObject; const Item: Variant);

{ Display directory and file information read from server }

begin
  GetFTPDir (ListView1, Item.FileName, Item.Size, RefreshStatus);
  RefreshStatus := False;
end;

procedure TForm1.FTP1ProtocolStateChanged(Sender: TObject;
  ProtocolState: Smallint);

begin
```

```
  case ProtocolState of

    { Indicate user id and password }

    ftpAuthentication: FTP1.Authenticate('anonymous', 'emailaddr');

    { Invoke list method to get current directory info. }

    ftpTransaction: FTP1.List('./');

    end;

end;

procedure TForm1.FTP1StateChanged(Sender: TObject; State: Smallint);

{ Get status of control and display in label }

begin
  case FTP1.State of
    prcConnecting   : Label1.Caption := 'Connecting to server...';
    prcResolvingHost: Label1.Caption := 'Resolving host...';
    prcHostResolved : Label1.Caption := 'Host resolved';
    prcConnected    : Label1.Caption := 'Connected to server';
    prcDisconnecting: Label1.Caption := 'Disconnecting...';
    prcDisconnected : Label1.Caption := 'Disconnected';
  end;

  { Use delay to see message status }

  Sleep (1000);
  Application.ProcessMessages;

end;

procedure TForm1.btnShowRootClick(Sender: TObject);

{ Show files on root of server }

begin
```

```
    Screen.Cursor := crHourGlass;
    RefreshStatus := True;
    FTP1.List('./');
    Screen.Cursor := crDefault;
end;


procedure TForm1.btnShowDirClick(Sender: TObject);

{ Show files in pub directory on server }

begin
    Screen.Cursor := crHourGlass;
    RefreshStatus := True;
    FTP1.List('./pub/');
    Screen.Cursor := crDefault;
end;


end.
```

NextControl

NextControl enables tabbing with the Enter key. Use it to provide users with an easier way of switching focus among controls and for fast data entry.

Syntax: `function NextControl (frmCtrl: TForm; KeyPressed: Char): Char;`

Parameters: frmCtrl: Current form name
              Key: Argument supplied from FormKeyPress event

Uses: LMScreen

Returns: Last key pressed

Example

STRPROC.DPR shows how to use the library routine. After typing a value in an edit control, when the user presses the Enter key, the next control in the tab order receives focus.

```
procedure TForm1.FormKeyPress(Sender: TObject; var Key: Char);

{ Move to next control when Enter key is pressed
```

```
      Note: This code must be placed in the FormKeyPress event
      handler. To enable tabbing with the Enter key, you must
      also set the KeyPreview property of the form to True }


begin
   Key := NextControl (Form1, Key);
end;
```

SearchListItem

SearchListItem searches a list box and returns the closest match to keys typed in an edit control. Use it to add an elegant touch to any of your programs.

Syntax: `procedure SearchListItem (ctrlEdit: TEdit; ctrlList: TListBox);`

Parameters: ctrlEdit: Edit component in which keystrokes will be entered
                    ctrlList: List box to search

Uses: LMUtil

Returns: Nothing

Example

LBOX1.DPR demonstrates the use of the library routine SearchListItem. When the user types in the Edit1 edit component, the program automatically returns the closest match to keys typed (see Figure 21.5).

```
procedure TForm1.Edit1Change(Sender: TObject);
```

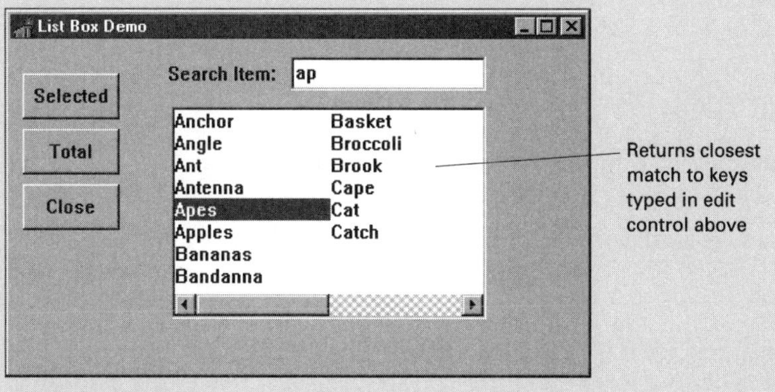

FIGURE 21.5
The SearchListItem procedure

```
{ Search through list box and return closest
  match to keys typed }


begin
   SearchListItem (Edit1, ListBox1);
end;
```

SendEMailMsg

SendEMailMsg sends a message over the Internet. The library routine is easy to use and reliable. This section provides a quick start to sending e-mail. For more information, see Chapter 13, "Delphi and the Internet."

Syntax:
```
procedure SendEMailMsg (ctrlSMTP: TSMTP; editSendTo, editFrom,
               editCC, editSubject: TEdit; ctrlMemo: TMemo);
```

Parameters: ctrlSMTP: Name of TSMTP component to use for sending mail

editSendTo: Name of edit control in which user types address (sender's address). This must be provided as an Internet address and not as a CompuServe, AOL, or other type of address. For example, if the sender's CompuServe account is 123456,7890, you would specify this as 123456.7890@compuserve.com.

editFrom: Edit control that provides your Internet e-mail address

editCC: Edit control that provides an optional e-mail address to which mail may be redirected

editSubject: Edit control indicating the title (description of the message)

ctrlMemo: Name of TMemo component containing memo to send

Uses: LMMail

Returns: Nothing

> **Note** *When mailing to a CompuServe account, be sure to replace the comma with a period as indicated in the Parameters example.*

Example

The following program demonstrates how to connect to an SMTP server and make transmissions. Figure 21.6 shows what controls are needed to run this example. For more information on how to send e-mail from Delphi, see Chapter 13, "Delphi and the Internet."

```
procedure TForm1.btnConnectClick(Sender: TObject);


{ Make connection to SMTP server }
```

```
begin

  Screen.Cursor := crHourGlass;

  if SMTP1.State = prcConnected then
    SMTP1.Quit
  else
    if SMTP1.State = prcDisconnected then begin
      SMTP1.RemoteHost := editServName.Text;
      SMTP1.Connect(GetNoParam, GetNoParam);
      Application.ProcessMessages;
      Screen.Cursor := crDefault;
      btnSend.Enabled := True;
      end;

end;

procedure TForm1.btnSendClick(Sender: TObject);

begin

  { Make sure user is connected }

  if not (SMTP1.State = prcConnected) then begin
    MessageDlg('Not connected to SMTP server', mtError, [mbOK], 0);
```

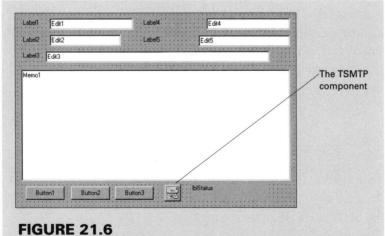

FIGURE 21.6
Controls for the SendEMailMsg library routine

```
      exit;
    end;


  while SMTP1.Busy do
      Application.ProcessMessages;

  { Send the message }

  SendEMailMsg (SMTP1, editSendTo, editFrom, editRedirectTo,
            editSubject, Memo1);

end;
```

ShowHelpTopic

ShowHelpTopic displays context-sensitive Help for an application. In order to show context-sensitive Help, you must indicate the Help topic name (*TopicName*) the same way it is defined in the .HLP file.

> **Note** *To create the .HLP file, you can use Microsoft Help Workshop (included with Delphi) or any third-party equivalent like Visual Help Pro by Winware, Inc., The Help Magician by Software Interface Inc., HelpGen by Rimrock Software, or others.*

Syntax:
```
procedure ShowHelpTopic (HelpFileName: String; HelpOption: Integer;
                          TopicName: String);
```

Parameters: HelpFileName: Name of .HLP file to display

HelpOption: 0 = Show main Help screen (Help Contents); 1 = Show Help Index; 2 = Show context-sensitive Help for a particular Help topic

TopicName: Help topic to show (applies only when *HelpOption* is set to 2)

Uses: LMUtil

Returns: Nothing

Example

The following code (taken from the SHOWHLP.DPR project) demonstrates how to display Help for an application. When the user clicks on the Help bitbtn control, the program invokes the Help Index page of DELPHI.HLP (see Figure 21.7).

```
procedure TForm1.btnHelpClick(Sender: TObject);
```

BitBtn with Kind
property set to
bkHelp

FIGURE 21.7
The SHOWHLP.DPR project

```
{ Demonstrate how to invoke Help using
  the library procedure ShowHelpTopic }

const
  HELP_INDEX = 1;

var
  HelpOption: Integer;
  HelpFileName, HelpTopicName: String;

begin

  HelpFileName := 'DELPHI.HLP';
  HelpOption := HELP_INDEX;
  HelpTopicName := '';

  ShowHelpTopic (HelpFileName, HelpOption, HelpTopicName);

end;
```

Appendix A
What's on the CD

Installing the CD

The CD-ROM included with this book contains 13 reusable code modules packed with dozens of reusable procedures and functions. These routines are designed to help you maximize your productivity as a developer and to make the most out of Delphi. The example files demonstrate how to incorporate library routines in projects. Before you can access these projects, you must install them to a hard drive. The install program on the CD, SETUP.EXE, will install these files for you. To run this program:

1 In Windows 95 or Windows NT4, choose the Start button.

2 Click on Run.

3 Enter your CD-ROM drive letter and the name of the setup program. For example, if your CD-ROM drive is D:\ then you would type D:\SETUP.

Afterwards, click on OK and follow the instructions in the setup program to install the library modules and example projects. Once installed, you can access these files by loading Delphi and opening one of the projects in the directory where you installed the examples. For instance, if you chose to install the library modules and example programs in the default path (C:\DLIB), you would switch to that directory and open one of the projects listed in the file Open window. To incorporate a library routine in a program, use the File|Add to Project… command in Delphi to add the module to your project and then type the name of the unit that references the library routine in the form's Uses clause. For more information on using the developers' library included with this book, see Chapter 5, "Working with Procedures and Functions."

The CD-ROM also includes a demo by Kai's Power Goo by Metatools and an associated text file. This video demonstrates how to apply real-time image warping effects in .AVI files (see Chapter 11 and the GOO.TXT file on the CD).

Troubleshooting the Install Program

In the unlikely event that you experience problems trying to install the files on the CD-ROM, the following steps can often be used to resolve most common problems:

▶ Be sure you have enough space on your hard drive to perform the install. The Setup program requires a minimum of 2.2MB of free disk space and 6MB for a complete install.

▶ Before running Setup, you may wish to turn off your screen saver and restart Windows. This will ensure that other programs running (or previously running) on your system will be less likely to conflict with SETUP.EXE.

▶ If the install program cannot create a directory on your hard drive for the sample projects/library modules, be sure that you have write permission to that drive and that no file on that drive has the same name as the directory you are trying to install to. Usually, installing the files to another drive/directory will resolve this.

If you still experience problems trying to install the example files after repeated attempts, refer to the README2.TXT file for manual instructions on how to install the CD.

Appendix B
Using the Formula One Component

The Developer and Client/Server Suite editions of Delphi include a special .OCX called the Formula One component which permits you to create and manipulate worksheets. The library includes four special routines to help you take advantage of this component. For example, with the CreateChart procedure, you can interactively generate a chart object in a worksheet. This appendix supplies additional information on using the control.

Performing Calculations

To enter an expression in a Formula One worksheet cell, you precede the formula with an equal sign (=). For example, to add the values in cells A1 and A2 you type =A1+A2. Once you press Enter, the answer will appear in the current cell. You can also add a range of cells the following way:

```
=SUM(C1:C7)
```

The **Sum** function totals the specified range (C1 to C7). Like Excel, you must use a colon to specify a range. You can also perform other common statistical operations using the **Average**, **Min,** and **Max** functions. For example:

=MAX(B3:B6)	Returns the maximum value contained in the range B3 to B6.
=MIN(B3:B6)	Returns the minimum value contained in the range B3 to B6.
=AVERAGE(B3:B6)	Returns the average value of the range B3 to B6.

Using Conditional Operators

Formula One worksheets can also contain conditional expressions to perform calculations based on varying parameters. To execute a conditional expression, you use the **If** function. The syntax of the **If** function is:

```
If (condition, true path, false path)
```

For example:

```
=IF(B1>B2,"Cleared","Uncleared")
```

compares the values in two cells and displays a string based upon the answer. If the value in cell B1 is greater than B2, then the message "Cleared" is displayed in the current cell. Otherwise "Uncleared" appears. You can also perform mathematical expressions using **If**. For example:

```
=IF(A1>100,C5*D5,0)
```

means that if cell A1 is greater than 100, the **If** function multiplies C5 times D5 and shows the answer in the current cell. Otherwise the function returns 0.

Writing Code to Interface with a Spreadsheet

In addition to its built-in functions, the Formula One component provides the ability to manipulate worksheets from programs. This extremely powerful feature permits you to customize the component in ways that would not be possible in Lotus or Excel. For example, you can define your own worksheet functions using native Object Pascal code, customize the environment to make working easier, and compile the spreadsheet program as a stand-alone executable application that runs without any external package to support it.

Determining the Active Cell

The Row and Col properties of the Formula One component allow you to get/set the current cell position. Each intersection of a row and column on the grid marks a different cell location. For instance, position 2, 6 refers to column 2, row 6 (or cell B6). The following example shows how this can be used in a program:

```
procedure TForm1.btnMoveToClick(Sender: TObject);

{ Display string in column 4, row 8 }

begin

  F1Book1.Col := 4;
  F1Book1.Row := 8;
  F1Book1.Text := 'Please wait...';

end;
```

In the preceding example, the current cell is set to column 4, row 8 (that is, cell position D8). Afterwards, a message is displayed in the cell. This next example shows how to retrieve the current cell coordinates:

```
procedure TForm1.btnCellPosClick(Sender: TObject);

{ Get current cell position }

var
  CurRow, CurCol: Integer;
  strCurrentRow, strCurrentCol: String;

begin

  CurRow := F1Book1.Row;
  CurCol := F1Book1.Col;

  Str(CurRow, strCurrentRow);
  Str(CurCol, strCurrentCol);

  ShowMessage('Row : ' + strCurrentRow + ' Column: ' +
              strCurrentCol);
end;
```

To determine the current cell, the CurRow and CurCol variables are set to the Row and Col properties respectively. Afterwards, the cell coordinates are converted to strings and displayed with **ShowMessage**.

Reading Cell Ranges

Like Lotus 1-2-3 and Excel, the Formula One component permits you to select a range of cells. To tag a cell range, click on a cell and hold the left button down while dragging the mouse cursor across the range. Then use the **SelStartRow**, **SelStartCol**, **SelEndRow**, and **SelEndCol** properties to determine the range of the selected area. For example:

```
procedure TForm1.btnAddRangeClick(Sender: TObject);

var StartRow, StartCol, EndRow, EndCol,
    Total, Cell_Value, I, Code: Integer;
    strTotal: String;

begin

  Total := 0;
  strTotal := '';
```

```
    { Get starting row and column }

    StartRow := F1Book1.SelStartRow;
    StartCol := F1Book1.SelStartCol;
    EndRow := F1Book1.SelEndRow;
    EndCol := F1Book1.SelEndCol;

    { Set active column }

    F1Book1.Col := StartCol;

    { Total value of selected range }

    for I := StartRow to EndRow do
        begin
          F1Book1.Row := I;
          Val(F1Book1.Text, Cell_Value, Code);
          Total := Total + Cell_Value;
        end;

    { Convert answer to string and display result }

    Str (Total, strTotal);
    ShowMessage (strTotal);

end;
```

This code will add the current cell values and display the answer in a modal dialog box. Using this technique, you can easily create your own standard handlers to automate many common worksheet tasks. For instance, you can define your own toolbar and use the buttons on the toolbar to automatically add columns, format cells, copy ranges, and more.

Saving and Retrieving Worksheets

The Formula One component allows you to save worksheets in both Excel 5 format and in its own native format. Worksheets saved in F1FileFormulaOne3 format can incorporate graphs (see Chapter 17, "Spreadsheet Routines"). Worksheets saved in

F1FileExcel5 format do not support charting but can be exported to Excel. The following example shows how to save a worksheet in Formula One's native format:

```
procedure TForm1.btnWriteClick(Sender: TObject);

{ Save worksheet }

var
  SSheetType: SmallInt;
begin
  SSheetType := F1FileFormulaOne3;
  F1Book1.Write ('Sheet1.xls', SSheetType);
end;
```

Once saved, the worksheet can be retrieved like this:

```
procedure TForm1.btnReadClick(Sender: TObject);

{ Retrieve worksheet }

var
  SSheetType: SmallInt;
begin
  SSheetType := F1FileFormulaOne3;
  F1Book1.Read ('Sheet1.xls', SSheetType);
end;
```

Note *For more information on using the Formula One component, see the VCF1.HLP Help file.*

Index

A

About dialog box, 60

Abs function, 107–108

accelerator keys, 121

active cells, 363–364

Active property, 156

ActiveX components, 62–63

actual parameters, 102

Add dialog box, 229

AddField function, 183, 257–258

Add file to project button, 5

addition, 73, 76

Additional page, 43, 46, 64

Add method, 183

Add to Repository command, 61

Add to Repository dialog box, 61

Add User command, 176

Add Watch at Cursor command, 140

aliases
for paths, 67, 170–171
for reports, 191

Alias Manager dialog box, 170

Align command, 18

aligning
components, 18–19
rich text format memos, 299–301

Alignment dialog box, 18, 318

ALTER TABLE statements, 180–181

ampersands (&) for accelerator keys, 121

ancestor type for components, 218

ANIMALS.DBF project, 159, 161

animated messages, 287–288

anonymous FTP login, 242

appearance of forms, 55–56

AppendRecord method, 163–164

applications
distributing on CD-ROM, 212–214
help for, 358–359

Application variable, 44

archiver, CD-ROM, 212–214

arcs on worksheets, 309

arithmetic
operators for, 73–75
for real numbers, 75–76

ARPANET, 231

array types, 88–90

ascending database sorts, 185, 262–263

Ascending order button, 192

assignment statements, 11–12

Assign new alias option, 191

asterisks (*)
for comments, 13
in InterBase, 178
for multiplication, 73

audio, 204–206, 275–276
for errors, 17
sound cards for, 286–287

authors for Object Repository items, 61

AutoOpen property, 204, 205

AutoSize property, 209

Average button, 192, 195

Average function, 362

.AVI files, 207–208, 214–215

B

Back button, 203, 204

Background Color property, 4

backing up files, 339–340

Baran, Paul, 231

BDE (Borland Database Engine), 151

begin statements
  for case, 81
  for procedures, 10

Berners-Lee, Tim, 231

Best fit button, 192

BETWEEN operator, 181

Bevel components, 208

BitBtn components, 43, 208

bitmaps
  in buttons, 43
  in directories, 270–273
  for thumbnails, 283–284
  tiled, 289–290
  transparent buttons over, 290–292

blinking messages, 233, 273–274

BLOB type, 177

BlockShadow procedure, 266–267

.BMP files. *See* bitmaps

body of procedures and functions, 98–100

BOF property, 169

Boldface button, 196

boldface text, 301

bookmarks, 169–170

Boolean type
  range and size of, 14
  for subranges, 86

borders
  and focus, 40
  for forms, 55–56
  for reports, 193, 195

Borders command, 193

BorderStyle property, 55–56

BOXOBJ.PAS file, 226

braces ({}) for comments, 12–13

Break on exception option, 144, 147

breakpoints, 138
  conditional, 139–140

deleting, 139
  setting, 138–139

Breakpoints list, 139

Bring to Front method, 211, 228, 291

browsers for World Wide Web, 232–237, 343–345

BrowseWebPage procedure, 233, 343–345

bsDialog value, 55

bsNone value, 55

bsSingle property, 56

bsSizeToolWin value, 55

bsToolWindow value, 55

BTNCLR.DPR project, 291–292

btn prefix, 9

BTNPRJ.DPR project, 43

bugs. *See* debugger

bullets
  for menu items, 127
  for rich text format memos, 301–302

Button button, 15

Button component, 30

buttons, 3
  adding, 6
  bitmaps in, 43
  hints for, 43–46
  moving, 6
  transparent, 290–292

Byte type, 14

C

calculator, sales tax, 20–23

Call Stack window, 142

Cancel button, 155

canceling Internet operations, 234

Cancel method, 234

CanClose parameter, 56

capitalizing words, 322–324

Caption property and captions
    changing, 6–7
    for labels, 15–16
    for pages, 58
    for radio buttons, 35
    for Start button, 4
CARTALK.AVI demo, 214–215
case sensitivity, 7, 176
case statements, 80–81
CD-ROM
    distributing applications on, 212–214
    installing, 360–361
cell ranges in Formula One, 364–365
Center button, 196
centering messages, 318–319
ChangeSearchPath function, 337–338
characteristics, 3
    of edit components, 17–18
    inheriting, 45–46
characters in strings
    deleting, 320–321
    replacing, 324–325
    reversing, 325–326
    right, 326–327
CHAR function, 177
charts for worksheets, 307–309
Chart Wizard, 308
Char type, 14
    in InterBase, 177
    for subranges, 86
CheckBox button, 15
CheckBox components, 3, 30, 33–35
Checked property
    for check boxes, 34
    for menu items, 127
    for radio buttons, 35
CHECKMARK cursor, 269
check marks for menu items, 127
CheckPentium function, 338–339
CHGCOLOR.DPR project, 38

Chr function, 124
circular unit references, 53
classes, 3
    names for, 9
    for user-defined components, 218
cleanup code, 56
clear buttons, 290–292
clearing string grid contents, 331–332
Close method, 8, 183
closing forms, 8
ClrStrGrid procedure, 331–332
Code Editor, 7, 137
coding
    databases, 159
    menu controls, 123–124
    procedures and functions, 98, 100–101
    queries, 183–184
    repeating, 68
    tracing and stepping over, 137–138
colons (:)
    in assignment operators, 11–12
    in syntax, 96, 98
color
    for help hints, 44
    inheriting, 45
    in messages, 267–269
    in rich text format memos, 303
    for Start button, 4
    for worksheets, 310
ColorMsg procedure, 267–269
color palettes, 209–211
Col property, 363
columnar style reports, 191
Column editing mode button, 192
columns
    in Formula One, 363
    for list boxes, 32
    for reports, 193, 199
Columns property, 32
ComboBox button, 15

ComboBox component, 30, 32–33

commands, extracting from strings, 321–322

commas (,) in syntax, 96

comments, 12–13

COMPARE.DPR project, 345

ComparePaths procedure, 345

compile errors, 135

Compiler tab, 136

compiling programs, 7

Component|Add Component Template command, 62

Component|Configure Palette command, 62

Component Expert, 217
    defining components in, 218–219
    generating units in, 219–220
    registering components in, 220–221

Component|Import ActiveX Library command, 63

Component Palette, 5–7, 15, 62

components, 15
    aligning, 18–19
    check boxes, 33–35
    combo boxes, 32–33
    deleting, 26
    edit, 16–18
    enabling and disabling, 41–42
    inheritance by, 45–46
    labels, 15–16
    list boxes, 29–32
    radio buttons, 35–37
    renaming, 8–9
    repeating, 18–19
    scroll bars, 37–39
    showing and hiding, 42
    tab order of, 19–20
    templates for, 61–62
    user-defined. *See* user-defined components

Component Template Information dialog box, 62

Comp type, 14, 75–76

conditional breakpoints, 139–140

conditional execution
    case statements, 80–81
    in Formula One, 362–363
    if statements, 77–80

configuring component palettes, 62

Connect method, 238, 248

constant parameters, 102–103

constants, 13–14
    vs. literals, 65–66
    for parameters, 96, 102–103

const reserved word, 96, 103

context-sensitive help, 115, 358–359

controls. *See also* components
    names for, 67
    referencing, 56–58
    sizing and moving, 64
    stacking, 63–65

control statements. *See* flow of execution

ConvertFraction function, 346–347

converting
    dates and time, 110–111
    enumerated types, 86
    floating-point numbers, 77, 97
    strings to upper case, 112

CoolBar components, 208

Copy function, 108

copying
    code, 68
    strings, 108

Count button, 192

counters in for loops, 83

CreateChart procedure, 307–309

Create method, 226

Create New Table Link dialog box, 199–200

Create Submenu command, 122

CREATE TABLE command, 176

Create Table dialog box, 171

Ctrl key with list boxes, 32

CUR32PRJ.DPR project, 277–279

CUR32.RES file, 269

Currency type, 75

cursors
running to, 137
user-defined, 269–270

CUSTCUR.DPR project, 269–270

CustomCursor procedure, 269–270

D

Data Access page, 152, 157

DataArrival event handler, 248

data aware controls, 155

databases, 151
adding records to, 163–166
bookmarks for, 169–170
coding for, 159
data modules for, 157–158
datasets in, 159–160, 184–185
deleting records from, 168, 181
editing records in, 166–167
empty, checking for, 168–169, 260–261
fields for, 257–258
inserting records into, 178–179
library routines for, 188, 257–263
program for, 151–155
queries for. *See* Structured Query Language
(SQL)
reports from. *See* ReportSmith report
generator
rich text format in, 156–157
searches in, 160–163
sorting records in, 262–263
tables for, 170–173, 176–178
updating records in, 167–168, 180–181

Data Controls page, 153, 155, 157

Data Definition Language (DDL) commands,
175

DataField property, 155

data fields in reports, 193

Data Manipulation Language (DML) commands,
175

data modules, 157–158

datasets, 183
navigating, 159–160
sorting, 184–185

DataSource components, 152

DataSource property, 155

data types. *See* types

dates
of files, 110–111
in InterBase, 177
in reports, 194

DateTimeToStr function, 111

DATE type, 177

day of week, retrieving, 89, 350–351

DayOfWeek function, 89

DBADDFLD.DPR project, 258

DBGrid components, 153, 156

DBImage components, 153, 208

DBNavigator components, 153, 155

DBPROJ.DPR project, 259, 261, 263, 273–274

DBRichEdit component, 156–157

.DCU extension, 27

debugger, 135–136
breakpoints in, 138–140
monitoring expression values in, 140–141
running to cursor in, 137
test values in, 141
tracing and stepping over code in, 137–138
viewing subroutine calls in, 142

decimal points in real numbers, 75

DECIMAL type, 177

declaring
multidimensional arrays, 89–90
record type, 85, 90–91
variables, 12

DecryptMsg function, 347–348

defaults
    for error sounds, 17
    for event handlers, 39
    for forms, 5
    for input values, 11
    for units, 24
Define by ReportBasic macro option, 197
Defined by SQL option, 197
defining
    hotspots, 115–117, 276–279
    user-defined components, 218–219
delays
    for help hints, 44
    for messages, 285–286
    pauses for, 111
Delete All Watches command, 141
Delete button, 155
Delete command
    for breakpoints, 139
    for menu items, 123
    for records, 181
Delete method, 168
Delete Watch command, 141
deleting
    bookmarks, 170
    breakpoints, 139
    characters from strings, 320–321
    columns in reports, 193
    components, 26
    file links, 200
    menu items, 123
    MultiPlayer buttons, 204
    records, 168, 181
    spaces from strings, 113, 327–328
    templates, 62
    watch expressions, 141
derived fields, 197–199
descending database sorts, 185, 262
Descending order button, 192
DESC keyword, 185

descriptions
    for Object Repository items, 61
    for packages, 229
    for templates, 124
design, programming mistakes in, 63
design-time vs. run-time, 10
detail section in reports, 192
DeviceType property, 204–205
.DFM extension, 27
dialog boxes, 7–8
    multi-page, 68–69
    working with, 10–12
directories
    bitmaps in, 270–273
    in FTP, 242–247, 351–354
    for Windows, 341
disabling
    components, 41–42
    menu items, 126–127
    watch expressions, 141
DisplayDirImage function, 270–273
displaying
    bitmaps, 270–273, 283–284
    button hints, 43–44
    components, 42
    forms, 51–52
    images, 46–49
    query results, 259–260
    screen savers, 279–282
    subroutine calls, 142
DisplayQueryRecs procedure, 259–260
distortion with graphics, 209
distributing applications, 212–214
division, 73–75, 76
div operator, 73–75
.DLL (Dynamic Link Library) files
    for ActiveX components, 63
    packages as, 228–229
dots (.). *See* periods (.)
Double type, 14, 75

DOUBLE PRECISION type, 177

.DPR extension, 26–27

DRAGFOLDER cursor, 269

dragging buttons, 6

DrawObject procedure, 309–310

drop-down menus, 5

drop shadow effects, 193, 195

Dynamic Link Library files
    for ActiveX components, 63
    packages as, 228–229

dynamic operations
    for controls, 64–65
    for menu items, 125–126

E

editable RichEdit components, 212

edit boxes, 3

Edit breakpoint window, 140

Edit|Bring to Front command, 211, 291

Edit button
    for Component Palette, 15
    for DBNavigator, 155

Edit components, 30
    adding to forms, 16–17
    properties of, 17–18
    searches in, 355–356

Edit|Cut command, 26, 193

Edit Derived Field dialog box, 197–198

editing
    file links, 200
    menu items, 123
    records, 166–167

Edit link option, 200

Edit method, 166

Edit|Tab Order command, 20

Edit Tab Order dialog box, 20

Edit|Undo command, 193

Eject button, 203, 204

else clauses
    with case, 80
    with if, 78

e-mail, 237–240, 249–253, 356–358

empty databases, checking for, 168–169, 260–261

empty strings, 11

Enabled property and enabling
    components, 41–42
    menu items, 126–127

EncryptMsg function, 92, 325–326, 348–349

end statements
    for case, 81
    for procedures, 10
    in units, 26

Enlarge method, 222–224

Enter key, tabbing with, 354–355

enumerated types, 84–86

Environment Options dialog box, 144, 147

EOF property, 161, 169

EOleError constant, 143

equal signs (=)
    in assignment operators, 11–12
    in Formula One calculations, 362

errors and error messages, 22
    from compilation, 7
    exception handlers for, 143–147
    input, 41
    out of memory, 67
    in Pentium processors, 338–339
    sounds for, 17
    in try..except blocks, 32
    types of, 135–136

Evaluate/Modify command, 141

Evaluate/Modify dialog box, 141

event handlers, 9–10, 39–41

EVENTS.DB table, 156

Events tab, 39

exceptions, 22
    handlers for, 143–145, 147
    reraising, 145–146

ExecSQL method, 183

executable files, 27

execution points, 137

.EXE extension, 27

expressions, 73–75

    absolute value of, 107–108

    evaluating, 141

    for fractions, 346–347

    monitoring, 140–141

    precedence order for, 76–77

    for real numbers, 75–76

Extended type, 14, 75

ExtractFileName function, 109

ExtractFilePath function, 109–110

extracting

    commands from strings, 321–322

    file names, 109

    paths, 109–110

F

F1FileExcel5 format, 366

F1FileFormulaOne3 format, 365

F1 key, 115

F5 key, 138

F7 key, 137

F8 key, 137

F9 key, 7, 22

Field editing mode button, 192

Field Editor command, 158

fields, 152

    for data modules, 158

    derived, 197–199

    editing, 166–167

    in file links, 199–200

    inserting, 257–258

    names for, 159

    in records, 91

    in reports, 193–195

    updating, 167–168

Field Selection Criteria dialog box, 196–197

FieldValues method, 165

File|Add to Project command, 106, 252

File|Close All command, 225

FileCopyList procedure, 327, 339–340

File|Create Database command, 176

FileDateToDateTime function, 110–111

FileGetDate function, 110–111

FileListBox button, 47

FileName property, 204

file names, extracting, 109

File|New command, 20

File|New Application command, 57

File|New Data Module command, 158

File|New Form command, 51

File|Object Repository command, 59

File|Print command, 200

File|Reopen command, 126

files

    backing up, 339–340

    dates of, 110–111

    links for, 199–200

    loading, 48

    paths to, 67

File|Save command, 200

File|Save As command, 24

File|Save Project As command, 26

File|Use Unit command, 54, 60

filters for reports, 196–197

finally statements, 142–143

finding records, 160–163. *See also* Structured
    Query Language (SQL)

Find Text dialog box, 33–34

First button, 155

First method, 160

floating-point numbers

    arithmetic for, 75–76

    converting to strings, 77, 97

FloatToStr function, 77

FloatToStrF function, 97

FLOAT type, 177

flow of execution
    case statements, 80–81
    for loops, 82–83
    in Formula One, 362–363
    GOTO statements, 68
    if statements, 77–80
    repeat..until loops, 84
    while loops, 83

focus, 9
    and borders, 40
    Enter key for, 354–355
    tab order of, 19–20

fonts
    inheriting, 45
    non-standard, 68
    for rich text format memos, 303
    for worksheets, 310

footers in reports, 194–195

Foreground Color property, 4

for loops, 82–83

formal parameters, 102

Format|Column Width command, 199

Format currency button, 196

Format general numeric button, 196

Format menu, 195

Format percent button, 196

formatted memo fields, 157

formatted strings, converting numbers to, 97

formatting
    headings in reports, 195–196
    reports, 192–193
    worksheets, 310–313

FormatWorksheet procedure, 310–313

FormCreate method, 29

forms
    ActiveX components on, 62–63
    appearance of, 55–56
    bitmaps on, 283–284
    block shadows on, 266–267
    buttons for, 6
    centering messages on, 318–319
    cleanup code for, 56
    closing, 8
    creating, 51
    delayed messages on, 285–286
    displaying, 51–52
    hotspots on, 115–117, 276–279
    Integrated Development Environment for, 59
    Object Repository for, 59–61
    referencing controls on, 56–58
    screen savers for, 279–282
    stacking controls on, 63–65
    tabbed notebook style, 58–59
    unit management for, 54–55
    unit references for, 52–54
    user-defined cursors on, 269–270

Forms tab, 68

Formula One component
    active cells in, 363–364
    calculations with, 362
    cell ranges in, 364–365
    conditional operators in, 362–363
    library routines for, 307–314
    saving and retrieving worksheets in, 365–366

formulas in Formula One, 362

forward directives, 105

forward slashes (/)
    for comments, 13
    for division, 73–74

fractions, expressions for, 346–347

FreeBookmark method, 170

FTP (File Transfer Protocol), 240–242
    directory information for, 242–247, 351–354
    with UNIX hosts, 247

FTP Client Control, 243

functions, 95
    body of, 98–100
    coding, 98, 100–101
    parameters for, 96, 98, 99, 101–103
    placement of, 103–106
    syntax of, 96–97
    user-defined, 97

G

GetDay function, 350–351

GetFTPDir procedure, 245–247, 351–354

GetNoParam function, 238

glass masters for CD-ROMs, 214

Glyph property, 43

GoToBookmark method, 170

GotoKey method, 161–163

GotoNearest method, 161

GOTO statements, 68

graphics, 208. *See also* bitmaps
    color palettes for, 209–211
    displaying, 46–49
    hotspots on, 276–279
    image controls for, 209–210
    size of, 209
    on worksheets, 309–310

Graphics unit, 44

GRIDPRJ.DPR project, 331–335, 350–351

grids, string. *See* string grids

GroupBox button, 15

GroupBox components, 30, 36

GUNSCOPE cursor, 269

H

hard-coded paths, 67

hard drive space for example files, 360

headings in reports, 193, 195–196

Height property
    for panels, 40
    for Start button, 4

help, 115, 358–359

HelpHint property, 44

help hints, 43–46

Help Search command, 115

hiding components, 42

High Color standard, 210

hints for buttons, 43–46

Hi-Sierra standard, 213

.HLP files, 358

hotspots, 115–117, 276–279

HTML (HyperText Markup Language), 232

HTML ActiveX components, 232

HTML documents, retrieving, 233–234

HTTP (HyperText Transmission Protocol), 232

hyphens (-) for separator bars, 120

I

Icon property, 4

icons
    for graphics, 283–284
    for Object Repository items, 61

if statements, 34, 77–80, 362–363

Image components, 3, 208. *See also* bitmaps; graphics

Image Editor, 269

ImageKnife toolkit, 210, 211

ImageList components, 208

implementation section in units, 25, 103–104

indentation for readability, 66

indexes
    for array types, 88–89
    in databases, 152
    for list boxes, 31

index values in for loops, 83

inequality in queries, checking for, 186–187

inequality operators (<>) with if statements, 80

infinite loops, 106

inheritance, 45–46

initializing
    arrays, 88–89
    list boxes, 30
    string grids, 332–333
    variables, 12

InitStringGrid procedure, 332–333

input
    anticipating errors in, 41
    edit components for, 16–18
InputBox function, 10–11, 95–96
Insert button, 155
INSERT command, 178–179
Insert crosstab button, 196
Insert|Field command, 193
Insert Field dialog box, 194
Insert footer button, 192
Insert From Template command, 124
Insert graph button, 196
Insert header button, 192, 194
Insert|Header/Footer command, 194
inserting
    fields, 193–195, 257–258
    records, 178–179
Insert method, 163–164
Insert picture button, 196
Insert text button, 196
installing
    ActiveX components, 63
    CD-ROM, 360–361
    user-defined components, 228–229
InstallSHIELD Express, 213
Integer type and integers, 12, 14
    dividing, 73–75
    in InterBase, 177
    for subranges, 86
Integrated Development Environment (IDE), 59
interactive queries, 187–188
InterBase Windows Interactive SQL utility, 175
    for adding tables, 176–178
    for deleting records, 181
    for inserting records, 178–179
    for queries, 179–180, 182–188
    for ranges, 181
    starting, 176
    for updating records, 180–181
interface section in units, 24, 26, 103–104

Internet
    canceling operations for, 234
    for e-mail, 237–240, 249–253, 356–358
    for FTP, 240–247
    history of, 231
    for network news, 248–249
    packages for, 249
    retrieving HTML documents on, 233–234
    with TCP/IP, 247–248
    viewers for, 232–237, 343–345
Internet Page, 250
IntToStr function, 86
IsEmpty function, 260–261
IS NULL operator, 186
IsNumEval function, 317–318
ISO 9660 standard, 213
Italicize button, 196
italic text, 304
ItemsIndex property, 31
Items property
    for list boxes, 30
    for radio groups, 36

K

Kai's Power Goo, 207–208
keys in databases, 152, 161–163
Kind property, 43

L

Label button, 15
Label components, 3, 15–16, 30, 193
large procedures, 67
Last button, 155
Last method, 160
lbl prefix, 16
LBOX1.DPR project, 355–356
LBOXPRJ.DPR application, 29–32

leading spaces, trimming from strings, 113

Left align button, 196

Left property, 4

length of edit components, 17

library routines
 accessing, 106–107
 for databases, 188, 257–263
 for multimedia, 211–212, 265–292
 for rich editing, 295–305
 for spreadsheets, 307–314
 for string grids, 331–335
 for strings, 317–328
 system, 337–341
 utility and Internet, 343–359

LIKE keyword, 179

lines on worksheets, 309

links for files, 199–200

ListBox button, 15

ListBox components, 29–32

ListItemNotify property, 243

List method, 242

ListView components, 246

literals vs. constants, 65–66

LMDB unit, 106, 257

LMMail unit, 239

LMMedia unit, 106

LMREdit unit, 106

LMScr32.PAS unit, 107, 269

LMSCREEN.PAS module, 234

LMString unit, 93

LMWEBBRW.PAS module, 234

LMWebBrw unit, 233

LoadFromFile method, 208, 209

loading
 files, 48
 images, 208–209
 queries, 261–262
 rich text format memos, 295–296

LoadQuery procedure, 261–262

logic errors, 135, 136

LongInt type, 14

long variable names, 67

loops
 for, 82–83
 infinite, 106
 repeat..until, 84
 while, 83

LowerCase function, 112

M

MainMenu button, 15

MainMenu component, 30

Mask property, 47, 339

Max function, 362

Maximum button, 192, 194

Max property, 39

MaxLength property, 17

Memo button, 15

Memo component, 30

memo fields
 aligning, 299–301
 boldface in, 301
 bullets in, 301–302
 formatted, 157
 italics in, 304
 loading, 295–296
 saving, 297–299
 style for, 303
 underlining in, 304–305
 undoing changes in, 305

menu bars, 120

Menu Designer, 119
 for accelerator keys, 121
 for creating menu items, 120
 for creating menu systems, 128–133
 for editing menu items, 123
 for programming menu controls, 123–124
 for separator bars, 120

for shortcut keys, 121–122
for submenus, 122–123
for templates, 124

menu items
adding, 123
check marks and bullets for, 127
creating, 120
deleting, 123
editing, 123
enabling and disabling, 126–127
run-time control of, 125–126

menus
Menu Designer for, 119–124
pop-up, 127–128
run-time control of, 125–126
submenus, 122–123

Merge reports button, 192

MessageBlink procedure, 233, 273–274

MessageBox function, 168

MessageDlg function, 123, 248

messages
animated, 287–288
blinking, 233, 273–274
centering, 318–319
color in, 267–269
decrypting, 347–348
delayed, 285–286
encrypting, 92–93, 348–349

methods
for actions, 8
testing, 226–228

Microsoft Video for Windows, 207

Min function, 362

Minimum button, 192, 194

Min property, 39

mistakes
anticipating, 41
programming, 63–68

modal dialog boxes and forms, 7–8, 51–52

mod operator, 74, 75

monitoring expression values, 140–141

MoveBy method, 160

moving
buttons, 6
controls, 64

multidimensional arrays, 89–90

multimedia
animated messages, 287–288
audio, 204–206, 275–276
block shadow effects, 266–267
CD-ROM for, 212–214
color messages, 267–269
delayed messages, 285–286
displaying bitmaps, 270–273, 283–284
graphics, 208–212
hotspots, 276–279
library routines for, 211–212, 265–292
MultiPlayer component for, 203–208
screen savers, 279–282
sound cards, checking, 286–287
tiled bitmaps, 289–290
transparent buttons, 290–292
user-defined cursors, 269–270
video, 207–208, 214–215, 274–275

multi-page dialogs, 68–69

MultiPlayer component, 203–204
for audio, 204–206
for video, 207–208

multiple-column list boxes, 32

multiplication, 73, 76

MultiSelect property, 32

mutual recursion, 106

N

NameList method, 242

Names property and names, 7, 9
for classes, 9
for components, 8–9
constants, 13–14
for data modules, 158
for executable files, 27

for fields, 159
for forms, 24–25
for labels, 16
long, 67
for menu items, 120, 123
for Object Repository items, 61
for pages, 58
for procedures and functions, 98
for subrange types, 87
for templates, 62
for units, 24, 219
variables, 11
nested menus, 122–123
Networking News Transfer Protocol, 248–249
New Component dialog box, 218
New Form button, 5, 51
New Items dialog box, 20, 51–52, 59
New Package dialog box, 229
New Page command, 58
New report button, 192
New tab, 59
Next button
for DBNavigator, 155
for MultiPlayer, 203
NextControl function, 354–355
Next method, 159, 160
Nil reserved word, 163
NNTODEMO.DPR project, 249
NNTP Client Control, 248
nodes for directory trees, 244
nonmodal forms, 51
non-standard fonts, 68
not operators
with if statements, 80
precedence of, 76
null values, checking for, 186–187
numeric strings, checking for, 317–318
NUMERIC type, 177
NumGlyphs property, 43

O

Object Inspector, 5–6, 9
for events, 39
for radio buttons, 36
for tab order, 19–20
Object Repository, 59
adding items to, 61
selecting items from, 60–61
objects, 3
as properties, 30
properties of, 3–4
reusing, 5
.OCX files, 63
OLEAutoUnit, 143–144
OnBusy event handlers, 243
OnChange event handlers, 39
OnClick event handlers, 34–35, 39
OnClose event handlers, 56
OnCloseQuery event handlers, 56
OnCreate event handlers, 30–31
OnDeactivate event handlers, 56
OnDestroy event handlers, 56
OnEndRetrieval event handlers, 234
OnError event handlers, 248
one-to-many links, 200
OnScroll event handlers, 38–40
OnStateChanged event handlers, 242
OnTimer event handlers, 233
OpenDialog components, 215
Open file button, 5
Open method, 183
Open project button, 5
Open report button, 192
Open Report screen, 191
OpenRichEdit function, 295–296
OpenStringGrid procedure, 333
operators
for arithmetic, 73–75
for derived fields, 198

with if statements, 79
precedence order for, 76–77
order
of component focus, 19–20
of precedence, 76–77
ORDER BY clause, 184–185
Ord function, 86
ordinal values, 80
out of memory errors, 67
ovals on worksheets, 309

P

Package Editor, 229
packages, 27
creating, 228–229
for Internet, 249
PageControl button, 58
PageControl components, 58
pages, renaming, 58
PaintBox components, 208
palettes
color, 209–211
configuring, 62
for user-defined components, 218
palettized images, 210
Panel button, 15
Panel components, 30
radio buttons on, 36
scroll bars for, 40–41
parameter queries, 187–188
parameters, 10
extracting from strings, 321–322
for forms, 57
for functions and procedures, 96, 98, 99, 101–103
for startup, 113–114
ParamStr function, 113–114
ParentColor property, 45
ParentFont property, 45

parentheses ()
for comments, 13
in expressions, 76–77
for procedures and functions, 10, 98
parent objects, 36
ParentShowHint property, 45–46
partial matches in InterBase, 179
.PAS extension, 24, 26
pass count breakpoints, 140
PasswordChar property, 18
passwords
for anonymous FTP login, 242
for edit components, 18
in InterBase, 176
paths
changing, 337–338
comparing, 345
extracting, 109–110
extracting file names from, 109
hard-coded, 67
for user-defined components, 219
Pause button
with MultiPlayer, 203
on toolbar, 5
pauses for delays, 111
PChar type, 112
Pentium processors, checking for errors, 338–339
percent symbols (%) in InterBase, 180
periods (.)
for array types, 88
in real numbers, 75
for record fields, 91
in units, 26
in UNIX, 247
Picture Editor, 116
picture viewer, 46–49
PICVIEW.DPR project, 271–273
placement of procedures and functions, 103–106
planning, programming mistakes in, 63
Play button, 203

Play method, 205

PLAYVIDEO.DRP project, 274–276, 287

PlayVideoFile procedure, 274–275

PlayWaveFile procedure, 275–276

plus signs (+) for addition, 73

PopupMenu button, 15

PopupMenu component, 30

PopupMenu property, 128

pop-up menus, 127–128

Popup method, 127

ports for FTP, 242

Pos function, 108, 297

position of Start button, 4

Post button, 155

Post method, 165, 166

precedence order in expressions, 76–77

precision of real numbers, 75

Pred function, 86

pre-masters for CD-ROMs, 213

Prev button, 203

Print dialog, 313

printing
   reports, 200–201
   worksheets, 313–314

Print report button, 192

PrintWorksheet procedure, 313–314

Prior button, 155

Prior method, 160

private section in units, 24, 220

procedures, 95
   body of, 98–100
   coding, 98, 100–101
   event handlers, 9–10, 39–41
   large, 67
   parameters for, 96, 98, 99, 101–103
   placement of, 103–106
   syntax of, 96–97
   user-defined, 97

ProcessMessages method, 111

programming
   common mistakes in, 63–68
   databases, 159
   menu controls, 123–124
   procedures and functions, 98, 100–101
   queries, 183–184
   repeating, 68

Project Manager, 54–55

Project|Options command, 136

projects
   creating, 57
   managing, 26–27

promotion of floating-point numbers, 77

prompts with InputBox, 11

properties, 3
   of edit components, 17–18
   inheriting, 45–46

Properties tab, 39

protected section in units, 220

public section in units, 24, 220

published section in units, 220

Q

Query components and queries, 182. *See also* Structured Query Language (SQL)
   code for, 183–184
   displaying results of, 259–260
   inequality checks in, 186–187
   interactive, 187–188
   loading, 261–262
   ranges in, 181
   for records, 179–180, 182–188

Quit method, 238

R

RadioButton button, 15

RadioButton components, 30

grouping, 36–37
using, 35–36
RadioGroup button, 15
RadioGroup components, 30
RadioItem property, 127
raise reserved word, 145–146
raising exceptions, 145–146
ranges
    checking, 86–87
    in Formula One, 364–365
    in queries, 181
{$R+} compiler directive, 87
readability
    comments for, 13
    indentation and spacing for, 66
read only RichEdit components, 212
real numbers, arithmetic for, 75–76
Real type, 14, 75, 76
Record button, 203, 204
records, 152
    adding, 163–166
    deleting, 168, 181
    editing, 166–167
    inserting, 178–179
    navigating, 159–160
    queries for. *See* Structured Query Language
        (SQL)
    searches for, 160–163
    sorting, 262–263
    type for, 90–92
    updating, 167–168, 180–181
rectangles on worksheets, 309
recursion, 106
references
    to controls, 56–58
    to objects, deleting, 26
    to units, 52–54
Refresh button, 155
registering components
    ActiveX, 63
    user-defined, 220–221

Register procedure, 221
remainder operator, 74, 75
RemoteHost property, 238
RemotePort property, 238
Remove file from project button, 5
Remove link option, 200
removing. *See* deleting
renaming
    components, 8–9
    pages, 58
    units, 24
repeating
    code, 68
    components, 18–19
repeat..until loops, 84
replacing characters in strings, 324–325
Report Query—Tables dialog box, 191–192, 199
reports
    managing. *See* ReportSmith report generator
    printing, 200–201
ReportSmith report generator, 191
    creating reports in, 191–192
    for derived fields, 197–199
    for drop shadow effects, 195
    fields in, 193–195
    for file links, 199–200
    for filters, 196–197
    formatting reports in, 192–193
    headings and columns in, 193, 195–196
    saving reports in, 200
Report styles button, 196
reraising exceptions, 145–146
resizing
    graphics, 209
    labels, 15
resource protection, 142–143
restoring string grid contents, 333
result sets, 183
retrieving
    HTML documents, 233–234
    worksheets, 365–366

reusing objects, 5

reversing characters in strings, 325–326

ribbon for reports, 195

RichEdit components, 212–213

rich text format memos, 156–157
 aligning, 299–301
 boldface text for, 301
 bullets in, 301–302
 italic text for, 304
 library routines for, 295–305
 loading, 295–296
 saving, 297–299
 style for, 303
 underlining in, 304–305
 undoing changes to, 305

Right align button, 196

right characters from strings, 326–327

rollback, transaction, 165–166

Row property, 363

RTE.DPR project, 156–157, 212, 296, 297, 300, 301, 302, 303, 304, 305

Run|Add Breakpoint command, 139, 140

Run|Add Watch command, 137, 140

Run button, 5, 7

Run|Evaluate/Modify command, 137, 141

Run|Parameters command, 114

Run parameters dialog box, 114–115

Run|Program Reset command, 55, 138

Run|Run command, 7, 138

Run|Run to Cursor command, 137

Run|Step Over command, 137–138

run-time
 vs. design-time, 10
 errors in, 135–136
 for menu item control, 125–126

Run to Cursor command, 137

Run|Trace Into command, 137

S

sales tax calculator, 20–23

Save all button, 5

Save As Template command, 124

Save file button, 5

Save report button, 192

SaveRichEdit function, 297–299

SaveStringGrid procedure, 334

saving
 menu templates, 124
 projects, 26
 reports, 200
 rich text format memos, 297–299
 string grid contents, 334
 worksheets, 365–366

SBLANKER.DPR project, 279–282

Scale Page Width button, 194

screen savers
 BorderStyle property for, 55
 displaying, 279–282

ScrollBar button, 15

ScrollBar components, 3, 30, 37–39

ScrollBox components, 36, 208

searches
 in databases, 160–163. *See also* Structured Query Language (SQL)
 in edit controls, 355–356

SearchListItem procedure, 355–356

search paths
 changing, 337–338
 comparing, 345
 extracting, 109–110
 extracting file names from, 109
 hard-coded, 67
 for user-defined components, 219

security
 encrypted messages, 92–93, 348–349
 in InterBase, 176

Select All option, 191

SELECT command, 178–179, 184–185

Select form from list button, 5

selecting Object Repository items, 60–61

selections

    combo boxes for, 32–33

    list boxes for, 29–32

    radio buttons for, 35–37

Selections dialog box, 196

selectors with case statements, 80

Select unit from list button, 5

SelEndCol property, 364

SelEndRow property, 364

SelStartCol property, 364

SelStartRow property, 364

semicolons (;)

    with if statements, 78

    as line terminators, 7

    in syntax, 98

SendData method, 248

SendEMailMsg routine, 239–240, 249, 356–358

sending e-mail, 237–240, 356–358

separator bars on menus, 120

SetAlignment procedure, 299–301

SetBlockStyle procedure, 303

SetBoldFace procedure, 301

SetBullet procedure, 301–302

SetFields method, 167–168

SetItalics procedure, 304

SetKey method, 162

SetListViewHeadings method, 246–247

SetUnderline procedure, 304–305

SETUP.EXE program, 360–361

shadow effects

    in forms, 266–267

    in reports, 193, 195

Shape components, 208

Shift key

    with list boxes, 32

    in repeating components, 19

shortcut keys, 121–122

ShortCut property, 121

ShortInt type, 14

ShowHelpTopic procedure, 358–359

SHOWHLP.DPR project, 358–359

ShowHotSpot procedure, 276–279

ShowMessage procedure, 7, 95–96

Show method, 52

ShowModal method, 54, 60

ShowScrSaver procedure, 279–282

ShowStr procedure, 98–100

ShowTNail function, 283–284

Simple Mail Transfer Protocol, 237, 250, 356–358

single quotes (') for messages, 7, 81

Single type, 14, 75

size

    of bitmaps, 283–284

    of charts, 308

    of columns in reports, 199

    of controls, 64

    of graphics, 209

    of labels, 15

    of panels, 40

    of real numbers, 75

    of reports, 194

    of Start button, 4

size handles

    for charts, 308

    and focus, 40

    for labels, 15

slashes (/)

    for comments, 13

    for division, 73–74

Sleep function, 111, 242

SlowPrint procedure, 285–286

SMALLINT type, 177

SMTP Client Control, 237

SMTP components, 250, 356–358

Sorted property

    for combo boxes, 33

    for list boxes, 32

sorting
combo boxes, 33
datasets, 184–185
list boxes, 32
records, 262–263
SortTable procedure, 262–263
sound, 17, 204–206, 275–276
sound cards, checking, 286–287
SoundEnabled function, 286–287
spaces in strings, deleting, 113, 327–328
spacing for readability, 66
SpeedButton components, 208
SpeedMenus
for Code Editor, 137
for databases, 158
for Menu Designer, 122
spreadsheets
charts for, 307–309
formatting, 310–313
in Formula One, 362–366
graphics on, 309–310
library routines for, 307–314
printing, 313–314
SQL. *See* Structured Query Language (SQL)
SquareVal function, 100–101
stacking controls, 63–65
Standard Page, 15
Start button, 3–4
Start|Programs command, 5
startup parameters, 113–114
State property, 238, 239
Step button, 203, 204
Step over button, 5
stepping over code, 137–138
Stop button, 203
StrCenter procedure, 318–319
STRCOLR.DPR project, 266–267, 268–269
StrDeleteAll function, 320–321
Stretch property, 47, 209
StrExtractCmd function, 108, 321–322

StrFormatUpper function, 322–324
string grids
clearing contents of, 331–332
initializing, 332–333
library routines for, 331–335
restoring contents of, 333
saving contents of, 334
weekly schedules on, 335
String List editor, 37
strings, 11
capitalizing words in, 322–324
centering, 318–319
converting floating-point numbers to, 77, 97
converting to upper case, 112
copying, 108
deleting characters from, 320–321
deleting spaces from, 113, 327–328
extracting commands from, 321–322
library routines for, 317–328
numeric, checking for, 317–318
replacing characters in, 324–325
reversing characters in, 325–326
right characters from, 326–327
String type, 11, 14
StrLower function, 112
STRPRJ.DPR project, 325–326, 347, 349
STRPROC.DPR project, 285–286, 320, 321, 323–324, 328, 341, 354–355
StrReplaceAll function, 324–325
StrReverse function, 325–326
StrRightChar function, 326–327
StrStripSpaces function, 327–328
Structured Query Language (SQL), 175–176
for adding tables, 176–178
for deleting records, 181
displaying query results in, 259–260
for inserting records, 178–179
for loading queries, 261–262
for queries, 179–180, 182–188
ranges in queries in, 181
for updating records, 180–181
Structured Query Language button, 192

structure of tables, updating, 180–181

StrUpper function, 112

Style extractor button, 196

style for rich text format memos, 303

submenus, 122–123

subrange types, 86–88

subroutine calls, 142

substrings
    copying, 108
    right characters, 326–327

subtraction, 76

Succ function, 86

Sum button, 192

Sum function, 362

summary fields, 194–195

Super VGA video, 210–211

syntax of procedures and functions, 96–97

SYS1.DPR project, 339–340

system fields in reports, 194

system library routines, 337–341

T

TabbedNotebook components, 58–59, 68–69

Tabbed pages option, 68

tabbing with Enter key, 354–355

Table components and tables, 152, 155
    adding to databases, 176–178
    bookmarks for, 169–170
    creating, 170–173
    deleting records from, 168, 181
    editing records in, 166–167
    empty, checking for, 168–169, 260–261
    fields for, 257–258
    inserting records into, 163–166, 178–179
    queries on. *See* Structured Query Language
        (SQL)
    sorting records in, 262–263
    updating records in, 167–168, 180–181

table definitions, updating, 180–181

Tab Order command, 20

tab order of components, 19–20

TabOrder property, 19–20

TApplication class, 44

Tasks|User Security command, 176

tax calculator, 20–23

TBitBtn components, 43

tbl prefix, 161

TBookmark components, 170

TBox components, 222

TButton class, 9

TCheckBox components, 33–35

TComboBox components, 32–33

TComponent class, 221

TCP/IP (Transmission Control Protocol/Internet
        Protocol), 232, 247–248

TDataSource components, 155, 157

TDateTime components, 111

templates
    for components, 61–62
    for menus, 124
    in Object Repository, 59–61

testing
    methods, 226–228
    user-defined components, 225–226

text. *See* rich text format memos; strings

Text property
    for combo boxes, 33
    for edit controls, 16–17

TForm class, 9

THTML components, 344

thumbnails for graphics, 209, 283–284

TicketTaker procedure, 287–288

TileBitmap procedure, 289–290

TileImage objects, 289

TILES.DPR project, 289–290

time delays
    for help hints, 44
    for messages, 285–286
    pauses for, 111

title bars, 11

TListBox components, 29–32

TListView components, 246

TMainMenu components, 119, 129

TMediaPlayer components, 214

Toggle Breakpoint command, 138, 139

Toggle form/Unit button, 5, 48, 130

toolbars, 5
  creating, 55
  for reports, 192

Tools|Alias Manager command, 170

Tools|Derived Fields command, 197

Tools|Field Selection Criteria command, 197

Tools|Options command, 144, 147, 229

Tools|Report Query command, 199

Tools|SQL Text command, 197

TOpenDialog components, 214

Top property, 4

TPageControl components, 63

TPopupMenu components, 128

TQuery components, 182, 197

Trace into button, 5

tracing code, 137–138

TRadioGroup components, 36–37

trailing spaces, trimming from strings, 113

Transmission Control Protocol, 247–248

TransparentButton procedure, 290–292

trees for directories, 244–247

TReport components, 200

Trim function, 113

TrimLeft function, 113

TrimRight function, 113

True Color standard, 210

try..except blocks, 32

try..finally blocks, 142–143

TScrollBar components, 37–39

TScrollBox components, 64

TShape components, 222

TStringGrid components, 129, 131

TTable components, 155–157, 161

TTICKET.DPR project, 288

TTreeView components, 244

type reserved word in units, 24

types, 14
  array, 88–90
  enumerated, 84–86
  in InterBase, 177
  record, 90–92
  subrange, 86–88
  in syntax, 96, 98

U

Underline button, 196

underlining in rich text format memos, 304–305

underscores (_) in InterBase, 180

UndoChange procedure, 305

unit file names, 219

units, 23–26
  managing, 54–55
  references to, 52–54
  for user-defined components, 219–220

UNIX hosts, FTP with, 247

UPDATE command, 180–181

updating records, 167–168, 180–181

UpperCase function, 112

URLs (Uniform Resource Locators), 232, 233

user-defined components
  benefits of, 217
  creating, 221–225
  defining, 218–219
  installing, 228–229
  registering, 220–221
  testing, 225–226
  units for, 219–220
  Visual Component Library for, 221

user-defined cursors, 269–270

user-defined procedures and functions, 97

user-IDs in InterBase, 176

user mistakes, anticipating, 41

uses clauses, 24
 for forms, 52–54, 57
 for library routines, 106–107
 for OLEAutoUnit, 144

Use Unit dialog box, 93

V

value parameters, 101–102

values
 assigning to variables, 11–12
 monitoring, 140–141
 ordinal, 80
 returned from functions, 95
 for scroll bars, 39

VARCHAR type, 177

variable parameters, 101–102

variables, 11
 assigning values to, 11–12
 monitoring, 140–141
 names for, 67
 for record types, 90–91
 in reports, 193
 for types, 85

var reserved word, 11, 102

VGA video, 210–211

video, 207–208, 214–215, 274–275

video drivers, 210–211

View|Breakpoints command, 139–140

View|Call Stack command, 142

View|Component List command, 15, 129, 131

viewers for World Wide Web, 232–237, 343–345

View|Project Manager command, 54

View Unit, 219

View|Units command, 54

Visible property
 for components, 42
 for menu items, 125
 for MultiPlayer, 205

VisibleButtons property, 204

Visual Component Library (VCL), 221

VNUMCHK.DPR project, 318

W

wallpaper, tiled bitmaps for, 289–290

Watch List window, 140–141

Watch Properties dialog box, 141

Watch Properties List, 140

.WAV files, 275–276

WeeklySchedule procedure, 335

while loops, 83

WHSHEET1.DPR project, 143

Width property and width
 of columns in reports, 199
 for panels, 40
 of reports, 194
 for Start button, 4

Win 3.1 tab, 47

Win95 page, 58

WinDir function, 341

Windows, directory for, 341

Winsock standard, 232

Winsock TCP Control, 247

with statements, 91–92, 165

words, capitalizing, 322–324

Word type, 14

worksheets
 charts for, 307–309
 formatting, 310–313
 in Formula One, 362–366
 graphics on, 309–310
 library routines for, 307–314
 printing, 313–314

World Wide Web, 231–237, 343–345

Z

Zoom 100% button, 192
Zoom page width button, 192
Zoom whole page button, 192
z-order, 211